ETHICAL ISSUES IN POLICING

Ethical Issues in Policing

SEUMAS MILLER
Centre for Applied Philosophy and Public Ethics, Charles Sturt University, Australia and the Australian National University

JOHN BLACKLER
Centre for Applied Philosophy and Public Ethics, Charles Sturt University, Australia

ASHGATE

Published by
Ashgate Publishing Limited
Gower House
Croft Road
Aldershot
Hants GU11 3HR
England

Ashgate Publishing Company
Suite 420
101 Cherry Street
Burlington, VT 05401-4405
USA

Ashgate website: http://www.ashgate.com

British Library Cataloguing in Publication Data
Miller, Seumas
Ethical issues in policing
1. Police ethics
I. Title II. Blackler, John, 1933 -
174.9'3632

Library of Congress Cataloging-in-Publication Data
Miller, Seumas.
Ethical issues in policing / by Seumas Miller and John Blackler.
p. cm.
Includes bibliographical references and index.
ISBN 0-7546-2244-4
1. Police ethics. 2. Police discretion. 3. Police shootings--Moral and ethical aspects. 4. Law enforcement--Moral and ethical aspects. I. Blackler, John. 1933 - II. Title.

HV7924.M544 2004
174'.93632--dc22

2004023402

ISBN 0 7546 2244 4

Printed in Great Britain by Antony Rowe Ltd, Chippenham, Wiltshire

Contents

Introduction

This book is a contribution to the literature on police ethics, and it is written from the standpoint of applied philosophy. One author, Miller, is a professional philosopher, the other, Blackler, is a former long-serving police officer in the New South Wales Police Service. It is hoped that by providing an integrated mix of ethico-philosophical analysis and practitioner knowledge and experience, the various ethical problems dealt with in this book will be better illuminated than otherwise would have been the case.

Many occupations exist to secure some fundamental *end* or goal, and this end is a human *good*. For doctors the end or goal is health, for lawyers justice, for journalists truth. In this book we argue that the central and most important end of policing is the protection of moral rights. The achievement of this fundamental end requires specialised skills, knowledge and individual judgment. However, there is a crucial further defining feature of policing, namely the routine and inescapable use of harmful methods, including coercive force, deception and the infringement of privacy. This combination of good ends and morally problematic means is, we argue, a distinctive feature of policing.

Ideally, members of occupations *internalise* the fundamental ends which define their particular profession. This process of internalisation may only be implicit. These ends may guide the actions of (say) doctors, even though they may not be very often explicitly aware that this is so.

Most important, members of such occupations, if they are to be successful practitioners, must identify with these defining ends. That is, their *self-worth* comes to depend in part on their capacity to realise these ends. The good teacher is one who not only has a capacity to impart knowledge, she also suffers a loss in self-esteem when she fails to successfully exercise this capacity. Similarly, the good police officer is one who not only has a capacity to detect crime and apprehend criminals, he also suffers a loss in self-esteem when he fails to successfully exercise this capacity.

Occupations are not only in part defined in terms of the end to which they ought to be directed, they are also in part defined in terms of the characteristic activities that members of the occupation engage in. In the case of the police, these characteristic activities are quite diverse, and include law enforcement activities, such as investigating and apprehending criminals, and peace-keeping activities, such as intervening in bar-room brawls or domestic disputes. When members of an occupation not only habitually engage in these activities, but do so skilfully and in a manner that secures the ends of the occupation, they are successful practitioners who can be said to possess the characteristic virtues of that occupation.

Individual police officers belong not only to an occupational group whose members have specialised knowledge and skills, they belong to a group which displays a high degree of solidarity and loyalty to one another. This is in part due to the trust that individual police officers need to be able to place in one another, given the dangers that they face in their work. Notoriously, the virtue of loyalty becomes a vice when it leads police to protect corrupt or incompetent colleagues.

In Chapter 1 of this book, we outline a distinctive philosophical theory of policing, according to which policing is an occupation and institution defined in part by the end of protecting moral rights and in part by the routine use of harmful methods, specifically coercive force. In this chapter we also criticise alternative accounts of the police role, including Egon Bittner's definition of policing purely in terms of the use of coercive force. Arguably, recent developments in human rights legislation in the European Union have given some impetus to conceptions of policing, such as our own, that emphasise the human rights dimension of police work.

In Chapter 2, we discuss and define the related notions of police authority and police discretion. The problematic concept of operational autonomy and its importance in relation to the need for investigatory independence of police from government – given individual politicians may themselves need to be the subjects of investigation – is explored, as is the concept of the original authority attaching to the office of constable in the United Kingdom and Australia. We offer a qualified defence of original authority in policing.

In Chapter 3, we turn our attention to one of the key harmful methods deployed by police, namely coercive force, and specifically deadly force. The use of deadly force in self-defence is distinguished from the use of deadly force to defend the rights of others, and both in turn from (the overlapping category of) the use of deadly force to enforce the law. The existence of this basic tripartite distinction has the implication that – contrary to much recent work in this area – there is a somewhat different moral justification for police use of deadly force than there is for the use of deadly force by ordinary citizens. The difference arises from the role that police have to *enforce* laws against serious crimes.

In Chapter 4, we consider another harmful method, or methods, deployed by police, namely surveillance, data-gathering, integrating and accessing of databases, and other like methods that have implications for the individual's right to privacy. In this connection, we discuss encryption and the ethical issues that it gives rise to in policing. We also consider in detail the various forms of entrapment, and the moral arguments in relation to the so-called "subjective" and "objective" tests for entrapment. We argue that entrapment is morally justified, but only under a quite restricted set of conditions.

Our focus in Chapter 5 shifts to police corruption. We begin by offering a new definition of the concept of corruption. We then detail various causes of police corruption in particular. There follows a distinctive account of noble cause corruption in policing.

In the final chapter of this book, Chapter 6, we discuss restorative justice in policing. Restorative justice techniques, such as conferencing and diversionary schemes for juveniles or first offenders, are a relatively recent development, and have arisen in part as a consequence of the perceived failure of reactive policing driven simply by the goal of investigating, apprehending, convicting and imprisoning offenders. Contrary to the views of many advocates of restorative justice methods, we argue that – properly understood – restorative justice implies, rather than contrasts with, retributive justice.

Earlier versions of some of the material in this book appeared in the following publications by Seumas Miller:

Issues in Police Ethics (Keon, 1996); *Police Ethics* (with John Blackler and Andrew Alexandra) (Allen and Unwin, 1997); *Corruption and Anti-Corruption* (with P. Roberts and E. Spence) (Prentice Hall, 2004); *Social Action* (Cambridge University Press, 2001); *Police Ethics* (*Vols. 1-4*: *Case Studies for Street Police*; *Cases Studies for Detectives*; *Case Studies for Police Managers*; *Bibliography*) (with J. Blackler) (Charles Sturt University and NSW Police Service, 2000); "Privacy and the Internet", *Australian Computer Journal*, Vol. 29, No. 1, 1997; "Corruption and Anti-Corruption in the Profession of Policing", *Professional Ethics*, Vol. 6, Nos. 3 & 4, 1998; "Authority, Discretion and Accountability: The Case of Policing", in C. Sampford, N. Preston and C. Bois (eds.), *Public Sector Ethics*: (London: Routledge, 1998); "Noble Cause Corruption in Policing", *African Security Review*, Vol. 8, No. 3, 1999; "Shootings by Police in Victoria", in T. Coady, S. James, S. Miller and M. O'Keefe (eds.), *Violence* and *Police Culture* (University of Melbourne Press, 2000); "Restorative Justice: Retribution, Confession and Shame", (with J. Blackler) in J. Braithwaite and H. Strang (eds.), *Restorative Justice* (Aldershot: Dartmouth Press, 2000); "Noble Cause Corruption in Policing Revisited", in P. Villiers and R. Adlam (eds.), *A Safe, Just and Tolerant Society: Police Virtue Rediscovered* (Winchester: Waterside Press, 2004); "Human Rights and the Institution of the Police", in T. Campbell and Seumas Miller (eds.), *Human Rights and the Moral Responsibilities of Corporate and Public Sector Organisations* (Dordrecht: Kluwer, 2004).

We would like to thank the following people for providing comments on earlier drafts of the book: Andrew Alexandra; Dean Cocking; Steve Coleman; John Kleinig; Martin Leonard; and Barbara Nunn. We also thank Ewen Miller for proofing, and for preparing the camera-ready copy of the book, as well as the bibliography and index.

Chapter 1

A Theory of Policing: The Enforcement of Moral Rights

In this chapter, we discuss the relationship between moral rights and the institution of the police.[1] We argue that the protection of moral rights is the central and most important moral purpose of police work, albeit a purpose whose pursuit ought to be constrained by the law. So while police institutions have other important purposes that might not directly involve the protection of moral rights, such as to enforce traffic laws or to enforce the adjudications of courts in relation to disputes between citizens, or indeed themselves to settle disputes between citizens on the streets, or to ensure good order more generally, these turn out to be purposes derived from the more fundamental purpose of protecting moral rights, or they turn out to be (non-derivative) secondary purposes. Thus laws against speeding derive in part from the moral right to life, and the restoring of order at a football match ultimately in large part derives from moral rights to the protection of persons and of property. On the other hand, service of summonses to assist the courts is presumably a secondary purpose of policing.[2]

It is important to state a number of things at the outset. First, this is a *normative* account of policing, not a *descriptive* account; it is an account of what policing *ought* to be about, not what it has been or is about. Moreover, it is a normative theory of the *institution* of the police, i.e. of the proper ends and distinctive means of the institution of the police. So it is not a theory about specific police methods or strategies; it is not a theory of, so to speak, best practice in policing. Accordingly, we will not here offer detailed arguments in relation to the disputes between "crime-fighter" and "peace-keeper" models of the role of police officers, or between "community-based" policing and "zero-tolerance" policing. That said, a

---

[1] See the *United Nations Code of Conduct for Law Enforcement Officials.* Most of the articles in this code specify the human rights constraints on police officers. However, Article 1 stresses the duty to protect persons, and the commentary (under c) notes the duty of police to provide aid in times of emergency. An earlier version of the material in the first two sections of this chapter appeared in John Blackler and Seumas Miller, *Police Ethics* (*Case Studies for Police Managers*) (Canberra: Charles Sturt University, 2000). Another version is to appear in Tom Campbell and Seumas Miller (eds.), *Human Rights and the Moral Responsibilities of Corporate and Public Sector Organisations* (Dordrecht: Kluwer, 2004).

[2] Naturally we acknowledge that many laws do not derive from moral rights, and also that those that do often do not do so in any straightforward manner.

normative theory of the institution of the police will have important implications for questions of police methods and strategies, though often these will not necessarily be straightforward or obvious. At any rate, such questions are not our concern in this chapter; rather, we take some of them up in later chapters.

Naturally, whether or not a descriptive theory of an institution is warranted depends on empirical facts. Moreover, the falsity of the *descriptive* theory would put pressure on the acceptability of any *normative* theory of institutions. If it turned out that no institution of that kind at any time or place *in fact* involved to any extent the pursuit of the moral good proposed in some normative theory of that institution, then this would make it implausible to claim that the institution, nevertheless, in general *ought* to aim at that good. That said, there is inevitably *some* mismatch or space between normative theory and descriptive theory. It is precisely this space that can and should be occupied by the work of those institutional designers seeking to apply or concretise an adequate normative theory of the institution in question.

Second, we are assuming a particular notion of moral rights. Moral rights are of two kinds. First, there are human rights; moral rights that individuals possess solely by virtue of properties they have as human beings, e.g. the right to life and the right to freedom of thought.[3] Second, there are institutional (moral) rights; moral rights that individuals possess in part by virtue of rights-generating properties that they have as human beings, and in part by virtue of their membership of a community or morally legitimate institution, or their occupancy of a morally legitimate institutional role. Thus the right to vote is an institutional right, since it exists in part by virtue of possession of the rights-generating property of autonomy, and in part by virtue of membership of a political community. Again, the right to arrest and detain someone for assault is a moral right possessed by police officers. This right is in part dependent on membership of a morally legitimate police institution, but it is also in part dependent on the human right of the victim not to be assaulted.

Moreover, we are assuming the following properties of moral rights. First, moral rights generate concomitant duties on others, e.g. A's right to life generates a duty on the part of B not to kill A. Second, human rights, but not necessarily institutional moral rights, are justifiably enforceable, e.g. A has a right not to be

[3] The intuitive idea is that there are certain properties that individual human beings possess that are at least in part constitutive of their humanity. Naturally there is room for dispute as to what these properties are; indeed, some putative properties might be criteria rather than defining properties. Moreover, while some putative properties, e.g. the capacity to reason, are more salient than others, e.g. the capacity for bodily movement, we do not have a worked-out theory to offer. However, the main point to stress here is that the properties in question are ones that are held to have *moral* value, e.g. individual autonomy or life. This conception is consistent with a view of human beings as essentially social animals. See Seumas Miller, "Individual Autonomy and Sociality", in F. Schmitt (ed.), *Socialising Metaphysics: The Nature of Social Reality* (Lanham, Maryland: Rowman and Littlefield, 2003).

assaulted by B, and if B assaults or attempts to assault A, then B can legitimately be prevented from assaulting A by means of coercion.[4] Third, bearers of human rights, in particular, do not necessarily have to assert a given human right in order for them to possess it, and for the right to be violated, e.g. an infant may have a right to life even though it does not have the ability to assert it (or for that matter to waive it).

Third, the conception of policing that we are offering is a teleological conception; it is a conception in terms of the ends or goals of policing.[5] Moreover, it is a teleological conception according to which the most important end or purpose of policing is the protection of moral rights.

Fourth, on the view that we are advocating, while police ought to have as a fundamental purpose the protection of moral rights, their efforts in this regard ought to be constrained by the law. In so far as the law is a constraint – at least in democratic states – then our view accommodates "consent" as a criterion of legitimacy for the police role.[6] However, on our view legality, and therefore consent, is only one consideration. For we are insisting that police work ought to be guided by moral considerations – namely, moral rights – and not simply by legal considerations. This enables us to avoid the problems besetting theories of policing cast purely in terms of law enforcement, or protection of the State, or even peace-keeping.[7] Such theories are faced with the obvious problem posed by authoritarian states, or sometimes even democratic states, that enact laws that

---

[4] Note that we are here asserting a *normative* conceptual connection between *human* rights and enforcement. We are not making the more familiar (and controversial) claim that for something to be a moral right, it must be able to be enforced. Here it is also useful to distinguish between different orders of rights and duties. For example, the right to life gives rise to the duty not to kill, but also the duty to protect someone from being killed.

[5] Miller has elaborated a teleological account of institutions in his *Social Action: A Teleological Account* (New York: Cambridge University Press, 2001), Chapter 6.

[6] We acknowledge that in common law countries the law reflects tradition, and therefore perhaps "consent" in another sense. See John Kleinig, *The Ethics of Policing* (Cambridge: Cambridge University Press, 1996), Chapter 2.

[7] John Alderson (*Principled Policing*, Winchester: Waterside Press, 1998) at times seems to advocate a view close to the one that we are proposing. However, at other times he seems to be elaborating the view that human rights are merely side constraints on policing, rather than a *raison d'être* for police work. (See especially Chapter 1.) By contrast, John Kleinig (Kleinig, *op. cit.*, p. 27) offers a social peace-keeping theory, and as such is vulnerable to the objection that he leaves the way open for authoritarian policing in the name of social pacification. Naturally Kleinig can qualify the social peace-keeping model by recourse to law. However, the problem is not thereby removed. For a legal system might itself simply be an instrument for authoritarian governmental control – as it was in Nazi Germany. In fact Kleinig qualifies his social peace-keeping account by recourse to democracy (Kleinig, *op. cit.*, p. 28). This still leaves open the possibility of social pacification in the service of the tyranny of the majority. What is called for is the constraint provided by some form of objective morality, e.g. moral rights.

violate human rights, in particular. Consider the police in Nazi Germany, Soviet Russia, or Iraq under Saddam Hussein. These police forces upheld laws that violated the human rights of (respectively) Jews, Soviet citizens, and Iraqi citizens (including Shi'ite Muslims' religious rights). By our lights, the officers in these police forces simultaneously violated human rights, and abrogated their primary professional responsibility as police officers to protect human rights.

Further, we reiterate that on the view that we are advocating, police engaged in the protection of moral rights ought to be constrained by the law, or at least ought to be constrained by laws that embody the will of the community in the sense that: (a) the procedures for generating these laws are more or less universally accepted by the community, e.g. a democratically-elected legislature, and; (b) the content of the laws are at least in large part accepted by the community, e.g. they embody general policies with majority electoral support or reflect the community's moral beliefs.[8] So we are in part helping ourselves to a broadly contractarian moral constraint on policing, namely the consent of citizens; although by our lights consent is not the *raison d'être* for policing, rather it provides an additional (albeit necessary) condition for the moral legitimacy of police work.[9] Moreover, we are refraining from providing police with a licence to pursue their (possibly only individually) subjective view of what counts as an enforceable moral right. What counts as an enforceable moral right is an objective matter. Nevertheless, some particular person or group has to specify what are to be taken to be enforceable moral rights and what are not to be so taken; and in our view ultimately this is a decision for the community to make by way of its laws and its democratically-elected government. Here we take it that in a properly constituted democracy, the law embodies the will of the community in the sense adumbrated above. Moreover, we can further distinguish between local, regional and national communities, especially in states that have sub-national elected bodies such as local councils. This enables us to give substance to notions of community-based policing or

---

[8] Here we are assuming that large fragments of a legal system can consist of immoral laws, and yet the system remain recognisably a legal system. See Ronald Dworkin's *Law's Empire* (Oxford: Hart Publishing, 1998), p. 101. We are also assuming that for a legal system to express the admittedly problematic notion of the will of the community, it is at least necessary that the overwhelming majority of the community (not just a simple majority) support the content of the system of laws taken as a whole – even if there are a small number of individual laws they do not support – and support the procedures for generating laws, e.g. a democratically-elected legislature. (See Miller, *Social Action*, pp. 141-151.) Finally, we are assuming that the fact that a party or candidate or policy or law secured (directly or directly) a majority vote is an important (but not necessarily decisive) consideration in its favour, and a consideration above and beyond the moral weight to be given to the existence of a consensus in relation to the value to be attached to voting as a procedure.

[9] See Howard Cohen and Michael Feldberg, *Power and Restraint: The Moral Dimension of Policework* (New York: Praeger, 1991), Chapter 2.

partnerships between police and local communities. For at the sub-national level, and especially the local level, it becomes feasible for police to consult and work with communities to address law enforcement issues in a consensual manner.[10]

There is a further point to be made here. The law concretises moral rights and the principles governing their enforcement, including human rights as well as institutional moral rights. To this extent, the law is very helpful in terms of guiding police officers and citizens in relation to the way that abstract moral rights and principles apply to specific circumstances. For example, there is a human right to life that can be overridden in accordance with certain moral principles, such as self-defence or defence of the lives of others. However, it is the laws governing the use of deadly force by police officers that provide an explicit and concrete formulation of these moral rights and principles, and thereby prescribe what is to be done or not done by police officers in specific circumstances.

In short, in our view police ought to act principally to protect certain moral rights, those moral rights ought to be enshrined in the law, and the law ought to reflect the will of the community. Should any of these conditions fail to obtain, then there will be problems. If the law and objective (justifiably enforceable) moral rights come apart, or if the law and the will of the community come apart, or if objective moral rights and the will of the community come apart, then the police may well be faced with moral dilemmas. We do not believe that there are neat and easy solutions to all such problems.[11] Clearly, if the law and/or the citizenry require the police to *violate* moral rights, then the law and/or the citizenry will be at odds with the fundamental purpose of policing. Accordingly, depending on the circumstances, the police may well be obliged to disobey the law and/or the will of the community. On the other hand, what is the appropriate police response to a citizen violating someone else's objective moral right in a community in which the right is not as a matter of fact enshrined in the law, and the right is not supported by the community? Consider, in this connection, women's rights to (say) education under an extremist fundamentalist religious regime such as the former Taliban regime in Afghanistan.[12] Under such circumstances, an issue arises as to whether police are morally obliged *qua* police officers to *enforce* respect for the moral right

---

[10] Moreover, community-based policing might reconstitute itself as problem-based policing, and thereby be more effective. See Herman Goldstein, *Problem-Oriented Policing* (New York: McGraw-Hill, 1990), and "Team Policing", in Steven G. Brandl and David E. Barlow (eds.), *Classics of Policing* (Cincinnati, OH: Anderson Publishing Co., 1996), p. 86f.

[11] See William C. Heffernan, "The Police and their Rules of Office: An Ethical Analysis", in William C. Heffernan and Timothy Stroup (eds.), *Police Ethics: Hard Choices for Law Enforcement* (New York: John Jay College Press, 1985).

[12] Regarding the role of the religious police of the Taliban in the Department of the Promotion of Virtue and Prevention of Vice, see Ahmed Rashid's *Taliban: The Story of the Afghan Warlords* (London: Pan Books, 2001), Chapter 8.

in question. Again, we suggest that they may well be obliged to intervene to enforce respect for such a moral right.

Normatively speaking then, the protection of fundamental moral rights – specifically *justifiably enforceable* moral rights – is the central and most important purpose of police work. As it happens, there is increasing recourse to human rights legislation, in particular, in the decisions of domestic as well as international courts. This is an interesting development. However, it must also be pointed out that the criminal law in many, if not most, jurisdictions already in effect constitutes human rights legislation. Laws proscribing murder, rape, assault and so on, are essentially laws that protect human rights. So it is clear that whatever the historical importance of a "Statist" conception of human rights – human rights as protections of the individual against the State – such a conception is inadequate as a *general* account of human rights. Human rights, in particular, and moral rights more generally, also exist to protect individual citizens from their fellow citizens, and individual citizens from organisations other than the organisations of the State. Moreover, tort law is also relevant here, e.g. tort law provides for compensation for the unintended infringement of human rights.

In this connection, please note that we do not say that the protection of (legally enshrined, justifiably enforceable) moral rights ought to be the *only* goal of policing; merely that it ought to be the *central and most important* goal, and that other important roles derive from it. Here it is important to note that we are rejecting the dichotomy sometimes offered between police as law enforcers and police as peace-keepers. Both roles are important, but our account shows why they are important. Law enforcement is important mainly because laws embody moral rights. Likewise, peace-keeping is important in large part because disorder typically consists of, or is a prerequisite for, violations of moral rights, including rights to security of person and of property.

Moreover, there are numerous service roles that police play, and ought to continue to play, because they consist of, or facilitate, their central and most important role of protecting moral rights. Consider, in this connection, police assistance in relation to missing persons who might have come in harm's way, or assisting drunks who might otherwise harm themselves[13] or be harmed.

Nevertheless, we do not hold that police are, or ought to be, preoccupied with seeing to it that *all* moral rights are secured. Roughly speaking, police are, or ought to be, engaged in moral rights work to the extent to which the moral rights in question are ones that justify and potentially require the use of coercive force for their protection.[14] Some moral rights are not justifiably enforceable, e.g. a wife's

---

[13] Note that on our view there are moral rights to assistance. So a drunk person in danger of (say) collapsing on his way home and freezing to death in the Finnish winter would have a moral right to assistance. Indeed, coercive force might need to be used to prevent such a person from endangering himself.

[14] Though no doubt all *human* rights need protection from time to time.

moral right to the sex her husband promised her when they got married. Other moral rights do not necessarily, or in general, require the use of coercive force for their protection. For example, a physically disabled person might have a moral right to appropriate access to public buildings such as libraries and government offices, and such access might necessitate the provision of sloping paths as opposed to stairs. But the securing of this right for the disabled might call only for action on the part of the local council; there might be no need for the police to be involved.

Here the distinction made by Henry Shue is relevant. Shue distinguishes between three sorts of duties that correlate with what he calls "basic rights".[15] These are the duties to: (a) avoid depriving; (b) protect from deprivation, and; (c) aid the deprived.

In relation to police work, (b) above, the duty to protect from deprivation, is especially salient. Police are typically engaged in protecting someone from being deprived of their right to life, liberty or property. Note that police provision of rights protection is distinctive in part by virtue of police use of, or more often the threat of the use of, coercive force. This is not, of course, to suggest police always or even typically use coercive force, or threaten to use it; rather the claim is that this recourse to coercion is a distinctive and routine feature of policing, and is in some sense "the bottom line" when it comes to realising the proper ends of policing.

At any rate, the account of the institution of the police that we are offering promises to display the distinctive defining features of the institution of the police; namely, its use of coercive force in the service of legally enshrined moral rights. On this account, the institution of the police is quite different from other institutions that are either not principally concerned with moral rights, or that do not necessarily rely on coercion in the service of moral rights. Consider business. Many business organisations do not have the securing of moral rights as a primary purpose; nor should they. On the other hand, moral rights are an important side constraint or stricture on business activity. Now consider welfare institutions. There is a human right to a subsistence living, and aiding the deprived (to use Shue's terminology) is a fundamental purpose of welfare institutions. However, aiding the deprived does not necessarily or routinely involve the use of, or threat of the use of, coercive force. Thus welfare institutions are different in kind from policing institutions.

It might be argued that contemporary military institutions meet our definition of the institution of the police. Consider so-called "humanitarian" armed intervention in places such as Somalia, Bosnia, Rwanda, Kosovo and East Timor. Whether or not each of these armed interventions was principally undertaken to protect human rights is a matter of controversy. At any rate, we make three points in response.

---

[15] Henry Shue, *Basic Rights* (Princeton: Princeton University Press, 1996), p. 52.

First, the nature and evolution of military and policing institutions is such that the lines have often been blurred between the two. For example, in the British colonies the police historically had a paramilitary role in relation to what was regarded as a hostile population, e.g. the Royal Irish Constabulary. Indeed, according to Richard Hill:

> Coercion by army and by police have always been distinguished by differences of degree, rather than kind, and through most of the history of policing there was no clear demarcation between the two interwoven strands of control situated towards the coercive extremity of the control continuum... Historically, constables were generally considered to be a reserve military body for mobilisation by the state in potential or actual emergency; conversely soldiers were frequently called upon to conduct duties generally considered to be of a 'policing' nature.[16]

But from this it does not follow that there are not good reasons for a *normative* theory of *contemporary* policing in liberal democracies to make distinctions between the fundamental role of the police and that of the military. Such reasons would include the well-documented and highly problematic character of paramilitary police forces, including in relation to the violation by such forces of individual moral rights, and the tendency for such forces to become simply the instrument of governments rather than the protectors of the rights of the community and the servants of its laws. (We will deal more directly with this issue in Chapter 2.)

Second, while contemporary military forces may undertake humanitarian armed interventions from time to time, this is not, or has not been, their fundamental purpose; rather, national self-defence has avowedly been their purpose.

Third, to the extent that military institutions do in fact take on the role of human rights protection by means of the use of coercive force, then they are being assimilated to police institutions. It is no accident that recent humanitarian armed interventions are referred to as episodes of "international *policing*."

There are some other objections to our account of the institution of the police. We try to deal with the most important of these later on in this chapter. In the following section of the chapter, we offer a brief account of moral rights and the cognate notion of social norms. In the section after that, we present our theory of policing as the protection of legally enshrined moral rights by means of coercive force. In the final section, we deal with some residual issues arising from the use of harmful methods in policing, including methods that under normal circumstances would themselves constitute human rights violations.

---

[16] Richard S. Hill, *Policing the Colonial Frontier: The Theory and Practice of Coercive Social and Racial Control in New Zealand, 1767-1867* (Wellington, NZ: Government Printer, 1986), Part One, p. 3.

Moral Rights and Social Norms

Moral rights are a basic moral category; but they are far from being the only moral consideration. Here we note that moral rights comprise a relatively narrow set of moral considerations. There are many moral obligations that are not, and do not derive from, moral rights, e.g. an obligation to assist a friend who is depressed, or not to cheat on one's boyfriend.

The point of human rights is to protect some basic human value or values. On James Griffin's account, human rights arise from the need to protect what he calls "personhood".[17] At the core of his notion of personhood is individual autonomy. Certainly, autonomy is a basic human value protected by a structure of human rights. However, we have some reservations about Griffin's account; specifically, it might turn out to be too narrowly reliant on autonomy. Perhaps the right not to be tortured does not simply derive from a right to autonomy; perhaps it derives, at least in part, from the right not to suffer extreme pain intentionally inflicted by another.[18]

Moreover, we want to suggest that there is a coherent notion of individual *identity* that: (a) underpins certain human rights, and; (b) is not reducible to individual liberty or autonomy.

According to the so-called "Stolen Generation Report" commissioned by the Australian government, in the 19th and 20th centuries thousands of aboriginal children were taken from their families by Australian state welfare officials and police and placed in white Australian families or non-indigenous institutions.[19] The official reasons given included that these children were at risk or neglected, and that these white families or institutions could provide better care for the children. The Report disputes the validity of these reasons.

Subsequently, many of these children who are now adults have come forward and expressed moral outrage at what happened to them; evidently the experience profoundly harmed them. It is now widely accepted that this policy was a violation of human rights. Let us accept that this is the case. The question that now arises is: By virtue of what property of parents and their children does this human right exist?

Presumably the right exists by virtue of an acknowledged deep relationship between parents and their children, and between siblings. To simplify, we will

---

[17] James Griffin, "Human Rights", in Tom Campbell and Seumas Miller (eds.), *Human Rights and the Moral Responsibilities of Corporate and Public Sector Organisations* (Dordrecht: Kluwer, 2004).

[18] This is a point made by Tom Campbell in discussion.

[19] *Bringing them Home: Report of the National Inquiry into the Separation of Aboriginal and Torres Strait Islander Children from their Families* (Commonwealth of Australia, 1997).

focus on the relationship between a mother and her young – say, five-year-old[20] – child, a relationship which has both a biological and an emotional dimension. If we focus on the child, as opposed to the mother, this relationship is in fact so central as to in part constitute the *identity* of the child. Small wonder then that removing young children from their mothers generated the degree of trauma that it in fact did.

However, the basis of the child's human right not to be removed from its mother can hardly be the child's autonomy. It is not the autonomy of the child that has been violated, since young children do not possess autonomy.

This suggests that we need to distinguish between individual autonomy and individual identity. Perhaps the term "autonomy" is sometimes used so as to embrace the notion of individual identity. If so, then we should distinguish between a "thick" and a "thin" sense of autonomy. An autonomous agent in the thin sense means something like a rational chooser; an autonomous agent in the thick sense means something like a rational chooser possessed of an individual identity, which identity the rational chooser takes into account in making his or her rational choices.

At any rate, whatever the correct theoretical account of human rights might be, we assume that Griffin is right to set out a relatively limited set of moral considerations as being human rights. These will include the right to life, to physical security, to freedom of thought, expression and movement, and to freedom to form human relationships, including freedom to choose one's sexual partner. They will also include the right to a basic subsistence; so they will include rights to food, water and shelter.

However, moral rights will include a range of rights that go beyond human rights and that, as mentioned above, might be termed "institutional moral rights". As said above, these are moral rights that depend in part on rights-generating properties possessed by human beings *qua* human beings, but also in part on membership of a community or of a morally legitimate institution, or occupancy of a morally legitimate institutional role. Such institutional moral rights include the right to vote and to stand for political office, the right of legislators to enact legislation, of judges to make binding judgements, of police to arrest offenders, and of patients to sue doctors for negligence.

Here we need to distinguish between: (a) institutional rights that embody human rights in institutional settings, and therefore depend in part on rights-generating properties that human beings possess as human beings (these are institutional *moral* rights), and; (b) institutional rights that do not embody human rights in institutional settings (these are not necessarily institutional *moral* rights, but rather *mere* institutional rights). The right to vote and the right to stand for

[20] We are assuming that five-year-olds are old enough to have established a very strong particular interpersonal relationship – indeed, an identity-conferring interpersonal relationship – with their mothers, but too young to be autonomous in any meaningful sense.

office embody the human right to autonomy in the institutional setting of the State; hence to make a law to exclude certain people from having a vote or standing for office, as happened under apartheid in South Africa, is to violate a moral right. But the right to make the next move in a game of chess, or to move a pawn one space forward, but not (say) three spaces sidewards, is entirely dependent on the rules of chess; if the rules had been different, e.g. if each player had to make two consecutive moves, or pawns could move sidewards, then the rights that players have would be entirely different. In other words, these rights that chess players have are *mere* institutional rights; they depend entirely on the rules of the "institution" of the game of chess. Likewise, (legally enshrined) parking rights, including reserved spaces, and one-hour parking spaces, etc. in universities, are *mere* institutional rights, as opposed to institutional *moral* rights.

A large question arises at this point as to the status of property rights. Are such rights institutional *moral* rights or *mere* institutional rights? It would seem that at least *some* property rights are institutional *moral* rights by virtue of being in part dependent on rights-generating properties that human beings have *qua* human beings. Specifically, some property rights depend on the rights-generating properties of: (a) the need to have exclusive use of certain physical material, e.g. *this* food and water, and physical space, e.g. *this* shelter, and; (b) individual or collective *labour*, including labour that *creates* new things, e.g. tools or ornaments that an individual or particular group has made. Some of these property rights might be individual rights, e.g. to personal effects, and some might be collective rights, e.g. to occupy a certain stretch of territory and exclude others from it. At any rate, we will assume that some property rights are institutional *moral* rights.

Some (but not all) moral rights, including many (perhaps all) human rights, are, or ought to be, embodied in the laws governing a community. This is most obvious in the case of many of the so-called "negative" rights, such as the right to life, the right to physical security, and the right to property. Murder, assault, rape, theft, fraud and so on, are criminal offences. Moreover, the police have a clear and central role to investigate and apprehend the perpetrators of these crimes – the rights violators – and bring them before the courts for trial and sentencing.

Obviously there are large fragments of the legal system concerned with matters other than criminality. For example, there are all manner of disputes of a non-criminal nature that are settled in the civil courts. These often involve important questions of *justice* that are not human rights issues. On the other hand, many of these disputes involve institutional moral rights, e.g. who gets what part of the estate of some deceased relative, or of the property formerly jointly owned by a husband and wife now involved in divorce proceedings. Moreover, in so far as a dispute is, or gives rise to, an issue of justice, then moral rights are involved, at least in the sense that the disputants have a moral right to a just outcome.

To the extent that law enforcement by police is enforcement of moral rights, whether enforcement of criminal law or not, the police are undertaking their fundamental role (on our account). On the other hand, the police do have a legitimate role in relation to law enforcement, where the laws in question do not embody moral rights. This is a matter to which we return later in this chapter. Suffice it to say here that the law enforcement role of the police in relation to matters other than the enforcement of moral rights is, in our view, either a derived role or it is a secondary role.

It is also the case that in Anglo-Saxon countries, in particular, there are some human rights that are not embodied in the law. And some of these are embodied in the law in some European countries. For example, in Australia, while it is a legal requirement that police assist someone who is drowning or starving, it is lawful for an ordinary citizen to refrain from providing such assistance. Yet the right to life is a human right, and therefore there is a concomitant moral obligation to assist someone who is drowning or starving, or at least to do so in situations in which assisting such a person would not put oneself at risk of harm, and in which police or others are not able to provide the needed assistance.

The moral and legal issues in this area are complex. However, in our view in general it ought to be unlawful for a person, A, to refrain from assisting another person, B, under the following conditions: (a) B's life is at immediate risk; (b) A's intervention is necessary if B is to survive, and; (c) A can assist with minimal cost to him or herself. Indeed, there ought to be a variety of so-called "Good Samaritan" laws, and the reason for this is that human rights ought to be protected, and some Good Samaritan laws protect human rights.

So we hold that in general violations of human rights ought to be criminalised. If this were the case – and it already is to a considerable extent – then the police would have a central role in relation to the enforcement of human rights by virtue of having a role in relation to the enforcement of the criminal law.

One of the interesting implications of this conception is that there would be a shift in the line of demarcation between the so-called "police service" role and the "law enforcement" role (especially criminal law enforcement role) of police. Typically, the police service role is contrasted with the law enforcement role; the rescue operations of Water Police, or of police dealing with dangerous mentally deranged persons, are supposedly service roles, not law enforcement roles. In one sense, the contrast here is already overdrawn; the law with respect to the safe utilisation of water craft needs to be enforced, as does the law in relation to dangerous mentally deranged persons. Moreover, questions of policing *methods* should not be confused with questions of what actions ought to be criminalised and what ought not. In relation to some criminal offences, e.g. juvenile gangs engaged in assaults, it might be more productive for police to engage in preventative strategies, such as restorative justice techniques, rather than simply arresting/charging and locking up offenders. (See Chapter 6.) More important, in so far as Good Samaritan laws with respect to so-called "positive" moral rights were enacted, then many police activities previously regarded as service roles would become in part law enforcement roles (indeed, roles of enforcing criminal laws). But it is important to stress here that the criminalisation of violations of certain positive moral rights is entirely consistent with an overall reduction in acts regarded as criminal, e.g. decriminalisation of laws in relation to cannabis and prostitution. After all, smoking cannabis and selling sex are not activities which in themselves necessarily violate anyone's moral rights.

Thus far we have sought to make a connection between moral rights and the law on the one hand, and law enforcement and the institution of the police on the other. This has enabled us to present, albeit in very general terms, the view that the fundamental point of policing is to enforce certain moral rights, viz. justifiably enforceable moral rights. However, there are other, competing views. One such influential contrasting view holds that the law embodies social morality in general.[21] On this view, in so far as the role of the police was to enforce the law, then their role would be to enforce social morality. Should this view be preferred to ours?

The notion of social morality is to be understood as connoting the framework of moral values and principles that a society accepts and conforms to; that is, the framework of *social norms*.

Elsewhere Miller has offered and defended a detailed account of the notion of a social norm.[22] Roughly speaking, according to that account a social norm is a regularity in behaviour among a group of individual persons such that: (a) each (or at least most) believes that each (including him/herself) morally ought to conform, and; (b) the belief of almost any individual that each (including him/herself) morally ought to conform is in part dependent on almost everyone else's belief that each morally ought to conform. So conformity to social norms is based on an interdependence of attitude – specifically, interdependence of moral beliefs.

Given the above account of social norms, it is easy to see why citizens feel that they ought to obey many of the laws of the land, and in particular criminal laws. For the criminal law is typically in large part an explicit formulation (backed by penal sanction) of a society's social norms. Citizens believe that they ought not to flout the laws against murder, theft, rape, assault and so on, because these citizens have internalised a system of social norms which proscribes such behaviour. Putting matters simply, for the most part any given citizen does not commit murder in part because s/he believes it is wrong for her/him to murder, and in part because others believe it is wrong for her/him to murder.

Unfortunately, there are some citizens who have not internalised the system of social norms, or who have not sufficiently internalised that system. Accordingly, there is a need to buttress the system of social norms by the construction of a criminal justice system. The latter system involves the detection of serious moral wrongdoing, and the investigation, trial and punishment of offenders.

---

[21] We take it that Lord Devlin's account is a version of this view (Patrick Devlin, *The Enforcement of Morals*, Oxford: Oxford University Press, 1965).

[22] Miller, *Social Action*, Chapter 4.

Accordingly, it is tempting to view the role of the police as the enforcement of social morality understood as the structure of social norms in force in the community. This picture is an appealing one. However, it is inadequate in two respects.

Firstly, the notions of a social norm, and of social morality, are relatively wide notions; considerably wider than the notion of a basic moral requirement that ought to be enshrined in the criminal law (or the legal system more generally). Note also that the notion of an action or omission required by a social norm is considerably wider than the notion of a duty correlative to a moral right. For the notion of a social norm – and therefore of social morality – embraces regularities in behaviour (including omissions) that are the subject of some moral attitude. So they include behaviour that is outside the purview of the criminal law, or indeed the law more generally. For example, social norms prescribe and proscribe sexual behaviour that is not necessarily, or even generally, the subject of any legal requirement. Moreover, there is a great danger in widening the law to embrace all of social morality. Consider, in this connection, the threats to individual autonomy posed by puritanical polities such as that of Calvin's Geneva or, as mentioned above, agencies such as the Department for the Promotion of Virtue and the Prevention of Vice under the Taliban regime in Afghanistan.[23]

Secondly, while behavioural conformity to a social norm is an objective social fact, social norms *qua* prescriptions are not necessarily objectively valid; everyone might be behaving in accordance with the social norm, but from this is does not follow that they *ought to be* conforming to it. That is, the notion of a social norm – and of social morality – is an essentially subjective notion; it refers to the values and principles that are *believed in* by the members of some presumably morally sentient community; but beliefs, including moral beliefs, are not necessarily *true* beliefs. So social morality stands in contrast with objective notions, such as the notion of human rights. Or at least there is a contrast here for those of us who believe that the notion of a human right is an objective notion. It might be thought, nevertheless, that the subjective character of social morality is no obstacle to its being deployed – via the notion of the criminal law in particular – to define the proper role of the institution of the police. After all, the criminal law is itself subjective in the above sense. The criminal law is a de facto set of laws; it is not necessarily the set of laws that *ought to* exist by the lights of some objective moral standard.[24] And it might be thought that the proper role of the police is to enforce the law in general, and the criminal law in particular, as it is, not as it morally ought to be.

---

[23] Rashid, *op. cit.*, Chapter 8.

[24] The criminal law is not simply a set of laws. For some theoretical accounts of the criminal law, see A. Duff (ed.), *Philosophy and the Criminal Law* (Cambridge: Cambridge University Press, 1998), and Dworkin, *op. cit.*

Once again, this is an issue to be addressed in more detail later in this chapter. Here we simply record our view that a normative account of the role of the police must be cast in terms of objective notions, not subjective ones. The de facto role of the police in apartheid South Africa was the enforcement of the laws of apartheid, and of the Serbian police, e.g. the so-called "Red Berets" of the Serbian Interior Ministry of Belgrade, the ethnic cleansing of Muslims in Bosnia, but these are not the morally legitimate roles of police forces.[25]

The upshot of the discussion thus far is that the view of police simply as enforcers of social morality is untenable. We cannot make a connection between the notion of social morality and the criminal law (especially) on the one hand, and the criminal law and the enforcement of the criminal law by the police on the other, and thereby erect a normative theory of the role of policing as the enforcement of social morality. Rather, we ought to prefer the related, but competing, view that the fundamental role of the police is to protect legally enshrined (justifiably enforceable) moral rights, and for two reasons. First, the notion of justifiably enforceable moral rights is a suitably narrow one to qualify as the fundamental purpose of policing, unlike the notion of social morality. Second, the notion of justifiably enforceable moral rights is an objective notion, again unlike the notion of social morality. Putting matters simply, justifiably enforceable moral rights are an *objective* set of *fundamental* (actual or potential) social norms that are capable of being enshrined in enforceable law. As such, justifiably enforceable moral rights are an appropriate notion to provide the moral basis for policing, or at least the central and most important moral basis for policing.

So much for the discussion of human rights and social norms, and their relationship to the institution of the police. In the next section, we consider in detail the relation between moral rights and the institution of the police.

Moral Rights and the Institution of the Police

As mentioned above, Miller has elsewhere provided a teleological normative account of social institutions.[26] According to that account, the ultimate justification for the existence of fundamental human institutions such as government, the education system, the economic system and the criminal justice system, is their provision of some moral or ethical good or goods to the community. The existence of universities is justified by the fact that the academics that they employ discover, teach and disseminate the fundamental human good, knowledge. The existence of an economic system, including the free-market system, is justified by the fact that it contributes to the fundamental human good, material well-being. The existence

[25] See Laura Silber and Allan Little, *Yugoslavia: Death of a Nation* (London: Penguin, 1997), p. 224.
[26] Miller, *Social Action*, Chapter 6.

of governments is justified by the fact that they provide the social good, leadership of the community, and thereby contribute to protection of human rights, order, prosperity, equitable distribution of economic goods, and so on. In short, the point of having any one of these institutions is an ethical or moral one; each provides some fundamental human or social good(s).

Moreover, these moral goods, or at least believed moral goods, are, normatively speaking, the *collective* ends of institutions, and as such they conceptually condition the social norms that govern, or ought to govern, the constitutive roles and activities of members of institutions, and therefore the deontic properties (institutional rights and duties) that attach to these roles. Thus, a police officer has certain deontic powers of search, seizure and arrest, but these powers are justified in terms of the moral good – legally enshrined human rights, say – that it is, or ought to be, the role of the police officer to maintain.

It is also worth noting here that there is no easy rights versus goods distinction. Human rights certainly function as a side constraint on the behaviour of institutional actors. But equally, the securing of human rights can be a good that is aimed at by institutional actors.

Further, a defining property of an institution is its substantive functionality (or *telos*), and so a putative institutional entity with deontic properties, but stripped of its substantive functionality, typically ceases to be an institutional entity, at least of the relevant kind; would-be surgeons who cannot perform surgery are not surgeons. Equally, would-be police officers who are incapable of conducting an investigation, or who cannot make arrests or exercise any form of authority over citizens, are not really police officers. Here, by "substantive functionality", we have in mind the specific defining ends of the institution or profession. In the case of institutions, including professions, the defining ends will be collective ends; they will not in general be ends that an individual could realise by his or her own action alone. In short, the theory of institutions, and of any given institution, is a *teleological* theory.

Moreover, as noted earlier, institutions in general, and any given institution in particular, require both a teleological *descriptive* theory, and a teleological *normative* theory.

Thus far we have spoken in terms of the theory of institutional action where institutions have been taken to be different and separate "entities". However, there is also a need for a theoretical account of the *interrelationships* between different institutions. It is clear that on our teleological account of institutions, any given institution is to be understood in terms of the collective end or ends to which its activities are and/or ought to be directed. However, there still remains the question of the relationships between institutions. One issue concerns the extent or degree of any required relationship. Another concerns the nature of the required relationship. As far as the extent of the relationships is concerned, in the post-Enlightenment West this interaction between institutional organisations belonging to the same society has typically taken place in the context of a commitment to a basic separation between them. Governments must stand apart from corporations lest public and private interests are confused, and corporations must stand apart from one another in the interests of competition. In communist regimes, by contrast, the doctrine of organisational (or at least institutional) separation, including separation of powers, has not been adhered to. Japan constitutes an interesting third model. While Japan is obviously in some sense a liberal democratic state, there has been an extent of government, corporation and bureaucracy linkage that is at odds with the notion of institutional separation. Moreover, there is some evidence that in recent years in the Western liberal democracies, the doctrine of institutional separation is under threat in the face of policies coming under the banner of so-called "economic rationalism". Such policies include the privatisation of law enforcement agencies and prisons, and the outsourcing of administrative functions.

As far as the *nature* of the relationship between institutions is concerned, this is presumably to be determined primarily on the basis of the extent to which the differential defining collective ends of institutions are complementary rather than competitive, and/or the extent to which they mesh in the service of higher-order ends. In this connection, consider the complementary ends of the institutional components of the criminal justice system, viz. the police (end or purpose to gather evidence and arrest suspects), the courts (to try and sentence offenders) and the prisons (to punish, deter and rehabilitate offenders). Consider also that certain institutions, e.g. the government and the police, might be meta-institutions in the sense that they have a role in relation to pre-existing institutions, e.g. the family and the economic system. That role might be to assist or to protect these pre-existing institutions, or at least their members.

Having discussed social institutions in general, we now need to turn to the institution of the police in particular.[27]

In times of institutional crisis, or at least institutional difficulty, problem-solving strategies and policies for reform need to be framed in relation to the fundamental ends or goals of the institution; which is to say they need to be contrived and implemented on the basis of whether or not they will contribute to transforming the institution in ways that will enable it to provide, or better provide, the moral good(s) which justify its existence. However, in relation to policing, as with other relatively modern institutions – the media is another example – there is an unclarity as to what precisely its fundamental ends or goals are. Indeed, it is sometimes argued that there can be no overarching philosophical theory or explanatory framework that spells out the fundamental nature and point of policing, and that this is because the activities that police engage in are so diverse.

Certainly the police are involved in a wide variety of activities, including control of politically-motivated riots, traffic control, dealing with cases of assault,

---

[27] An earlier version of the material in this section and the one following it appeared in Seumas Miller, "Corruption and Anti-Corruption in the Profession of Policing", *Professional Ethics*, Vol. 6, Nos. 3 & 4, 1998.

investigating murders, intervening in domestic and neighbourhood quarrels, apprehending thieves, saving people's lives, making drug busts, shooting armed robbers, dealing with cases of fraud, and so on. Moreover, they have a number of different roles. They have a deterrence role as highly visible authority figures with the right to deploy coercive force. They also have a law enforcement role in relation to crimes already committed. This latter role involves not only the investigation of crimes in the service of truth, but also the duty to arrest offenders and bring them before the courts so that they can be tried and – if found guilty – punished. And police also have an important preventative role in relation to crime and disorder. How, it is asked, could we possibly identify any defining features, given this diverse array of activities and roles?

One way to respond to this challenge is to first distinguish between the activities or roles in themselves and the goal or end that they serve, and then try to identify the human or social good served by these activities. So riot control is different from traffic control, and both are different from drug busts, but all these activities have a common goal, or at least a delimited set of goals. Moreover, this common goal or set of goals is a human or social good, or at least a delimited set of such goods. The human or social goods to be aimed at by police will include upholding the law, maintaining social order, and preserving human life.[28]

Indeed, policing seems to involve an apparent multiplicity of ends or goals. However, some ends, such as the enforcement of law and the maintenance of order, might be regarded as more central to policing than others, such as financial or administrative goals realised by (say) collecting fees on behalf of government departments, issuing speeding tickets, and serving summonses.

But even if we consider only so-called "fundamental" ends, there is still an apparent multiplicity. For example, there is the end of upholding the law, but there is also the end of bringing about order or conditions of social calm, and there is the end of saving lives. Indeed, Lord Scarman relegates law enforcement to a secondary status by contrast with the peace-keeping role.[29] Moreover, the end of enforcing the law can be inconsistent with bringing about order or conditions of social calm. As Skolnick says: "Law is not merely an instrument of order, but may frequently be its adversary".[30]

Can these diverse and possibly conflicting ends or goals be reconciled? As discussed above, we suggest that they can, and by recourse to the notion of justifiably enforceable moral rights. The first point here is that the criminal law in particular is, or ought to be, fundamentally about ensuring the protection of certain moral rights, e.g. the right to life.

---

[28] Different theorists have seen one of these goals as definitive. See, for example, J. Skolnick and J. Fyfe, *Above the Law: Police and the Excessive Use of Force* (New York: Free Press, 1993), and D. Bradley, N. Walker and R. Wilkie, *Managing the Police* (Brighton: Harvester Press, 1986), p. 62f.

[29] Lord Scarman, *The Scarman Report* (London: Penguin, 1981).

[30] Jerome Skolnick, *Justice Without Trial* (New York: Macmillan, 1966).

The second point is that social order, conditions of social calm and so on, which are at times contrasted with law enforcement, are in fact, we suggest, typically necessary conditions for moral rights to be respected. A riot or bar-room brawl or violent domestic quarrel is a matter for police concern precisely because it involves the violation of moral rights, including the rights to protection of person and property. Consider, in this connection, interregnum periods of disorder between the ending of military hostilities and the establishment of civil order, such as the looting, revenge killings and so on, that took place on a large scale at the US-proclaimed close of the most recent war in Iraq.

The third point to be made here pertains to the enforcement of those laws that do not appear to embody justifiably enforceable moral rights. Many of these laws prescribe actions (or omissions), the performance (or non-performance) of which provides a social benefit. Consider the laws of taxation. The benefits provided by taxation include the provision of roads and other services to which arguably citizens do not have a moral right, and certainly not a justifiably enforceable moral right. On the other hand, taxes also enable the provision of benefits to which citizens do have justifiably enforceable moral rights, e.g. medicine for life-threatening diseases, basic welfare, and so on.

The fourth point to be made here pertains to the justification for enforcement of the law by police. We have argued that certain legally enshrined moral rights are justifiably enforced by police, as are laws that indirectly contribute to the securing of these rights. The moral rights in question are justifiably enforceable moral rights. Now clearly there are laws that are not of this sort. Many of these laws are fair and reasonable, and the conformity to them enables collective goods to be provided. But what is the justification for their enforcement by police? We suggest that the fact that they provide collective benefits, and/or that they are fair and reasonable, do not of themselves provide an adequate justification for their enforcement. Perhaps consent to the enforcement of just and reasonable laws that enable the provision of collective benefits provides an adequate moral justification for such enforcement. Here there is an issue with respect to the degree and type of enforcement that might be in this way justified; deadly force may not be justified, even if it is consented to in relation to fair and reasonable laws that enable collective benefits to be provided. Moreover, as is well-known, there is a problem in relation to consent. Evidently there is not in fact explicit consent to most laws, and the recourse to tacit consent seems not to offer a sufficiently strong and determinate notion of consent.

At any rate, we want to make two points here in relation to what is nothing more than a version of the traditional problem of the justification for the use of coercive force by the State to enforce its laws.[31] First, self-evidently there is no

---

[31] See Dworkin, *op. cit.*, p. 190. There are questions here in relation to the *exclusive* right of the State to enforce moral rights. Arguably, the State only has an exclusive right to punish,

obvious problem in relation to the enforcement of laws that embody *justifiably enforceable* moral rights, including human rights. Moreover, there may well be other laws that can justifiably be enforced (up to a point) on the grounds that not only are they fair, reasonable and productive of social benefits, but in addition citizens have consented to their enforcement (up to that point). Second, we want to suggest that, notwithstanding our first point, there are fair, reasonable and socially beneficial laws with respect to which enforcement is not morally justified. Further, there may not be an adequate justification for enforcement of some of these laws, even if enforcement were to be consented to. The reason for this is that the nature and degree of enforcement required to ensure compliance with these laws – say, use of deadly force – is not morally justified.[32] Certainly recourse to deadly force – as opposed to non-deadly coercive force – is not justified in the case of many unlawful actions; specifically, unlawful actions not regarded as serious crimes. Indeed, this point is recognised in those jurisdictions that have made it unlawful for police to shoot at many categories of "fleeing felons".[33] It is more often than not now unlawful, because immoral, to shoot at (say) a fleeing pickpocket.

At any rate, we cannot pursue these issues further here (but see Chapter 3). Rather, we will simply assume that the general human and social good that justifies the institution of the police is the protection of justifiably enforceable moral rights. Accordingly, such moral rights ought to be respected by social norms, and ought to be enshrined in the law, especially the criminal law.

But policing has a further important distinguishing feature. The end or moral good to be secured by the institution of the police is the protection of justifiably enforceable moral rights. But that is not all that needs to be said; we need also to speak of the *means* by which this end is to be achieved.[34]

Egon Bittner has propounded a very different theory of policing to the one we have suggested. However, his account is insightful. Bittner focuses attention on the means deployed by police to secure their ends. He has in effect defined policing in terms of the use or threat of coercive force.[35] He offers the following definition of policing: "a mechanism for the distribution of non-negotiable coercive force

---

but not an exclusive right to enforce in the narrow sense of protection against rights violations.

[32] This is consistent with there being a moral obligation to obey these laws; we are speaking here of the justification for the *enforcement* of such laws. For an account of the moral justification for obeying the law, see Miller, *Social Action*, pp. 141-51. See also David Luban, *Lawyers and Justice: An Ethical Study* (Princeton: Princeton University Press, 1988), Chapter 3.

[33] See Seumas Miller, "Shootings by Police in Victoria: The Ethical Issues", in T. Coady, S. James, S. Miller and M. O'Keefe (eds.), *Violence and Police Culture* (Melbourne: Melbourne University Press, 2000).

[34] See Miller, "Corruption and Anti-Corruption in the Profession of Policing", *op. cit.*, p. 88.

[35] Egon Bittner, *The Functions of Police in Modern Society* (Cambridge, Mass.: Gunn and Hain, 1980).

employed in accordance with the dictates of an intuitive grasp of situational exigencies".[36]

Bittner's account of policing is inadequate because it fails to say anything about the goals or ends of policing. Moreover, coercion is not the only means deployed by the police. Other typical means include negotiation, rational argument, and especially appeal to human and social values and sentiment. Moreover, whole taxonomies of police roles have been constructed on the basis of different mixes of methods, e.g. negotiation, and proximate ends of policing, e.g. maintaining peace. Consider Kleinig's taxonomy in terms of peace-keepers, crime-fighters, "social enforcers" and "emergency operators".[37] Here we need to stress that we are not advocating one or other of the possible configurations of these mixes. Hitherto, we have spoken of the ends of policing, and especially the fundamental purpose of ensuring the protection of justifiably enforceable moral rights. Now we are speaking of the means by which to achieve that purpose, and also of different roles (comprised of means and proximate ends) by means of which that ultimate purpose might be realised. Clearly there are different ways to achieve a given end; and there are different means, including different roles, by which to realise the fundamental and ultimate end of policing as we have described it. Whether to emphasise the crime-fighter or the peace-keeper role, for example, ought to be settled in large part on the basis of which is the most efficient and effective means to ensure the protection of (justifiably enforceable) moral rights. To this extent, our theory of policing is – at least in principle – neutral on questions of police methodology, and in relation to disputes between advocates of law enforcement roles and service roles for police.

To return to Bittner: in drawing attention to coercion, he has certainly identified a distinctive feature of policing, and one that separates police officers from (say) criminal justice lawyers and politicians.

Further, in stressing the importance of coercion, Bittner draws our attention to a fundamental feature of policing, namely its inescapable use of what in normal circumstances would be regarded as morally unacceptable activity. The use of coercive force, including in the last analysis deadly force, is morally problematic; indeed, it is ordinarily an infringement of human rights, specifically the right to physical security and the right to life. Accordingly, in normal circumstances the use of coercive force, and especially deadly force, is morally unacceptable. So it would be morally wrong, for example, for some private citizen to forcibly take a woman to his house for questioning or because he felt like female company.

Use of coercive force, especially deadly force, requires special moral justification precisely because it is in itself at the very least harmful, and possibly an infringement of human rights; it is therefore in itself morally wrong, or at least, so to speak, a prima facie moral wrong. Similarly, locking someone up deprives

---

36 Bittner, *op. cit.*

37 See, for example, Kleinig, *op. cit.*, p. 22f.

them of their liberty, and is therefore a prima facie moral wrong. It therefore requires special moral justification. Similarly with deception. Deception, including telling lies, is under normal circumstances morally wrong. Once again, use of deception requires special moral justification because it is a prima facie moral wrong. Intrusive surveillance is another prima facie moral wrong – it is an infringement of privacy. Therefore, intrusive surveillance requires special moral justification. And the same can be said of various other methods used in policing.

The point here needs to be made very clear lest it be misunderstood. Police use of coercion, depriving persons of their liberty, deception and so on, are morally problematic methods; they are activities which considered in themselves and under normal circumstances are morally wrong. Therefore, they stand in need of special justification. In relation to policing there is a special justification. These harmful and normally immoral methods are on occasion necessary in order to realise the fundamental end of policing, namely the protection of (justifiably enforceable) moral rights. An armed bank robber might have to be threatened with the use of force if he is to give himself up, a drug-dealer might have to be deceived if a drug ring is to be smashed, a blind eye might have to be turned to the minor illegal activity of an informant if the flow of important information he provides in relation to serious crimes is to continue, and a paedophile might have to be surveilled if evidence for his conviction is to be secured. Such harmful and normally immoral activities are thus morally justified in policing, and morally justified in terms of the ends that they serve.

The upshot of our discussion thus far is that policing consists of a diverse range of activities and roles, the fundamental aim or goal of which is the securing of (justifiably enforceable) moral rights; but it is nevertheless an institution the members of which inescapably deploy methods which are harmful; methods which are normally considered to be morally wrong. Other institutions which serve moral ends, and necessarily involve harmful methods, or prima facie wrongdoing, are the military – soldiers must kill in the cause of national self-defence – and political institutions. Australia's political leaders may need to deceive, for example, the political leaders of nations hostile to Australia, or their own domestic political enemies.

We have suggested that policing is one of those institutions the members of which need at times to deploy harmful methods; methods which in normal circumstances are morally wrong. In response to this, we need first to ask ourselves why it is that morally problematic methods such as coercion and deception are inescapable in policing. Why could not such methods be wholly abandoned in favour of the morally unproblematic methods already heavily relied upon, such as rational discourse, appeal to moral sentiment, reliance on upright citizens for information, and so on?

Doubtless in many instances morally problematic methods could be replaced. And certainly overuse of these methods is a sign of bad police work, and perhaps of the partial breakdown of police-community trust so necessary to police work.

However, the point is that the morally problematic methods could not be replaced in *all* or even *most* instances. For one thing, the violations of those moral rights which the police exist to protect are sometimes violations perpetrated by persons who are unmoved by rationality, appeal to moral sentiment, and so on. Indeed, such persons, far from being moved by well-intentioned police overtures, may seek to coerce or corrupt police officers for the purpose of preventing them from doing their moral and lawful duty; hence the truth of the claim that the use of coercive force in particular remains the bottom line in policing, no matter how infrequently coercion is in fact used. For another thing, the relevant members of the community may for one reason or another be unwilling or unable to provide the necessary information or evidence, and police may need to rely on persons of bad character or methods such as intrusive surveillance.

So the use of harmful methods cannot be completely avoided. It remains important to realise that these methods are in fact morally problematic; to realise that coercion, depriving someone of their liberty, deception, invasion of privacy and so on, are in fact in themselves harmful. Indeed, these methods constitute prima facie wrongdoing, and some of them constitute – under normal circumstances – human rights violations. In the final section of this chapter, we consider some of the elements of this means/end problematic in policing.

Moral Rights in Policing: Means and Ends

In drawing attention to the use of harmful methods by police, we are far from denying the moral acceptability of these methods. The key point is that the use of any particular harmful method may be morally justified in the circumstances.[38] When police officers act in accordance with the legally enshrined and morally justified principles governing the use of harmful methods, they achieve three things at one and the same time: they do what is morally right; their actions are lawful; and – given these laws are the result of properly conducted democratic processes – they act in accordance with the will of the community.

Nevertheless, the use of harmful methods in the service of moral ends – specifically the protection of (justifiably enforceable) moral rights – gives rise to a number of problems in policing. Here we will mention only four.

Firstly, the working out of these moral principles and the framing of accompanying legislation is highly problematic in virtue of the need to strike a balance between the moral rights of victims and the moral rights of suspects.

Obviously suspects – people who are only suspected of having committed a crime, but who have not been tried and found guilty – have moral rights. Suspects have a right to life, a right not to be physically assaulted, and a right not to be

---

[38] We are here speaking of morally acceptable harmful methods. Torture, for example, is a morally harmful method which arguably ought never to be used by police.

subjected to undue psychological harassment or intimidation. More generally, suspects have a right to procedural justice, including the right to a presumption of innocence and a fair trial.[39]

On the other hand, the police and the criminal justice system do not principally exist to protect the rights of suspects. They exist to protect the rights of victims and to ensure that offenders are brought to trial for appropriate disposition.[40] Accordingly, if the police believe on the basis of adequate evidence that a particular person is guilty of a serious crime, then the police are obliged to do their utmost to arrest and charge the suspect, and provide sufficient evidence to enable his or her successful prosecution.

However, there is inevitably a certain tension between these two moral requirements of the police – the requirement to respect the moral rights of suspects (including the duty to make available evidence that may assist a suspect) and the requirement to apprehend, and provide evidence to ensure the conviction of, offenders. And the procurement of such evidence may inevitably involve the kinds of justified, but harmful, actions we have been speaking of.

This tension has to be somehow resolved by framing laws that strike a moral balance between, on the one hand, ensuring that the rights of suspects are protected, and on the other, providing the police with sufficient powers to enable them to successfully gather evidence and apprehend offenders (especially rights violators).

This tension, and any resolution of it, is further complicated by the social, institutional and technological contexts in which they operate. A set of laws might be thought to have struck an appropriate ethical balance between the moral rights of suspects and the provision of necessary powers to police, until one considers the criminal justice institutional context. For example, if putting young offenders into the system merely has the effect of breeding criminals, then this needs to be a factor taken into consideration in framing laws, including laws governing the nature and extent of police powers. Similarly, technological developments, such as surveillance technology and high-level encryption products, can justify either restrictions on police powers or extensions to police powers.

A second problem in this area has already been mentioned. It arises when the three desiderata mentioned above come apart. That is, a problem arises when what the law prescribes is not morally sustainable, or at least is not morally acceptable to the community or significant sections of the community. Dramatic examples of the gap between law and the morality of significant sections of the community include the discriminatory race laws in South Africa under apartheid, the laws against

---

[39] Here we are assuming that rights to procedural justice are institutional *moral* rights.

[40] This is putting things simply, even simplistically, but it makes no difference to the main point we are seeking to make here. Consider, in this connection, the restorative justice movement; it sees itself as an alternative to punishment-oriented conceptions of the criminal justice system. (See Chapter 6 below.)

homosexuality in Britain earlier this century, and the current laws in relation to prostitution and cannabis in parts of Australia. Other kinds of examples include obvious loopholes and deficiencies in the law. For example, legislation in relation to telephone interception in this country might be thought to reflect appropriate moral principles, yet other forms of surveillance using new technology are not yet subject to laws reflecting these principles.

In all these kinds of situations, police are placed in an invidious position, and one calling for discretionary ethical judgement. It is a lose/lose situation. In the first kind of example, while they are under a moral obligation to enforce the law, they may be unsure that the laws they are enforcing are in fact morally justifiable. Certainly they are aware that the laws in question are regarded as immoral by significant sections of the community. Recourse to justifiably enforceable moral rights, including human rights, is helpful in this context. For in so far as such rights provide an objective moral standard, and in so far as this objective moral standard comes to be widely accepted, then the uncertainty arising from subjective moral standards will cease to be a problem.

In the second kind of example, the law may allow police to engage in activities they believe to be immoral, and which the community believes to be immoral, and yet engaging in these activities may enable them to secure convictions they would otherwise be unable to secure. Clearly the resolution of this problem lies in bringing the law into line with objective moral principles.

A third problem in this area remains even after the provision of laws that strike the appropriate moral balance mentioned above, and even when laws are not in need of revision. This problem seems to arise out of inherent features of police work.

There is a necessity for police to be given a measure of professional autonomy to enable them to exercise discretion. Thus, individual police officers have a significant measure of legal authority.[41] A police officer is legally empowered to "intervene – including stopping, searching, detaining and apprehending without a warrant any person whom he, with reasonable cause, suspects of having committed any such offence or crime"[42] – at all levels of society.

Moreover, the law has to be interpreted and applied in concrete circumstances. There is a need for the exercise of discretion by police in interpretation and application of the law. Further, upholding and enforcing the law is only one of the ends of policing; others include maintaining of social calm and the preservation of life. When these various ends come into conflict, there is a need for the exercise of police discretion, and in particular the need for the exercise of discretionary *moral* judgement. (See Chapter 2 for a more detailed discussion of police discretion.)

---

[41] On general issues of autonomy and accountability in policing in Australia, see David Moore and Roger Wettenhall (eds.), *Keeping the Peace: Police Accountability and Oversight* (Canberra: University of Canberra, 1994).

[42] *NSW Crimes Act*, no. 40, section 352, sub-section 2(a) (1990).

The unavoidability of the exercise of discretionary moral judgement in policing means that it will never be sufficient for police simply to learn, and act in accordance with, the legally enshrined moral principles governing the use of harmful methods. On the other hand, our normative teleological account of policing in terms of the goal of protecting (justifiably enforceable) moral rights provides the theoretical means to satisfactorily resolve some of these dilemmas requiring discretionary moral judgement.

A fourth, and final, problem concerns the proper scope of the institution of the police. It is evident that trans-national crime is on the increase. Accordingly, national law enforcement agencies are increasingly involved in trans-national (and therefore trans-jurisdictional) law enforcement collaboration. Further, there has been a growth in private policing, including in the area of criminal investigations of fraud and white-collar crime. It might be thought that these developments threaten an institutional conception of policing. Given these developments, does it still make sense to talk of the *institution* of the police? We suggest that it does still make sense. Very briefly, while the notion of an institution is tied to the realisation of certain ends, it is not necessarily the notion of a compartmentalised entity unrelated to other like institutions. We can still think of a specific organisation as an institution, notwithstanding the fact that it has strong and important collaborative connections with like institutions, and notwithstanding the fact that other somewhat dissimilar organisations perform similar roles. Of course, this says nothing about the desirability of these developments. On the teleological account of institutions that we are offering, whether or not trans-national collaboration and/or private-sector policing is to be welcomed or spurned depends on its contribution to the moral good that justifies the institution of the police, namely the protection of legally enshrined, justifiably enforceable, moral rights.

Chapter 2

Authority and Discretion in Policing[1]

In Chapter 1, *inter alia*, we offered a (normative) teleological account of the institution of the police. Institutions consist of individual persons who occupy roles defined in terms of tasks, and rules, regulations and procedures. Normatively speaking, these roles are related to one another in terms of their contribution to the goal(s) or end(s) or function(s) of the institution, and also (usually) hierarchically. In the case of the institution of the police, the end or function is the protection of (justifiably enforceable) legally enshrined moral rights. The relationship between the constitutive roles of an institution can be referred to as the "structure" of the institution.

Aside from the explicitly stated or defined tasks, rules, regulations and procedures, there is an important implicit and informal dimension of an institution roughly describable as "institutional culture". This notion comprises the attitudes, values, norms, and the ethos or "spirit" which pervades an institution. Culture in this sense determines much of the activity of the members of that institution, or at least the manner in which that activity is undertaken. So while the explicitly determined rules and tasks may say nothing about being "secretive" or "sticking by one's mates come what may" or having a hostile or negative attitude to particular social groups, these attitudes and practices may in fact be pervasive; they may be part of the culture. Notoriously, police culture has negative, as well as positive, elements, e.g. the so-called "blue wall of silence".

While the structure, function and culture of an institution provide a framework within which individuals act, they do not fully determine the actions of individuals. There are a number of reasons for this. For one thing, rules and regulations, norms and ends cannot cover every contingency that might arise; for another, rules, norms and so on, themselves need to be interpreted and applied. Moreover, changing circumstances and unforeseeable problems make it desirable to vest individuals with discretionary powers to rethink and adjust old rules, procedures and norms, and sometimes elaborate new ones.

Inevitably, the individuals who occupy roles have varying degrees of discretionary power in relation to their actions. These discretionary powers are of different kinds and operate at different levels. For example, senior and middle-level public servants have discretion in the way they implement policies, in their

[1] An earlier and much briefer version of this chapter was authored by Seumas Miller and appeared as "Authority, Discretion and Accountability: The Case of Policing", in C. Sampford, N. Preston and C. Bois (eds.), *Public Sector Ethics: Finding and Implementing Values* (London: Routledge, 1998), pp. 37-53.

allocations of priorities and resources, and in the methods and criteria of evaluation of programs. Indeed, senior public servants often exercise discretion in relation to the formulation of policies. Consider that Gordon Chase, the New York Health Services Administrator, conceived, developed and implemented the methadone program in New York in the early 1970s, notwithstanding political opposition to it.[2] Lower echelon public servants also have discretionary powers. Police officers have to interpret rules and regulations, customs officers have the discretionary power to stop and search one passenger rather than another, and so on.

Moreover, it is not only the individual actions of institutional actors that are not fully determined by structure, function and culture. Many joint or cooperative actions that take place in institutions are not determined by structure, function or culture. For example, a senior public servant might put together a team of like-minded people and they may pursue a specific agenda which is not one determined by the prevailing institutional structure, function or culture, and is even in part inconsistent with them. We take it that some of the post-Wood Royal Commission initiatives within the NSW Police Service, e.g. team policing and intelligence-driven policing methods, are examples of such internal joint or collective discretionary activity.[3]

It should also be noted that legitimate individual or collective discretionary activity undertaken within an institution is typically facilitated by a rational internal structure, including role structure and policy and decision-making procedures, and by a rational institutional culture. By "rational", it is here meant both internally consistent and rational in the light of the institution's purposes. Arguably, the police structure and culture in many contemporary police services are not rational in this sense. In particular, a culture of secrecy and solidarity amongst street cops is – from the standpoint of this rationality, as opposed to the rationality of self-interested factions – inconsistent with a hierarchical organisational structure preoccupied with accountability. Accordingly, it is likely that many (individual and collective) discretionary judgements will be ones that do not contribute to the realisation of the institution's purposes, even if they do facilitate the narrow self-interest of individuals and factional elements.

Aside from the internal dimensions of an institution, there are its external relationships, including its relationships to other institutions. In particular, there is the extent of the independence of an institution from other institutions, including government. Here it should be noted that, strictly speaking, independence is not the same thing as autonomy, but is rather a necessary condition for it. An institution possessed of independence from other institutions might still lack autonomy, if it lacked the kinds of rational internal structure and culture noted above. Indeed, internal conflicts can paralyse an institution to the point where it becomes incapable of pursuing its institutional purposes.

---

[2] D. P. Warwick, "Ethics of Administrative Discretion", in J. L. Fleishman (ed.), *et al.*, *Public Duties: The Moral Obligations of Public Officials* (Cambridge, Mass.: Harvard University Press, 1981), p. 93.

[3] Justice James Wood, Royal Commission into Corruption in the New South Wales Police Service, 1994-7.

Police Independence

The extent to which an institution – as distinct from an individual member of an institution – ought to have independence from government turns in large part on the function of that institution, and the extent to which it is necessary for that institution to have independence in order to properly carry out its function(s) or end(s). For example, the judiciary needs a high level of independence from the legislature and the executive, if it is to properly carry out its specialised tasks of interpreting and applying the law.

Institutional independence needs to be seen in the context of the so-called "separation of powers". Specifically, the executive, the legislature and the judiciary ought to be kept separate; otherwise too much power is concentrated in the hands of a unitary state agency. It is highly dangerous for those who make laws also to be the ones who apply those laws. Politicians, for example, need to be subject to laws adjudicated by judges who are institutionally independent of politicians, on pain of undue influence on judicial processes and outcomes.

Historically, the proper extent of independence of one institution from another has been problematic, and is in any case a matter of striking a balance between competing considerations. To what extent should the public service be independent of the government of the day? The public service exists to serve the public interest by implementing the policies of the government. So on the one hand, the public service must be responsive to the elected government of the day. Yet on the other hand, the public service must have a degree of independence in order to ensure that proposed policies are lawful and fully and accurately costed, and that government ministers are provided with "frank and fearless" advice in relation to their policies.[4]

There is inevitably a tension arising from the sometimes disparate commitments of public servants to the policies and therefore interests of the government of the day, on the one hand, and to the public interest on the other. But this does not mean that it is not capable of more or less satisfactory resolution by means of striking a balance between these commitments when they come apart. Any attempt to resolve this tension once and for all is problematic. For here there are apparently only two options, neither of which is palatable. Firstly, the public interest as interpreted by public servants might be allowed to override the directives of the government – resulting in a public service unresponsive to the elected government. Secondly, and alternatively, the public service could be denied any latitude to provide bottom-up, independent input to government – resulting in a politically motivated, slavishly loyal, public service that unhesitatingly implements policies it knows to be unjust, unworkable, not financially viable, unlawful or otherwise against the public interest. Such a public service might even engage in cover-ups and improprieties on behalf of the government.

---

[4] For discussions of public service accountability in a range of different countries, see J. G. Jabbra and O. P. Dwivedi, *Public Service Accountability: A Comparative Perspective* (Kumarian Press, 1988).

Although police services in contemporary liberal democracies are public-sector agencies, they provide a somewhat different kind of example.[5] Certainly there is an important and difficult issue in relation to the institutional independence of the police. Evidently police need to have a considerable degree of operational autonomy, if they are properly to discharge their functions of upholding the law, maintaining the peace, and thereby securing the moral rights of citizens. This is partly a matter of efficiency and effectiveness; the police are, or should be, the experts. It is also in part a matter of the separation of powers doctrine mentioned above; politicians, for example, need to be subject not only to an independently adjudicated law, but also to an independently enforced law. If a powerful politician, or powerful group of politicians, act unlawfully, appropriately authorised police must investigate, arrest and charge them. In order to ensure that the police effectively carry out these tasks in relation to government, they need to have a substantial degree of independence from government.

Moreover, the police must not simply come to be the instrument of government policies. For the priority of the police is to serve the law, and on our account, to protect moral rights enshrined in the law. The police states of communist Eastern Europe, Nazi Germany, Iraq under Saddam Hussein, and the like, are testimony to the importance of a substantial degree of police independence from government in favour of serving legally enshrined moral rights. Indeed, police operational autonomy has on occasion been abridged by democratically-elected governments in order, for example, to create and preserve a manageable level of public disorder from which the incumbent political party and their supporters may politically or materially benefit. This is evidently what happened in the 1970s in Queensland, Australia, during the premiership of Joh Bjelke-Petersen.[6] The point to be made here is that the police ought not to be used for narrow political purposes. Such use is an infringement of the operational autonomy of the police. It is also an inappropriate function for the police to be performing; the police should be above politics, at least in this sense of politics.

Direct ministerial control of policing was eschewed in Mr. Justice Lusher's 1981 Report of the Commission to Inquire into New South Wales Police Administration:

> ...a distinction is to be drawn between the function of government in the administration of justice and possibly law enforcement on the one hand, and most, if not all, other areas of the government function. In the latter, whilst subject to the law in the broad sense, the area of policy and the views and intentions of the government of the day are necessarily reflected quite commonly and properly. The keeping of the peace, preventing of crime, and the detection of offenders and bringing them to justice are singularly related to the

---

[5] For a useful introductory discussion of this issue, see Keith Bryett, Arch Harrison and John Shaw, "Police and Government in a Democracy", in their *An Introduction to Policing*, Vol. 2 (Butterworths, 1994), pp. 39-57

[6] Evan Whitton, *The Hillbilly Dictator: Australia's Police State* (Sydney: ABC Enterprises, 1988).

> law and its application in practice, and the activity is governed by the law, to be carried out within it and always subject and answerable to it.[7]

Acknowledgment of the formally autonomous nature of policing has (largely) ensured its operational autonomy from direct party-political control in New South Wales. This convention, and the thread of legal reasoning that supports it, informed Mr. Justice Lusher's interpretation of Section 4 of the *Police Regulation Act, 1899*. The Lusher Report suggested the Commissioner of Police's governance of the NSW Police Force was "subject to the directions of the Minister...", but such "direction" must not limit the Commissioner's unreviewable discretionary authority. The Report distinguished the Minister's authority from that of the NSW Police Commissioner as: "...the responsibility [of the Minister for Police] for the provision of resources and for ensuring that police act efficiently and effectively and according to law from the responsibility of the police themselves for law enforcement."[8]

Justice Lusher's concept of police operational autonomy reflected the 1962 findings of the United Kingdom's Royal Commission on the Police:

> The duties which it is generally agreed in the evidence should be performed by chief constables unhampered by any kind of external control are not capable of precise definition, but they cover broadly what we referred to earlier as 'quasi-judicial' matters; that is, the enforcement of the criminal law in particular cases involving, for example, the pursuit of enquiries and decisions to arrest or prosecute...
>
> We entirely accept that it is in the public interest that a chief constable, when dealing with these quasi-judicial matters, should be free from the conventional processes of democratic control and influence.[9]

Were one to accept the concept of the "quasi-judicial" nature of policing, one might then agree with the notions of Lusher and others, that policing should stand to some extent separate from direct ministerial control in an analogous manner to the judiciary.[10] Here it is important to stress that this quasi-judicial nature of policing pertains to evidence-gathering in relation to crimes, arrest of suspects, and the like. It does not pertain to the adjudication of cases; to this extent, it does not conflict with the judicial role.

Notwithstanding the acceptability of this notion of the quasi-judicial nature of policing, and the consequent need for a degree of police independence, the precise nature and extent of that required independence remains unclear. The 1994-7 *Royal Commission into the New South Wales Police Service: Final Report*, Vol. II, Chapter 3, pp. 243-5, concerned itself with the ministerial direction of the police. At Paragraph 3.26, it invoked a distinction between *policy* matters and *operational*

---

[7] The Hon. Mr. Justice Lusher, *Report of the Commission to Inquire into New South Wales Police Administration* (Sydney: NSW Government Printer, 1981), p. 680.

[8] *ibid.*, p. 183.

[9] *The Royal Commission on the Police*: *Cmnd. 1728: Final Report*, 1962, paras. 87 and 88.

[10] For a contrary view, see Laurence Lustgarten, *The Governance of the Police* (London: Sweet and Maxwell, 1986), p. 24.

matters, and indicated that the latter were the preserve of the police, the former of the Minister.

However, this distinction is problematic. It is at the very least an oversimplification to claim that policing can be divided into two parts, one designated "policy", the other "operations". The further notion that the part determined to be "policy" can be unproblematically handed to a political figure is doubtful. Lawrence Lustgarten, writing from the British experience, points out the difficulties inherent in trying to make out this distinction:

> The precise pedigree of the distinction is unclear. It appears by implication in the [British] Police Authorities (Powers) Bill introduced by Jack Straw MP in 1980, attracting some bipartisan interest. This would enable police authorities to determine "policies". Lawyers will recall its appearance in the speech of Lord Wilberforce in *Anns v. London Borough of Merton [1978] A.C. 728, 754-755*. It is possible that the rigid division can coherently be maintained in the relatively uncontentious area of negligence law but a glance at... executive decisions shows that it breaks down entirely in relation to policing.
>
> More precisely some of the crucial "policy" decisions are about "operations". The method of policing, for example, will determine whether the force relies upon computerised information collected by various forms of pressure upon those at the edges of criminal involvement, leading to isolated "swoops" upon subjects but otherwise remaining aloof from the public, or an intensive commitment to street patrols leading to personal knowledge of most people in the area, involvement in community welfare projects and coordination with other "care and control" agencies in crime prevention. The choice could be described as policy, but its concrete manifestations are in the day to day contact with the public – abrasive or supportive – and it is these which may produce dissatisfaction and demands for change. "Swamp 81"[11] in Brixton is only the most spectacularly disastrous example; public strip-searching, excessive force in dealing with youths congregating on the street, or attempts to gain access to confidential school records of a particular pupil are more typical examples of causes of antagonism.
>
> The distinction becomes even less tenable when one examines the decision to set up a drug squad. This involves allocation of manpower and related resources that would otherwise be used in alternate ways. In other words, it represents a decision that drugs deserve greater or increased attention when compared to traffic control, burglary or rape. It may also have serious consequences for relations with various groups within the community – innocent persons feel harassed by searches; women or householders who feel that the safety of the streets or their property is not receiving sufficient protection. The decision is highly controversial and a classic example of political choice. Yet it could equally well be categorised as "operational" – it merely involves reassignment of a limited number of constables to particular duties.[12]

We have been discussing institutional independence in the context of the interface of police and the government of the day. Enough has been said by way of demonstrating that the notion of the police as simply the instrument of government

---

[11] In 1981, "Operation Swamp" was undertaken in Brixton, London, by the Special Patrol Group of the London Metropolitan Police. It involved saturation policing, and riots ensued. It was the subject of *The Scarman Report*.

[12] Lustgarten, *op. cit.*, pp. 20-21.

is unsustainable. On the other hand, determining the precise nature and extent of police independence has turned out to be extremely difficult. We have emphasised the importance of maintaining a degree of police independence from government. However, it is equally important to point to the dangers of high levels of police independence. After all, the police are the coercive arm of the State, and historically the abuse of their powers has been an ever-present threat. Specifically, the police institution as the coercive arm of the State does need to be subjected to (at least) the constraint and influence of the community via democratically-elected bodies, notably the government of the day.

As is the case with the independence of other institutions, there is a need to strike a balance between, on the one hand, the independence of the police, and on the other hand, the need for: (a) community and government control of the police, and; (b) police accountability for their methods and actions.

Police Accountability

If an institution has substantial independence from other institutions, and if that institution has a very hierarchical structure, then those who occupy the upper echelons will have a relatively high degree of discretionary power. Military commanders, especially in time of war, are a case in point. Police Commissioners in times of emergency are a further case in point. But now consider the extraordinary powers possessed by police in authoritarian regimes, such as former Soviet Union. Indeed, the power of the one-time head of the secret police, Beria, became so great as to be thought to be a threat to the de facto head of state, Stalin, who had Beria murdered as a consequence.

Evidently the power of the police needs to be constrained, and there are a number of ways to achieve this. One way is to devolve police authority in a quasi-federated structure, as is the case in the UK, where the police are still to an extent a function of local government; there is no national police as such.[13] Another way is to delimit their sphere of operational autonomy in favour of the policies, including policies in relation to police methods, of democratically-elected government; although, as we have seen, this can be counterproductive. A third, and much favoured, method is to ensure accountability by way of oversight bodies, such as Ombudsmen, Police Boards, and the like.

Institutional independence stands in some tension with this highly desirable feature of institutions, accountability. Accountability is clearly a matter of great importance when it comes to institutions with great power, and especially institutions, such as the police and the military, that are possessed of near monopolistic powers of physical coercion in relation to their citizens.

---

[13] In fact police are subject to central government via the Home Office, as well as to local government via the Police Authority. However, the authority of local government has been diluted by the 1995 requirement that the Police Authorities have a significant number of members nominated by the Home Secretary. See Peter Neyroud and Alan Beckley, *Policing, Ethics and Human Rights* (Cullompton, Devon: Willan Publishing, 2001), p. 97.

The notion of accountability is not the same as, but yet should go hand in hand with, the notion of responsibility. Here we need first to distinguish some different senses of responsibility. Sometimes to say that someone is responsible for an action is to say that the person reasoned or deliberated concerning some action, then formed an intention to perform that action, and finally acted on that intention and did so on the basis of those reasons. However, on other occasions what is meant by the expression "being responsible for an action" is that the person in question occupies a certain institutional role, and that the occupant of that role is the person who has the institutionally-determined right and duty to decide what is to be done in relation to certain matters. If the matters in question include directing the actions of other agents, then the occupant of the role is not only responsible for what transpires, he or she is a person in authority. So being in authority is a species of being responsible in our second sense of that term. We will come back to the notion of authority later on in this chapter.

If a person is responsible in this second sense for some action or sphere of activity, then typically that person is, or at least ought to be, accountable for it. To say that someone is accountable in this sense is to say that he or she is able to be, or ought to be able to be, called to account for and to justify the action or actions in question. Sometimes accountability brings with it liability, and an adverse judgement on the part of those to whom one is accountable can result in the infliction of punishment. Given the opportunity in policing for wrongdoing, and the historical tendency to corruption in police services, accountability is obviously of great importance.

The notion of accountability is complex. There are different kinds of accountability and different persons to whom one can be accountable. Personal accountability is accountability to oneself, and typically involves the provision of justifications to oneself for one's actions. With the possible exception of psychopaths, each of us has moral standards and values. There are some things we simply would not do, and there are other things we regard as so important we ought to do them even if it is not in our interest. Accountability is not to be equated with liability, but it typically implies liability, especially punishment. In relation to personal accountability, if we fall short of our own moral standards and values, we suffer shame or remorse, or at the very least are disappointed with ourselves.

As members of a community or society, we are also accountable to others in a number of ways. Obviously we are legally accountable. Some of our actions are subject to legal scrutiny and judgement. Moreover, sanctions, including punishment in the form of imprisonment, can flow from adverse legal judgements. But we are also held morally accountable by the other individuals and groups. Our actions are judged as unfair, weak and so on, by our friends, spouses and the members of the community to which we belong. Moreover, adverse judgement is typically followed by expressed attitudes and actions that signal disapproval and even contempt. Such judgement-making and expressed disapproval constitutes a process of holding individuals accountable. And while this process is informal and carries no legal sanctions, it is one that can powerfully influence our behaviour.

As members of an institution, we are not only morally and legally accountable, we are of course administratively accountable, and in police institutions there are typically an elaborate array of institutional mechanisms to ensure accountability. In recent times, the number and kinds of these mechanisms has increased markedly, to the point where the costs, as well as the benefits, of accountability mechanisms are beginning to become an issue of concern. For example, the existence of a plethora of both internal and external administrative accountability mechanisms in Australian police services is a matter of concern to some Australian police.[14]

A particular problem for accountability procedures arises in institutional contexts. Obviously a person ought to be held accountable for his or her own actions. However, in institutional contexts there are many actions, outcomes and spheres of activity to which many different persons in fact contribute.

Because of the cooperative nature of activity in institutions, it is often unclear who is actually responsible for some untoward outcome, and the extent of their contribution to that outcome. This issue in moral philosophy is known as the "problem of many hands". An example that comes to mind in the recent history of policing is the investigation of former Police Superintendent Harry Blackburn of the New South Wales Police.[15] After a lengthy police investigation, Blackburn was falsely accused of being a sex offender. However, in the course of the investigation, hypotheses were accepted without adequate testing, evidence eliminating Blackburn as a suspect was discredited, witnesses were extensively prompted, and so on. The point of interest here is that these errors, acts of negligence and so on, were not committed by one person, but by quite a large group of individuals, each of whom was supposedly being guided by their own judgement. So the question arises as to how moral responsibility is, as it were, to be parcelled out. And of course there are the corresponding questions as to how accountability and liability are to be ascribed to these different individuals.

Authority and Discretion in Policing

Thus far we have discussed the institutional independence and accountability of police services *qua* institution. In this section, we turn directly to the consideration

---

[14] For example, arguably the system for handling complaints against NSW police officers is unwieldy, resource intensive and ineffective. The complaints system involves a multiplicity of internal and external agencies, including the internal affairs department of the police, local area police commanders and various of their committees, as well as the independent bodies, the NSW Ombudsman and the Police Integrity Board. There is evidence that too many complaints are investigated, and too many of these inadequately investigated, i.e. efficiency and effectiveness would require that there were fewer, but better quality, investigations of complaints. (Seumas Miller, David Biles, Tracey Green and Jerry Ratcliffe, *Report on Drug-related Complaints Against the NSW Police* (Australian Research Council-funded SPIRT Grant, 2001), and Jerry Ratcliffe, David Biles, Tracey Green and Seumas Miller, "Drug-Related Complaints against Police: Some Findings from a NSW Study", *Policing: An International Journal of Police Strategies and Management*, March, 2005.)

[15] Frank Davis, *Blackburn: A Forensic Disaster* (Sydney: Harry the Hat Publications, 1990).

of the authority and discretion of individual police officers.[16] In order to set the stage for our discussion, we first present four case studies that exemplify the exercise of authority and discretion.

Case Studies[17]

Case Study 2.1 The Screaming Skull

A hawkish former Israeli general is invited by Australian Jewry to speak at Sydney Town Hall. The Arab community obtains a street march permit to protest his presence in Australia; a thin line of police separate the marchers and the arriving audience. The protest is passing off without incident, although National Front members are in the crowd on the footpath. Also present, a well-known self-proclaimed Nazi, "The Screaming Skull". "The Skull" is using offensive, anti-Semitic language.

Present also, a police sergeant with a reputation for poor judgement in public-ordering situations. He peremptorily orders a constable to arrest The Skull and charge him. Operationally, this is a bad call; this action may create a "flashpoint" for disorder and a widespread disturbance – the very situation police have been posted there to prevent. The constable tells the sergeant he will assist him to make the arrest – if he is ordered to – but will not arrest or charge The Skull himself.

Case Study 2.2 Missing the Boat

Police are called to a liner at the overseas terminal, Sydney; a customs officer has found a small amount of marijuana in a plastic envelope, maybe enough for half a joint, in a boarding crew member's jacket pocket. The seaman explains that he bought a "deal" for personal use at Kings Cross the evening prior whilst drunk, and thought he'd consumed it; at the time of boarding, he was unaware of the residue in his jacket.

Prosecution for "possession" of a drug, including marijuana, will involve his dismissal by the shipping company; the ship will leave Sydney that afternoon, stranding him in Australia. A conviction will result in the seaman's union withdrawing his membership, losing him his livelihood. He'd been flown to Australia to take the place of another crew member – and will become indebted to the shipping company for air-fares. He is penniless, having spent the remainder of

---

[16] For a useful selection of articles on police discretion, see John Kleinig (ed.), *Handled with Discretion: Ethical Issues in Police Decision Making* (Lanham, Maryland: Rowman and Littlefield, 1996). See also Kenneth Culp Davis, *Discretionary Justice: A Preliminary Inquiry* (Baton Rouge, LA: Louisiana State University, 1969), and Edwin Delattre, *Character and Cops: Ethics in Policing* (Washington, DC: American Enterprise Institute, 1994), Chapter 4.

[17] Case Studies 2.1 and 2.2 and some of the ensuing discussion originally appeared in Seumas Miller, John Blackler and Andrew Alexandra, *Police Ethics* (Keon, 1995).

the travelling expenses advanced him by the shipping company. He will become subject to detention and deportation from Australia – at some cost to the Commonwealth – as an inadvertently illegal immigrant. He is the sole support of his wife and child in the UK – they have been living on relief and this is his first ship in six months.

Case Study 2.3 Grand Theft Auto

CID officers were frequently asked to a factory to arrest and charge (as was the company policy) employees caught stealing the little cast-metal scale model autos (the 50p Corgi Matchbox type) the company manufactured. These arrests were, however, a source of some discussion amongst the DCs, since the value of the items was small and the crime insignificant.

A call was received by CID asking officers to come to the boardroom of the same factory to make an arrest. The officers learned that it was alleged that one of the managers had altered the production instructions in the plant, substituting inferior materials and selling the high-quality metal specified for the casting of the cars. By so doing, he had accumulated and sold some £20,000-worth ($AU50,000) of metal. The Board of Directors of the company was meeting to decide whether to file a legal charge against the manager. The CID, as they sifted the facts, were convinced of his guilt. They waited outside the boardroom, were served dinner and drinks, but were finally informed by the Chairman of the Board that the company had decided not to prosecute. It was suspected by the police that since the manager held stock in the company, they had decided to drop the case to avoid public embarrassment and possible financial loss.

Soon thereafter, the same company called to have an arrest made for stealing one of the 50p model cars, and were informed they would have to proceed in the matter by private summons.[18]

Case Study 2.4 David Martin

David Martin was a dangerous criminal being pursued by police in an underground subway in England in 1982. Cornered in the underground subway by armed police, Martin was persistently ordered by police to give himself up, but refused to do so. However, he made no hostile movements against the police. It was a case of passive non-compliance. The police were concerned that he might have a gun and might use it against them. Certainly his history indicated he was capable of this kind of action. On the other hand, if the police were to allow him to go free, his history indicated the lives of others would be at risk. Finally, the police decided not to shoot him but to rush and disarm him. He was found to be unarmed.[19]

---

[18] Peter K. Manning, "Rules, Colleagues and Situationally Justified Actions", in R. Blakenship (ed.), *Colleagues in Organisations* (New York: Wiley Press, 1978), pp. 263-89.
[19] P. A. J. Waddington, *The Strong Arm of the Law* (Clarendon Press, 1991), p. 62

Police Discretion

As noted in Chapter 1, individual police officers have a significant measure of legal power. They are legally empowered to stop, search, detain and so on, any person whom they with reasonable cause suspect of having committed a crime. Moreover, in exercising this authority, they interfere with the most fundamental human rights. Arresting someone is necessarily depriving the person of his or her liberty. And should a suspect attempt to evade or resist arrest, that person can under certain circumstances lawfully be deprived of his or her life by a police officer. For example, in some jurisdictions around the world, police officers are legally entitled to shoot fleeing persons suspected of serious crimes.

These substantial legal powers are to some extent discretionary.[20] For example, the decision whether to arrest a suspect, or merely issue him with a summons, is by law a matter of police discretion. Naturally it is required that such discretion be exercised on the basis of considerations such as the seriousness of the suspected offence, the likelihood that the suspect will abscond if merely summonsed, and so on. Although the police have considerable discretionary powers, they are also accountable for these actions to their superiors, to their departments of internal affairs, to the courts, and so on.

The discretionary powers of the police – including their implicit or explicit legally-granted powers – include the following.

First, the law has to be interpreted and applied in concrete circumstances. There is a need for the exercise of discretion by police in the interpretation and application of the law. Notoriously, police can (lawfully) choose not to enforce some laws in some circumstances, e.g. they can issue a caution in relation to a minor infringement, if they judge the outcome of an arrest to be deleterious to the peace.

In so far as it is legally permissible for the police not to enforce a given law in some circumstance, e.g. because to enforce it might prevent them from meeting a more important legal requirement, it is misleading to say that the police are in effect usurping the role of the legislature by ignoring the law. On the other hand, where the police do deliberately choose not to enforce a law because they believe it is immoral and/or the community does not accept it, then this creates ethical problems. Consider, in this connection, the police in South Africa under apartheid who refused to enforce the *Mixed Marriage and Immorality Act* outlawing sex and marriage across the colour bar. However, this problem is not one of a discretionary

---

[20] We do not mean to imply that there are not sometimes great differences in the discretionary powers of police from one jurisdiction and from one country to another. For example, generally speaking, UK and Australian police have greater discretionary powers than police in the US, where there is no concept of original authority and where "full enforcement" legislation exists in many states and at a federal level. See William C. Heffernan, "The Police and their Rules of Office: An Ethical Analysis", in William C. Heffernan and Timothy Stroup (eds.), *Police Ethics: Hard Choices in Law Enforcement* (New York: John Jay Press, 1985). See also Ian K. McKenzie and G. Patrick Gallagher, *Behind the Uniform: Policing in Britain and America* (Brighton, UK: Harvester/Wheatsheaf Press, 1989), p. 125.

judgement arising out of the need to apply or interpret the law in specific circumstances. Rather, it is an issue of determining when it is morally incumbent on police to refuse to enforce bad laws.

Concerning interpretation: in a well-known South African case, a policeman arrested a man for speaking abusively to him over the phone, claiming the offence had been committed in his presence. The court ruled that the place at which the offence was committed was in the house of the defendant and that therefore the crime had not been committed in the presence of the policeman. So the ruling went against the police officer. But it was not obvious that it would. At any rate, our point is that the interpretation and application of the law is not always a straightforward matter.

Second, the law does not, and cannot, exhaustively prescribe. Often it grants discretionary powers, or has recourse to open-ended notions such as that of the "reasonable man" or "reasonable suspicion". Accordingly, a number of police responses might be possible in a given situation, and all of them might be consistent with the law. Police discretion is involved at most stages of their work. It is often involved in the decision to investigate or not investigate a possible crime; this is in part because there are simply not enough resources to investigate all reported crimes. It is sometimes involved in the decision to arrest or not arrest. And it is sometimes involved in the decision to lay charges or not. Notoriously, police can lawfully use their discretion to target certain individuals or groups, e.g. members of minority racial groups, and leave themselves open to accusations of discrimination in so doing.

Third, upholding and enforcing the law is only one of the ends of policing, others include the maintaining of social calm and preservation of life. When these various ends come into conflict, there is a need for the exercise of police discretion. Consider, in this connection, Case Studies 2.1, 2.2 and 2.4. On our account of the ultimate ends of policing as the protection of (justifiably enforceable, legally enshrined) moral rights, there is a criterion in terms of which to resolve these conflicts between proximate ends. Nevertheless, there remains a need for discretionary judgement; such a criterion is far from being a mechanical procedure for determining "correct" actions in specified situations.[21]

Fourth, there is often a hard choice to make in relation to using specific means to achieve the ends of policing. This arises because of the nature of some of the methods deployed by police, including the routine use of coercion. Our theory of policing points to a distinctive feature of policing – the protection of moral rights by means of harmful methods – that gives rise to moral dilemmas. In general, these dilemmas need to be resolved by recourse to objective moral principles enshrined in laws, and therefore sanctioned by the community. However, inevitably such laws

---

[21] Howard Cohen ("Overstepping Police Authority", *Criminal Justice Ethics*, 6 (2), Summer/Fall 1987, p. 54) offers a plausible reasoning procedure for means/end decision-making in policing. However, by our lights, typically the inconsistent ends in the sorts of examples Cohen describes would either turn out to be competing moral *rights* in need of logical ordering, or the logical ordering in effect would have been done by the legislators – in which case the ends would presumably not be in competition.

are not sufficiently fine-grained to satisfactorily resolve what ought to be done in situations involving unique or unusual combinations of considerations; hence the need for discretionary judgements on the part of police.

Fifth, policing involves unforeseen situations and problems requiring an immediate, on the spot solution. It is therefore necessary to ensure that police have discretionary powers to enable them to provide such solutions.

Granted the inevitability of some discretionary powers of police, what further issues can be identified in relation to police discretion? One set of issues concerns the conceptual analysis of the concept of police discretion. What is police discretion? How does police discretion differ from related concepts, such as the concept of so-called "original authority"? More specifically, what is the proper extent of police discretion? We have seen that some degree of police discretion is *inevitable*, but this does not settle the question as to what extent of police discretion is *desirable*.

Another set of issues concerns the precise nature and extent of *particular* discretionary powers actually possessed by the police. Consider, for example, the discretionary power of the police to arrest or not arrest a murder suspect, as opposed to a person suspected of a minor theft. A further set of issues concerns the correctness or incorrectness of particular exercises of police discretion. The police officer in Case Study 2.1 has the power to arrest The Skull, but would it be correct for him to do so in the circumstances? A final set of issues concerns the accountability of police in relation to the exercise of their discretionary powers.

We will consider two matters. Firstly, we will look at the concept of original authority and its relation to police discretion. Second, we will consider the structure of some of the situations confronted by police and calling for the exercise of discretion.

Original Authority of the Police

Police officers need to exercise authority on a daily basis. But the notion of authority is a difficult one. We must distinguish between legal authority and moral authority. A police officer might have legal authority, but in virtue of his lack of credibility in a community, he might have no moral authority. Consider the moral authority of white police officers in a black South African township in the days of apartheid. Authority involves a relation between at least two people. In the case of legal authority, for example, the person *in* authority has a *right to command* the person *over* whom she has authority (to show their driver's licence, say), and correspondingly, that person has a *duty to obey* such lawful commands.

We also need to distinguish between power and authority. A large man might have power over a smaller one, but it would not follow that he had either legal or moral authority in relation to the small man. In some instances, de facto coercive power is a necessary condition for the holding of authority. This is true of police. If, for instance, police did not have the de facto power to apprehend criminals because (say) the criminals were too well-armed, then not only the effectiveness but also the authority of the police would be undermined. At the same time, it seems unlikely that effective policing could rely purely on the exercise of coercive force. Past a certain point, the exercise of coercive force is actually likely to undermine the authority of police; they come to be seen as a group who will try to have their way irrespective of the wishes and opinions of the community that they are supposedly serving, and ultimately irrespective of what they have been authorised to do. This is a disastrous outcome in two respects. First, the police will find it difficult to perform their legitimate role, given the dependence of the police on the community for achieving the defining purposes of police work. Second, the police will be engaged in activities that they are not authorised to undertake; they will be abusing their authority.

A further task to be performed here is to clarify the relationship between authority and the related notion of responsibility. In this connection, we must invoke our above-mentioned distinction between two different kinds of responsibility. Sometimes to say that someone is responsible for an action is simply to say that the person had a reason for performing the action, that the person had an intention to perform the action, and that the person actually performed the action. This is the ordinary everyday sense of "responsible", and we are responsible for most of our actions in this sense of being responsible.

However there is a different sense of responsibility. What is meant by the expression "being responsible for an action" in this second sense is that the person in question occupies a certain institutional role, and that the occupant of that role is the person who has the institutionally- or organisationally-determined legal and moral right, and duty, to decide what is to be done in relation to certain matters. So, for example, a mechanic in a workshop might be responsible for fixing all problems to do with brakes. Notice that even if the mechanic did not in fact fix any brakes – and therefore was not responsible for fixing brakes in our first sense of being responsible – he can still be said to be responsible for fixing brakes in our second sense of being responsible.

The notion of authority is a special case of being responsible in our second sense. We saw that the occupant of an institutional or organisational role who has a legal and moral right, and duty, to decide what is to be done in relation to certain matters is responsible for those matters. However, if those matters involve directing the actions of other persons, then the occupant of the role is said to be the person in authority in relation to these people he/she is directing. Thus, a police officer not only has responsibility in the sense in which the mechanic has responsibility, the police officer also has *authority*. For example, police officers have the authority to direct motorists or to arrest an offender.

Consider Case Study 2.4. The police officer who arrested Martin can be said to possess responsibility in all of our senses of that term. Firstly, the officer actually and intentionally arrested Martin, and did so for a reason, namely the fact that Martin was a dangerous offender. So the police officer was responsible for Martin's arrest in the ordinary sense of being responsible for an action.

Secondly, each of the police officers was – in virtue of being a sworn officer of the law present at that place at that time – responsible in our second sense for arresting Martin. It was the officer's responsibility to arrest Martin, and he would have been responsible in this sense even if he did not in fact arrest Martin, but rather simply let him go free. Further, since this responsibility involved directing or controlling the action of another person, namely Martin, it was not only an exercise of the officer's responsibility, it was an exercise of his authority.

In relation to the concept of original authority, we need to distinguish compliance with laws from obedience to the directives of men and women, especially one's superiors. Thus, according to the law, an investigating officer must not prosecute a fellow police officer if the latter is self-evidently innocent. On the other hand, he might be ordered to do so by his superior officer. Now individual police officers are held to be responsible to the law as well as their superiors in the police service. However, their first responsibility is to the law. So a police officer should disobey a directive from a superior officer that is clearly unlawful. However, the admittedly controversial doctrine of original authority goes further than this. It implies that there are at least some situations in which police officers have a right to disobey a superior's otherwise *lawful* command, if obeying it would prevent them from discharging their own obligations to the law.[22]

Consider Case Study 2.1. According to the doctrine of original authority, there are at least some actions, including the decision to arrest or not arrest (at least in some contexts), which are ultimately matters for the decision of the individual officer, and decisions for which he is, or might be, individually legally liable.[23] Accordingly, the police officer in Case Study 2.1 may be legally entitled to disobey his commanding officer to the extent of refusing to arrest The Skull, although not to the extent of refusing to assist the sergeant in the sergeant's arresting of The Skull. It is not that the sergeant has issued an obviously unlawful directive. Rather, the sergeant's authority to direct is overridden by the authority of the individual police

---

[22] Relevant legal cases here are the "Blackburn cases", principally *R v. Metropolitan Police Commissioner; Ex parte Blackburn [1968] 2 Q. B. 118* (cited in Bryett, *op. cit.*, p. 43), in which Lord Denning considered the Commissioner of the London Metropolitan Police "to be answerable to the law and to the law alone" in response to a demand for *mandamus* from a plaintiff seeking to get the courts to require police intervention, and *Fisher v. Oldham Corporation [1930] 2 K.B. 364* (cited in Bryett, *op. cit.*, p. 42), in which the court found the police service was not vicariously liable in virtue of the original authority of the office of constable. Concerning the exercise of original authority in decisions to arrest: In some jurisdictions proceeding by summons has increased significantly and officers do not possess original authority in respect of any part of the summons process. To this extent their original authority has diminished.

[23] A concept very close to original authority is sometimes referred to as a species of discretionary power, namely the concept of a discretionary decision that cannot be overridden or reversed by another official. See Ronald Dworkin, *Taking Rights Seriously* (Cambridge, Mass.: Harvard University Press, 1977), p. 32. Here we need to distinguish a decision that cannot as a matter of fact be overridden, e.g. the use of deadly force by a lone officer in the field, and a decision that cannot be overridden as a matter of law. Only the latter can be referred to as a species of authority.

officer in respect of the police officer's power to arrest, at least in some contexts. The contexts in question are ones in which the action of arresting a given person would prevent the police officer from discharging his obligations to the law, and (in this instance) his obligation to keep the peace, in particular. If this is indeed the legal situation, then it reflects a commitment to the ethical notion of professional autonomy. Police are being held to be akin to members of professional groups such as doctors. In the case of a surgeon, for example, it is up to the surgeon – and not the surgeon's employer – to decide whether or not to operate on a patient who might suffer complications if operated on.

Now consider Case Study 2.4. Could, or ought, one of these police officers have been required to shoot Martin, if he had been ordered to do so? Could, or ought, one of these police officers have been required to put his life at risk by rushing at Martin, if he had been ordered to do so? It is not clear that either of these directives would have been unlawful. What is evident is that, according to the doctrine of original authority, the authority of a superior officer to direct his subordinate police officer in this kind of case is overridden by the authority of the otherwise subordinate police officer to choose to put his or her own life at risk or to shoot (and face the possibility of a murder charge).

Concomitant with their first responsibility being to the law, individual police are held legally liable for their actions. This liability is both civil and criminal. Hence the police officer in Case Study 2.1 may have a real concern that he might be sued and be held liable for damages in a civil court, if his arrest of The Skull turned out to be unjustified in the circumstances, and led to (say) damage to persons and property.

Consider now Case Study 2.4, in which police officers are confronted with a situation of passive non-compliance by a criminal known to be dangerous. On the one hand, if they shoot him and he turns out to be unarmed, they might be up on a murder charge. On the other hand, they put their own lives at risk by rushing him and trying to overpower him. After all, there is reason to believe that he might be armed. Faced with this unpleasant dilemma, it might seem that a third option is preferable, namely the option to let him go free. Certainly this is an option available to ordinary members of the public when they confront armed and dangerous persons. But matters are somewhat different for the police. They have a moral and a legal duty to apprehend such persons. Failure to try to apprehend an armed and dangerous offender would amount to serious neglect of duty on their part. Indeed, if they simply allowed him to go free, and he went on to (say) murder some innocent person, then this neglect of duty might be held by a court to be criminal negligence.

Moreover, if a senior and superior officer issued an apparently lawful directive to these subordinate officers to shoot the offender, on the grounds that the evidence indicated that he was probably concealing a dangerous weapon and was highly likely to use it, the subordinate police officers might well be acting within their legal rights to refuse to do so. For they might disagree with the senior officer's judgement, and hold that they might find themselves liable for wrongful killing if it turned out that the offender was unarmed.

Perhaps the general moral principle underpinning this apparent legal right of individual police officers, including subordinate officers, to refuse to comply with apparently lawful directives to shoot is the moral enormity that we attach to taking someone else's life. The specific moral principle governing these actions of police dictates that if a certain police officer is to do the killing, then that very police officer (and not, for example, his superior) ought to be the one to decide whether or not he himself does that killing. If this is so, then the autonomy of police officers in these kinds of situation is not simply a species of professional autonomy deriving from the particular ends of the profession. Rather, it is a species of personal autonomy possessed by all human beings, viz. the moral right to decide for oneself whether or not one kills or refrains from killing a fellow human being in circumstances in which killing would be morally justified.[24]

The above-described individual civil and criminal liability of police officers stands in some contrast with military combatants. A civilian would in general sue the military organisation itself, rather than the soldier whose actions resulted in harm to the civilian. Moreover, presumably soldiers do not reserve a general institutional right to refuse to shoot to kill when (lawfully) ordered to do so by their commanding officers.[25] In keeping with the absence of such a general right, criminal liability in relation to negligence and many categories of wrongful killing is generally sheeted home to the military officer who issued the command, rather than his subordinates who were his instrument.

This notion of individual police officers' responsibility to the law, as opposed to their superior officers, and the concomitant legal liability of individual police officers, is known as "original" authority in order to differentiate it from mere "delegated" authority. An office with delegated – as opposed to original – authority is an office whose powers have been delegated by a higher authority. For example, person A might delegate her authority to make payments from her bank account to person B. Perhaps A does this for a brief period while she is overseas, and does it to enable her bills to be paid. Naturally, since B's authority to operate A's bank account is delegated authority only, A is in a position to remove that authority from B or to override B's decisions. Again, consider the role of supervisor in a large organisation. It might be that the supervisor of all staff in the Department of Philosophy is the Head of the Department. However, these powers to supervise

[24] If this is indeed the case, then it raises the question of whether a police officer would be morally entitled to refrain from killing an offender if there was a clear duty to kill the offender because this was the only way to protect the life of a third innocent person. The issue here is that of role (moral) obligations versus one's moral rights as an individual human being.

[25] On the other hand, perhaps they do reserve a moral right to refuse to shoot to kill; perhaps this is an inalienable moral right. If so, then the contrast drawn between the police and the military would be much less sharp. It could, however, still be drawn at the institutional level in terms of, for example, the notion of presumption. The presumption might be that an individual soldier would not be the one to decide whether or not he or she would shoot to kill in cases where he or she was directed by a superior to do so (or not to do so); rather the superior would be the one to decide. In the case of police officers, this would not be the case – there would be no such presumption in favour of a superior officer; rather the individual police officer about to do the shooting would be the one to decide. The situation is further muddied by the existence of paramilitary police roles, such as police snipers.

have been delegated by a higher authority, namely the Dean of the Faculty. Accordingly, in principle the decisions of the Head of the Department can be overridden by the Dean.

It is important to note that both the Dean and the Head of Department are subject to the law and to university regulations. Deans cannot override decisions of the Head of Department in a manner that infringes laws or regulations. For example, the Dean could not override a decision by the Head of Department to report a case of assault within the Department to the police. Similarly, the person in whose name the bank account is cannot override the decisions of the person with delegated authority in a manner that infringes laws or regulations. For example, even if it is A's bank account, A cannot override a decision of B's – as A's delegate – not to make a payment to a heroin dealer.

As already mentioned, the authority attaching to the office of constable is allegedly original, and not merely delegated, authority. In particular, the legal basis of an officer's discretionary power to arrest or not arrest a suspect, or to use deadly force in relation to a suspect, is the original authority attaching to the office of constable. Accordingly, certain decisions of police officers (allegedly) cannot be overridden by their superiors. In certain circumstances, if a police officer chooses not to arrest someone, a superior officer might not be legally entitled to insist that she do so. Again, if a police officer chooses not to shoot a suspect, a superior officer might not be legally – let alone morally – entitled to insist that he do so.

This notion of the original authority of individual police officers also needs to be distinguished from the distinct, albeit correlative, notion discussed above of the quasi-judicial independence of police forces from other institutions, including especially government. Police forces in Anglo-Australian liberal democracies have traditionally jealously guarded their independence from government on the grounds that they principally exist to uphold the law, and not simply to implement the political policies of the government of the day.

At any rate, the legal situation in relation to the doctrine of original authority in those countries in which it has been claimed to exist, namely the UK and Australia, seems unclear. While there is evidently in Anglo-Australian law this notion of the individual policeman or woman's original authority, there is also some legal support for the opposite view. For example, there is some legal support for the right of Police Commissioners to order their subordinates to arrest or not arrest people, irrespective of whether it is desirable or otherwise problematic for the subordinates to make those arrests.[26]

As far as the factual situation of police officers' exercise of this original authority is concerned, it can be argued that there is a contradiction between this notion of the individual police officer's independence on the one hand, and the reality of the hierarchical and militaristic structure of actual police forces, and the powerful strictures of police culture, on the other. Notionally, individual police

---

[26] See R. Hogg and B. Hawker, "The Politics of Police Independence", *Legal Service Bulletin*, Vol. 8, No. 4, 1983, and papers by Alderston, Goldring and Blazey, and Plehwe and Wettenhall, in David Moore and Roger Wettenhall (eds.), *Keeping the Peace: Police Oversight and Accountability* (Canberra: University of Canberra, 1994).

officers might have original authority, but in practice, it is sometimes suggested, they do what their superiors tell them, and they conform to conservative police cultural norms, including the norm of not reporting a fellow officer's misdemeanour. Moreover, there is the matter of organisational policy. For example, following a spate of shoplifting court cases being lost, a policy might be adopted within a police service that police officers were not to be content with a "reasonable cause to believe" standard as justifying the arrest of shoplifters, but should rather seek to establish a *prima facie* case before arresting people for shoplifting offences.

In addition to the legal and factual questions, there is a normative or value question concerning police original authority: this is the question whether it is desirable for individual police officers to have and to exercise original authority.

This question amounts to asking whether it is desirable: (a) for individual officers to have the legal right to make decisions on the basis of their judgement of what the law requires – and to do so, at least in some circumstances, even in the face of the commands of superior officers; (b) for individual officers to be legally liable for the untoward outcomes of these judgements, and; (c) for the administrative structures and cultural norms within the police services to be such that individual police officers in fact act on that original authority in a significant number of situations.

This is a vexed and complex issue. On the one hand, if the police officers in the lower echelons are in fact the most competent to make decisions in a variety of circumstances – more competent than their superiors – then establishing original authority may be for the good. For when there is a clash between the judgements of such officers and their superiors in relation to *certain* actions the subordinate officers are to perform or not perform, it is likely that acting on the judgements of lower echelon police officers will lead to the best outcomes. Case Study 2.1 provides backing for this line of argument. Moreover, vesting individual police officers with original authority entrenches their independence in relation to, for example, the undue influence that senior police or members of government might seek to have if senior police or members of government were themselves engaged in unlawful activities. In addition, original authority implies liability, and liability is a disincentive to abusing one's powers. On the other hand, since authority brings with it power, giving individuals authority creates the *possibility* of abuse of power. In particular, it might be thought that the history of police abusing their powers demonstrates that the power of individual police officers needs to be curtailed, rather than entrenched. Moreover, handing authority to individual police officers at the expense of their superiors brings with it an increased possibility of bad consequences flowing from the poor judgements of inexperienced junior officers. Further, if an officer's authority is merely delegated, then he may escape, for example, onerous financial liabilities of a kind he or she is unable to meet.

The question of removing original authority needs to be distinguished from the issue of curtailing discretionary powers. In the case of original authority, but not police discretion, officers have a legal right on occasion to override the lawful orders of their superiors in favour of complying with their obligation to the law as they understand it, and may be held liable for the untoward consequences of their actions, irrespective of whether these actions were performed in compliance with the directives of their officers.

Accordingly, at least in principle, police officers could lose their original authority without their sphere of de facto discretionary powers being substantially curtailed. Moreover, the extent of their de facto discretionary powers could be reduced while they retained their original authority. This is because discretionary powers can be based on delegated authority or they can be based on original authority. If the former, then their exercise can be overridden by the authority that delegated these powers, e.g. a superior officer. If the latter, then they cannot be overridden in this way, since there is no person in authority who has delegated these powers to them.

On the other hand, it is probable that curtailment of discretionary powers would go hand in hand with the elimination of the original authority of police officers. One scenario here would be the authority of individual police officers being taken in law to derive from the Minister of Police, and the enactment of more and more laws to restrict the areas of police discretionary powers.

By way of summation, the following points can be made. Firstly, whether or not individual officers are in fact *legally* vested with original authority, and if so, in relation to which powers, is a matter for the judiciary to determine; and we have indicated that there appears to be some confusion in the law on this matter, at least in the UK and in Australia. Secondly, whether or not individual officers have in fact been, or will be, vested with original authority was, or is, substantially a decision for the community and/or the government to make. Thirdly, whether or not individual officers *ought to be* vested with original authority is a matter for informed rational argument; and we have sought to provide some of the relevant considerations here. Fourthly, if police officers have been legally invested with original authority, then it will be up to police officers to exercise the relevant discretionary powers, and to do so in the knowledge that their decisions cannot normally be overridden by their superiors – as would be the case if they were merely delegated powers. Finally, such exercise of discretionary powers based on original authority goes hand in hand with individual liability – as opposed to vicarious liability. When it comes to the accountability of police vested with original authority, the buck stops with the individual police officer.[27]

Individual Authority and Police Pursuits

We have seen that there are some grounds for preserving the original authority of individual police officers. Nevertheless, there are clearly cases in which this authority needs to be curtailed. One such kind of case appears to be police pursuits.

In a discussion of police pursuits, Alpert and Dunham wrote:[28]

---

[27] This is consistent with limiting the liability of police officers possessed of original authority (say) for practical considerations, such as their inability to make large payments.

[28] Geoffrey P. Alpert and Roger G. Dunham, *Police Pursuit Driving: Controlling Responses to Emergency Situations* (New York: Greenwood Press, 1990), p. 9.

One important element concerning the usefulness of pursuit driving is the rate of immediate apprehension of law violators. Generally, less than 10% of the crime reported in the United States is reported either in progress or within a few seconds after the crime was committed, and only a small percentage of these offenders are apprehended immediately (Bureau of Justice Statistics, 1988). Increasing police pursuits may increase the number of offenders arrested immediately, but may have little effect on the overall apprehension rate. Furthermore, any increase in pursuit driving will substantially increase the risk of accident, injury, or death to the public. Pursuit policies must address these issues and do so in one of three models:

1. Judgemental: allowing officers to make all major decisions relating to initiation, tactics and termination.
2. Restrictive: placing certain restrictions on drivers' judgements and decisions.
3. Discouraging: severely cautioning or discouraging any pursuit, except in the most extreme situations.

In New South Wales, Australia, instructions require a police officer initiating a pursuit to call police radio VKG and advise the DOI (Duty Operations Inspector), who will direct and if necessary terminate that pursuit. The response of the police NCOs' (non-commissioned officer) industrial representative, the Police Association of NSW, had initially addressed a number of matters, including the previously unaddressed one of the abridgment of police officers' original authority, which remains a concern. The NSW Police Service's use of a DOI reflects public concerns regarding road trauma resulting from police pursuits. Whilst not reflective of the 1991 Australian National Police Research Unit's report on police pursuits, the US statistics should be a matter of concern:

> Findings in this study demonstrate that about one third of all pursuits end in an accident outcome, which is fairly close to what has been reported in the literature... The consequences of police car chases are being felt across the United States. In 1995, according to figures released by the National Highway Safety Administration, more Americans died as a result of high-speed police pursuits than were shot and killed by officers, showing that police cars are more deadly than their firearms – 383 people died in pursuits as against 380 shot dead by law officers.[29]

Police initially had difficulty with the notion of a distant DOI "second guessing" them in operational matters, especially in areas such as car chases – an ideal area for examining the sense of "mission" that empowers/justifies/excuses police:

[29] David Hay, "Halt: It may be the end of police car chases", *The Age*, March 21st, 1998, p. 30.

> The powerful, conventional sense of justice most police share mixes with the hedonic experience of chase and capture – few things match the visceral thrill of the manhunt – creating for participants enterprises of undoubted pleasure, satisfaction, and worth.[30]

Eventually, accustomed to a "rule-making" model of police management, police came to accept the DOI, the restrictions on vehicular pursuits seeming from a public safety viewpoint to share much in common with the Commissioner's directions on the use of firearms in circumstances that placed the public at risk, and in those terms, becoming acceptable to police.

Extension of the DOI notion into other areas of operational policing created problems; a disgruntled constable argued:

> "I can wear calling off a car chase: mostly it's kids; if you do catch them, they just get a bond [recognisance], and that's not worth risking you and your mate's life for, or the life of some innocent party – or even the car thief's life – and I don't need some DOI with goodness knows what street experience, if any, to tell me that. But this other stuff?"
>
> "DOIs are calling off the foot pursuits of kids throwing stones at passing cars or even bag-snatchers. Now it seems you mustn't chase them into some areas for fear of creating a wider "breach of the peace". This DOI idea fits with the "boss culture" of police management, but it will end up reducing operational police to puppets and de-skilling us; all we will provide is the muscle – the decisions will be all made for us by allegedly expert bosses. How long will it be until we have non-police DOIs directing us? And what of my tertiary-level education and supposed "professionalism" and "original authority"? DOIs – and soon, duty officers too – will be making all the operational decisions; that makes a nonsense of any pretence of workforce professionalism. Pretty soon, the unsupportable notion of police professionalism will just go."[31]

Subordination of the original authority of individual operational police officers to the directions of a distant "duty officer" was the point of a UK case, *R. v. Oxford. ex parte Levey [1987] 151 LG Rev. 371.*[32] Police were in hot pursuit of robbers who were in possession of the property of Levey when the pursuit was called off by an inspector in the radio control room before they could follow the robbers into the London suburb of Toxteth, an area subject to racial tension and civil disturbance.

Levey sought a declaration from the court that it was *ultra vires* for the Chief Constable to adopt a policy which declared Toxteth a "no-go area" for police, and that it was also *ultra vires* for the pursuit to be called off. Further, Levey sought *mandamus* against the Chief Constable, portraying his Toxteth policy as a breach of his statutory duties.

---

[30] John Blackler and Seumas Miller, *Police Ethics: Case Studies for Street Police* (Charles Sturt University and NSW Police Service, 2000) p. 214. This work also contains an earlier version of the material in this section.

[31] Authors' interview with General Duties police officer, Sydney metropolitan area, 1999.

[32] See also *The Times,* November 1st, 1986, pp. 16-18.

The subject matter was never resolved; the court held that *in this case*, because a truculent group of people was present in the street, the pursuit was called off allegedly on the grounds of officer-safety, not because of any no-go policy:

> Arguably such a policy would amount to a total abdication from the duty to enforce the law, with which the courts have consistently said they would interfere. The policy to inform the control room was intended to ensure that any law enforcement activities in the sensitive area of Toxteth could take full account of the current situation there. This was a matter about the appropriate methods for enforcing the law, a choice over which 'Chief Constables have the widest discretion' (per Sir John Donaldson MR).[33]

Evidently, curtailing original authority – or at least operational autonomy – even in the area of pursuits is not without problems.

Changes to the Tortious Responsibility of the Police

As noted above, the other side to original authority is tortious responsibility. The thread of legal reasoning begun in Britain in *Stanbury v. Exeter Corporation [1905] 2 K.B. 838*, and continued in the Australian cases *Enever v. R. [1906] 3 CLR 969* and *Fisher v. Oldham Corporation [1930] 2 K.B. 364,* produced the concept that police constables, acting in the performance of their duties, exercise an original authority inherent in the office of constable. This notion, restated in *Attorney-General for NSW v. Perpetual Trustee Company [1955] A.C. 457,* is based on civil actions against the police-employer (and in the case last mentioned, *by* the police employer), and has incrementally established the principle that master-servant law, the law of "agency", did not apply to police officers in the execution of their duty. Police officers individually, not their police employer, bear tortious responsibility for their actions.

This tortious responsibility might be said to be basic and essential to the concept of constabulary autonomy. Consider then the effect of recent New South Wales legislative change.[34] It reads:

> A member of the Police Service is not liable for any injury or damage caused by any act of omission of the member in the exercise by the member in good faith of a function conferred or imposed by or under this or any other Act or law with respect to the protection of persons from death or injury or property from damage.

This should be read down against the *Law Reform (Vicarious Liability) Act 1983*, No. 38, Section 8, 'Further vicarious liability of the Crown', which reads:

---

[33] Robert Reiner, *Chief Constables: Bosses, Bobbies or Bureaucrats?* (Oxford: Oxford University Press, 1992), p. 21.

[34] Section 213 (1) 'Protection from personal liability' of the *Police Service Act 1990*, No. 47 (reprinted as in force at January 24th, 1994 to include all amendments up to the *Statute Law (Miscellaneous Provisions) Act (No. 2) 1993*, No. 108).

> Notwithstanding any law to the contrary, the Crown is vicariously liable in respect of the tort committed by a person in the service of the Crown in the performance or purported performance by the person of a function (including an independent function) where the performance or purported performance of the function:
>
> (a) is in the course of his service with the Crown or is incident of his service (whether or not it was a term of his appointment to the service of the Crown that he perform the function), or
> (b) is directed to or is incidental to the carrying out of any business, undertaking, or activity of the Crown.

These amendments affecting the police officers' tortious responsibility did not arise out of decisions regarding the constabulary function – they originated mainly in the area of corporate actions, commencing with the appeal of *Lister v. Romford Ice and Cold Storage Co. Ltd., HL (E) 1956* (reported in the *Commonwealth Law Reports, 1984-5, Vol;. CLR 156*, at p. 555), and continued in the appeal of *McGrath v. The Council of the Municipality of Fairfield* (*ibid., CLR 156*, at p. 672), and *Ocean Crest Shipping Co. v. Pilbara Harbour Services Pty. Ltd., (1986) 160 CLR: 626, 66 ALR 29.*[35]

Given the reciprocal relation between authority and liability – and specifically between the original authority of the police and their civil liability – the original authority of police in Australia has been significantly undermined by these developments. The question remains as to whether this is desirable or not. It might be thought to be desirable on the grounds that individual police officers are thereby protected from having to suffer the consequences of their mistakes. Doubtless, this kind of reasoning appeals to police unions concerned with the welfare of their members. Moreover, given the liability of the police organisation or the State, inevitably the responsibility of individual police officers for their actions – their original authority – is diminished, and a justification provided for limiting and controlling their discretionary powers. Doubtless this kind of reasoning appeals to those seeking to exercise greater control over individual police officers, including some police managers and some distrustful members of the government.

While these two lines of reasoning have some weight, neither gets to the heart of the matter. Specifically, neither addresses the issue of police independence, and in particular the need for a quasi-judicial role for the police. Police independence, and specifically the quasi-judicial role of police in relation to, for example, the investigation, arrest and charging of powerful members of the community, including politicians and senior police, requires that a substantial degree of authority be vested in individual police officers, and not simply in the police institution (in practice, the Chief Constable or Police Commissioner), much less in the government of the day. It remains unclear how this required police

---

35 A coverage of these developments in tort law is available in Susan Kneebone, "The Independent Discretionary Function Principle and Public Officers", *Monash University Law Review,* Vol. 16, No. 2, 1990, pp. 184-210.

independence is to be preserved once the original authority of individual police officers is extinguished in favour of delegated authority.

Exercising Police Discretion

Case Studies 2.2, 2.3 and 2.4 evidence the complexities inherent in the exercise of police discretion. In each case there are competing ethical considerations. In Case Study 2.4, the human right to life is at issue, as is the concomitant moral obligation to preserve life, including not only the life of the police officers and of the dangerous criminal Martin, but also the lives of citizens who might be threatened if Martin were to escape. On the other hand, there is the end of law enforcement, in the sense of the requirement that Martin be apprehended so that he can be brought before the courts and – if found guilty – punished for his serious crimes; the serious crimes in question are violations of legally enshrined, justifiably enforceable, moral rights. In the event, the police officers chose to risk their own lives to ensure that Martin was apprehended. As it turned out, Martin was unarmed and this ethically-informed decision was vindicated.

In Case Study 2.2, there is the illegality to consider. The seaman has been found in possession of an illegal substance, namely marijuana. On the other hand, there is the disproportionate harm that he will suffer if he is convicted of this offence.

The structure of the ethical problem in Case Study 2.2 is as follows: (a) an illegal action has taken place, although it is not the violation of a moral right; (b) other things being equal, police have as an obligatory moral duty the enforcement of the law, and; (c) the consequence of enforcing the law in this instance is a state of affairs which is morally undesirable.

In Case Study 2.2, an individual will be disproportionately harmed, even though he has brought this upon himself. Perhaps the police have a general obligation, as do ordinary citizens, to avoid contributing to bringing about an injustice, the injustice of disproportionate harm for wrongdoing. However, the particular feature of this situation is that the law is the instrument whereby the disproportionate harm will be done. Yet a fundamental aim of the law is to protect moral rights, and (more broadly) to ensure that justice is done; and the police have a particular obligation to ensure that the law not be used to infringe moral rights or to bring about an injustice. Moreover, in addition to the matter of the possible infringement of the rights of the seaman, or at least of the injustice to him, there are the following consequentialist considerations: if the law is used as an instrument of injustice, let alone of infringement of moral rights, this will have a criminalising effect on those unjustly penalised, and it will tend to undermine public support for the law.

Case Study 2.3 seems to involve contradictory behaviour on the part of the police and the company. Initially the police are prepared to arrest those responsible for the petty theft of 50p model cars, but after the company refuses to press charges against the manager for a much more serious crime, the police discontinue their practice of arresting those who steal the 50p model cars. For their part, the Board of Directors of the company is prepared to pursue petty thieves, but not a manager guilty of a serious crime.

The apparent inconsistency in the behaviour of the Board of Directors is easy to explain. They want legal action to be taken against anyone who steals from them, unless taking legal action would go against their business interests.

The police use their discretion in relation to time and resources invested in pursuing particular crimes, and petty theft is a low priority. However, one ethical consideration in play here might be the extent to which members of the public are prepared to assist the police in achieving police ends, such as law enforcement in relation to property rights. Perhaps when the company demonstrated that it put its business interests above enforcing the law against those who steal its property, the obligation on the part of the police to pursue those who offend in minor ways against the company is diminished. This suggests that there is a cooperative relationship between the police and those they protect. This cooperation generates moral obligations. The terms of the cooperative arrangement seem to be that the police are obligated to protect the moral rights of the public and the public to assist the police to do so. However, if some members of the protected community fail to discharge their obligation, in that they are not prepared to assist the police to apprehend and punish those who offend against them and others – and especially if the reasons that they do not assist are self-interested ones in conflict with the community's larger interest – then those individuals have broken the terms of the arrangement and can no longer expect police discretionary judgements to go in their favour.

The term "police discretion" is used rather loosely, but it has at least three distinct senses: (a) de facto discretionary power (actual power, whether lawful or unlawful); (b) *de jure* discretionary power (legal discretion), and; (c) lawful de facto discretionary power, i.e. a de facto power the exercise of which is legally permissible (but not legally required). We will use the term "discretionary power" to refer to (c). So discretionary power is the power that individual police officers actually have to make decisions within legally delimited areas; a discretionary power of a police officer is an actual power the officer has that is also legally permissible for him or her to exercise. So it might be a matter of a police officer's lawful discretionary power that he can detain a disorderly member of a crowd; but he might be physically unable to do so. So he lacks discretionary power in our sense. On the other hand, it might be a matter of an officer's de facto discretionary power that he can throw someone out of the window, but it would be unlawful to do so. Again, the officer lacks discretionary power in our sense. On the other hand, if it is legally permissible – though not legally required – for an officer to detain a member of the crowd, and the officer is actually able to do so, then he has discretionary power in our sense.

In summation: on this account of police discretion, a police officer does not exercise discretion in respect of performing or not performing an action if he is in fact unable to perform it. Moreover, in breaking the law, as distinct from (lawfully) refusing to enforce it, a police officer does not exercise police discretion. It follows from this that there are two ways of reducing the discretionary powers of police. The first way is to use the law to restrict their powers, e.g. make it legally impermissible for police officers to shoot fleeing felons. The second way is to reduce their de facto powers, e.g. by not issuing guns to police except in special circumstances.[36]

The proper extent of police discretionary powers is a matter of controversy. Some argue that in order to reduce police abuse of power, their discretionary powers should be significantly curtailed. Such abuse of power in relation to the rights of suspects is well-established in many, perhaps most, countries, and of course discretionary powers have enabled or facilitated corrupt police activities in police forces throughout the world. An alternative view is that, by and large, the reduction of police discretionary powers is a mistake; rather what is called for is increased accountability in relation to the exercise of those powers. The idea is not to reduce the powers of police, but rather to reduce their ability to abuse those powers. Whether or not to reduce the discretionary powers of police, or to increase police accountability, or to do both, is to ask a simple question in relation to a complex issue. A better approach might be to adopt a more piecemeal approach, and ask with respect to some specific discretionary power, or with respect to a set of discretionary powers in a given area of police work, whether or not that power, or that set of powers, ought to be discretionary and/or subject to greater accountability.

Here we need also to recall our distinction made earlier in this chapter between individual discretionary action and joint or collective discretionary activity. We have been principally concerned with the discretionary powers of individual police officers. However, there is also the issue of the discretionary powers of police organisations, or specific cohorts of police officers, taken as collectives making joint decisions, as opposed to collectives doing as they are directed by the most senior officer. For example, it might be legally permissible for a police department to make a collective discretionary judgement in relation to not enforcing laws against the use of cannabis under certain circumstances.[37]

We have distinguished police discretion from police accountability and from the original authority of police; and we have also distinguished joint or collective discretionary activity from individual discretionary actions.

Our general point here is that the decision whether to reduce or increase police discretion in relation to any specific discretionary powers, or area of police work, ultimately needs to be settled by recourse to the fundamental purpose of policing, viz. the enforcement of morally justifiable, legally enshrined, moral rights. If specific discretionary powers are not needed, and indeed are potentially counterproductive in relation to the direct or indirect realisation of this purpose,

---

[36] The existence of social norms adhered to by police, but not legally enshrined, complicates the picture, e.g. a norm according to which police always give priority to assisting officers in trouble. Such norms, if they are consistent with the law but place further strictures on the police officer's actions, might be regarded as reducing the officer's discretionary power, especially if these norms embody objective moral principles. On the other hand, if such norms are at times inconsistent with the application of the law, then arguably they should not be regarded as limiting the discretionary power of police; or at least, we now need a further sense of the term "discretionary power" that is sensitive to normative constraints other than the law.

[37] Such a judgement might be held to pertain to a policy, as opposed to an operational, issue.

then presumably they should not be granted. Thus, the power of police to arrest ought not to be discretionary in relation to an offender who has committed a serious crime, such as murder or rape, and where the police have overwhelming evidence that the offender has committed this offence

If, on the other hand, a specific discretionary power is needed, then other things being equal, it should be granted. (Other things might not be equal; the police power in question might be inconsistent with the moral rights of citizens.) Naturally, if a specific discretionary power is needed, but there is a tendency for it to be abused, then perhaps police should retain the power, but also be subject to increased accountability in relation to their use of the power. In relation to violent street crime in a given area, police may well require discretionary powers to stop and search for weapons. Obviously they cannot, and ought not, stop and search everyone; yet for their own protection, and in order to realise the ends of protecting the property and persons in the area, stopping and searching on the basis of discretionary judgement might be necessary. Suppose it now came to light that a certain minority group within the community, namely young black men, was being systematically harassed as a consequence of the overuse of this discretionary power; suppose also that objective evidence indicated that a majority of offenders in fact came from this group. This situation might call for at least two additional responses on the part of the police hierarchy. Firstly, there might need to be greater accountability in relation to police use of their discretionary power, e.g. recording and monitoring of police use of this power in relation to young black males. Secondly, steps might need to be taken to reduce the level of police reliance on this power, e.g. increased community interaction and greater emphasis on intelligence-gathering in relation to specific individuals and gangs responsible for the offences, and the targeting by police of those individuals.

In relation to reducing the discretionary powers of individual police offices, James Doyle suggests that investigative and peace-keeping roles could constructively sustain a fairly high degree of police discretion, whereas law enforcement involving coercion and curtailing of freedom cannot. He argues that in these latter areas, the possibility and complete unacceptability of abuse of police power is very great, and hence there is a need to curb individual police discretion in these areas. By contrast, in the areas of investigation and peace-keeping, police need and "usually have other powers and responsibilities that make them more comparable to professionals on whom society bestows a relatively high degree of autonomy".[38]

Given that the autonomy of professionals, such as doctors, lawyers – and in a somewhat different way, academics – consists in part in original, and not merely delegated, authority, Doyle's line of argument suggests the possibility that police ought to have not only discretionary powers, but original authority, in certain areas of policing, e.g. investigation, but not necessarily in all. For example, perhaps police on patrol ought not to have original authority in relation to pursuits; it ought

---

[38] James Doyle, "Police Discretion, Legality and Morality", in William C. Heffernan and Timothy Stroup (eds.), *Police Ethics: Hard Choices in Law Enforcement* (New York: John Jay College, 1985), p. 63

not to be up to them whether or not to embark on, or whether or not to abort, a police pursuit.

Once again, we would seek to resolve such questions by recourse to our normative theory of the ends of policing as the protection of (justifiably enforceable, legally enshrined) moral rights. In the case of police pursuits, perhaps the protection of moral rights, including the right to life, is best served by depriving police officers in patrol cars of the right to pursue without express permission. It remains an open question whether, and to what extent, general areas of policing, such as investigation or peace-keeping – as opposed to particular policing tasks such as arresting drunk and disorderly citizens – might justify the granting of original authority and/or discretionary powers to police.

Chapter 3

The Moral Justification for Police Use of Deadly Force[1]

In Chapter 1, we argued that the protection of moral rights is the central and most important purpose of police work, albeit a purpose whose pursuit ought to be constrained by the law. We further argued that policing inescapably deploys methods that are harmful, e.g. coercion and deception; methods which are normally considered to be morally wrong.

Moreover, we assumed the following properties of moral rights. First, moral rights generate concomitant duties on others, e.g. A's right to life generates a duty on the part of B not to kill A. Second, human rights, but not necessarily institutional moral rights, are justifiably enforceable. Third, bearers of human rights, in particular, do not necessarily have to assert a given human right in order for the right to be violated, e.g. an infant may have a right to life even though it does not have the ability to assert it.

What does the second-mentioned property, justifiable enforceability, amount to in relation to deadly force? Consider enforcement of the right to life. Person A has a right not to be killed by B, and so B has an obligation not to kill A. But what if B ignores his obligation and attempts to kill A? In that event, A has a right that B be prevented by someone (either A or some other person, C) from killing A; A's right to life is justifiably enforceable. Here the means of prevention would include the use of deadly force, if it was necessary. In short, A has a right to use deadly force against B in self-defence, and C also has a right to use deadly force against B to protect A's life. Indeed, on this account, C may well have an *obligation* to kill B to protect A, given it was necessary and given that C could do so without threat to C's own life. Consider, in this connection, a situation in which A is C's child or spouse who is being threatened by B. Surely C is under an obligation to A to kill B, if this is the only means of preventing B from killing C's child or spouse.

So there are justifiably enforceable moral rights, and it is the central and most important purpose of police to protect legally enshrined, justifiably enforceable, moral rights. However, there are laws that are not of this sort. Many of these laws are fair and reasonable, and the conformity to them enables collective goods to be provided, e.g. anti-litter laws. But what is the justification for their enforcement by

---

[1] An earlier version of this chapter was authored by Seumas Miller and appeared as "Shootings by Police in Victoria: The Ethical Issues", in T. Coady, S. James, S. Miller and M. O'Keefe (eds.), *Violence and Police Culture* (Melbourne: Melbourne University Press, 2000).

police? We suggest that the fact that they provide collective benefits, and/or that they are fair and reasonable, do not of themselves provide an adequate justification for their enforcement. Perhaps consent to the enforcement of just and reasonable laws that enable the provision of collective benefits provides an adequate moral justification for such enforcement. Here there is an issue with respect to the degree and type of enforcement that might be in this way justified; deadly force may not be justified, even if it is consented to in relation to fair and reasonable laws that enable collective benefits to be provided. Certainly recourse to deadly force – as opposed to non-deadly coercive force – is not justified in the case of many unlawful actions; specifically, unlawful actions not regarded as serious crimes. Indeed, this point is recognised in those jurisdictions that have made it unlawful for police to shoot at many categories of "fleeing felons". It is more often than not now unlawful, because immoral, to shoot at (say) a fleeing pickpocket.

At any rate, in this chapter we examine in detail the moral justification for police use of deadly force. We do so in the context of the assumption that, quite independently of the existence of police services, individual persons have a right to life, and there is a derived right to kill in self-defence, and a derived obligation to kill in defence of others. With the establishment of police services in modern societies, the responsibility for defending oneself, and especially for protecting others, has to a large extent devolved to the police. Crudely, the idea is that if someone's life is threatened, whether my own or someone else's, the first step should be to call the police. However, this in no way entails that the rights of ordinary citizens to self-defence and to defend the lives of others have been forfeited.

We see our rights-based account of the moral justification of police use of deadly force as standing in some contrast with *some* versions of contract theory.[2] On our conception, the rights to self-defence and to the defence of others are logically prior to police services, and indeed government. Moreover, objective moral principles governing the exercise of these rights, e.g. the principle of necessity and proportionality, are also logically prior to police services and governments. Indeed, these rights and the moral principles governing their exercise constrain, or ought to constrain, the actions of police and the laws enacted by governments. So there is no question of a "state of nature" in which everyone is entitled to use force at his own subjective discretion or whim, and in accordance with his own subjectively chosen rules. Accordingly, persons do not renounce this freedom when they come to embrace the State. The reason for this is twofold. First, no-one ever had, or could have had, a moral right to use force solely at their own

---

[2] While some contractarians would concede retention of the right to self-defence, they may well not do so in relation to the right to defend others. Thus, according to Hobbes, "A Covenant not to defend my self from force, by force, is alwayes voyd" (Thomas Hobbes, *Leviathan*, Chapter 14, any edition). For one influential recent contractarian view, see Jeffrey Reiman, "The Social Contract and the Police Use of Deadly Force", in Frederick Elliston and Michael Feldberg (eds.), *Moral Issues in Police Work* (Totowa, NJ: Rowman and Allanheld, 1985), pp. 237-49. See also John Kleinig, *The Ethics of Policing* (Cambridge: Cambridge University Press, 1996), p. 109.

subjective discretion, i.e. independently of objective reasons. Or at least no-one could have had a moral right to use *deadly* force solely at their own subjective discretion. Second, whatever *objective* moral right to use deadly force individual persons could have had (e.g. the right to kill in self-defence) they retain, notwithstanding the existence of governments and police services.

Note that our rights-based account in relation to the use of deadly force is consistent with citizens reasonably accepting that governments and, more specifically, the police, have a near-monopoly on the use of coercive force within their communities, and that the police reasonably have *some additional* powers and duties in relation to the use of deadly force that are not possessed by ordinary citizens. What precisely these powers and duties are is a matter we discuss in some detail below. Here we simply note that citizens might reasonably grant special powers to police on the basis of the need for a partial division of labour in relation to the protection of legally enshrined, justifiably enforceable, moral rights. However, such a division of labour is consistent with citizens retaining enforcement rights, such as the right to the defence of others. Indeed, it is because citizens retain such rights that it is permissible, indeed obligatory, that they protect themselves and others, given the unavailability of police to do so on occasion. Moreover, the retention of these rights in the context of a partial division of labour serves to explain why it is that citizens have a moral duty to assist the police in the enforcement of the moral rights in question, e.g. a duty to assist a police officer to arrest an escaping murderer, if it be required.

Accordingly, we do not accept some of the main arguments that might be thought to be available to a contractarian theory of police use of deadly force. Specifically, we do not accept the claim that an individual person, A, can somehow *grant* to others the right to *kill* A, if A fails to do certain things he promised to do.[3] This is in part because there are at least some rights that are inalienable, specifically the right to life, the right to autonomy, and the (derived) rights to self-defence and the defence of others.[4] And it is in part because, to the extent that others have a right to *kill* A for things that A has done or failed to do, e.g. the right to kill A in self-defence, they do not need to be granted that right by A. Human rights, in particular, are not granted to others; rather they are possessed, and only possessed, by virtue of properties one has as a human being.[5]

---

[3] *ibid.* One can of course grant to others the right to such things as one's property, and one can grant the right to enforce contracts one has entered into. But we are denying that one can straightforwardly *grant* the right to use deadly force to enforce such contracts.

[4] Inalienable rights are not necessarily absolute rights; the right to life is inalienable, but it does not follow that it is absolute. The existence of a right to self-defence demonstrates that the right to life is not absolute.

[5] This is consistent with a human right taking on a particular form in one institutional setting that is to some extent different from the form it takes in a different institutional setting, and that there be room for decision-making in relation to the precise character of such institutionalised human rights. For example, the human right to autonomy can underpin a variety of different voting arrangements.

Here we need to stress the role of human rights in relation to practical moral reasoning. The first point is that the social activities of promise-making, contracts and consenting take place against a background assumption of *inalienable* human rights, especially the rights to life and to autonomy. What is not up for potential agreement is the very capacity to be a contractor; contracts to enter into slavery or hand over one's right to life to another are self-nullifying. Secondly, while human rights are not absolute rights, human rights nevertheless normally "trump" other considerations, such as social utility; in general, a decision to infringe a human right can only be justified by recourse to other human rights considerations. So human rights ought not to be overridden for the sake of other benefits to the community, such as social order. Here it should be remembered that while social order is a necessary condition for human rights being respected, it is far from sufficient. Totalitarian states are characterised by high levels of social order, notwithstanding the massive human rights violations that they involve.

On our account, there is a justifiably enforceable right to life, and this right gives rise to a right to self-defence and a right to the defence of others. It follows that police officers, like ordinary citizens, have a right to use deadly force in self-defence and in defence of others. Moreover, it is widely assumed that the only two morally acceptable justifications for police use of deadly force are self-defence and the defence of others. For example, according to the Australian National Committee on Violence's Recommendation 85.1, 'Uniform laws throughout Australia regarding the use of firearms and other lethal force by police', "These laws should reflect the principle that lethal force should only be used as a last resort, involving self-defence or the defence of others".[6] However, we will argue that the matter is more complex than this, and that there is an additional possible moral justification for police use of deadly force. But first we need to provide a more detailed account of the right to self-defence.[7]

Killing in Self-Defence

There are a number of criteria of adequacy for any account of justifiable killing in self-defence.[8] First, the justification of killing in self-defence is not simply that there is a deadly threat, or that there is a deadly threat which can only be removed

[6] *Violence: Directions for Australia* (Canberra: National Committee on Violence, 1990).

[7] For discussions of the moral justification for killing in self-defence, see J. J. Thomson, "Self-defence", *Philosophy and Public Affairs*, September, 1991, S. Uniacke, *Permissible Killing*, (Cambridge: Cambridge University Press, 1994), Seumas Miller, "Killing in Self-defence", *Public Affairs Quarterly*, Vol. 7, No. 4, 1993, and Seumas Miller, "Judith Jarvis Thomson on Killing in Self-defence", *Australian Journal of Professional and Applied Ethics*, Vol. 3, No. 2, 2001.

[8] The material in this section is taken from Seumas Miller, "Killing in Self-defence", *Public Affairs Quarterly*, Vol. 7, No. 4, 1993. For arguments defending this account, see that article.

by killing the person who constitutes the deadly threat. Fault is involved in the justification of self-defence.

Second, any right to life or right not to be killed that an individual might have is dependent on, or in some way linked to, that individual discharging his or her obligation not to kill others. In other words, the moral value of an agent's life is partly dependent on the value that agent puts on the lives of others.

Third, the linkage has to be such that the right not to be killed is suspended, and not cancelled or overridden.

Fourth, the linkage has to be relativised to some extent to the defender and his attacker. The defender is not obligated to respond to the life-threatening attack in the way that a third person is obligated to respond. One's legitimate interest in one's own life, and the responsibility for it, is different from another person's legitimate interest in, or responsibility for, one's life.

Fifth, the attacker's reason for attacking is a morally relevant consideration.

Sixth, whether or not the attacker forced the choice is a morally relevant consideration.[9]

Given these criteria of adequacy, we suggest the following fault-based internalist (suspendable) rights-based theory (or "FIST").[10] X has a right not to be killed by Y, and Y has a concomitant obligation not to kill X. However, X suspends X's right not to be killed by Y, if X comes to have all of the following properties: (a) X is a deadly threat to Y; (b) X intends to kill Y, and X is responsible for X having this intention to kill Y; (c) there is not in fact a strong and decisive moral justification for X to kill Y, and; (d) it is not the case that X believes with good reason that X has a strong and decisive moral justification to kill Y.

Accordingly, each person, X, has a set of suspendable rights not to be killed; X has a right not to be killed by Y and a right not to be killed by Z, etc. X also has a set of suspendable obligations not to kill; X has an obligation not to kill Y and an obligation not to kill Z, etc. Here X's right not to be killed generates an obligation on the part of Y, Z and so on, not to kill X.

There are four conditions on the suspension corresponding to four features of the attacker, it being understood that the attacker himself suspends his right in virtue of possessing these four features: condition (a) simply states what being an attacker consists in, namely being a deadly threat; condition (b) expresses the requirement that the attacker must be responsible for the fact that he is a deadly threat; condition (c) signals the relevance to justified killing in self-defence of the attacker's reason for his attack, and; condition (d) makes the point that suspension would be unjustified if the attacker falsely, but with good reason, believed he had a strong and decisive moral justification for his attack.

These rights are such that when one member of the set of rights is suspended, the other rights (and concomitant obligations) remain in force. Thus if A's right not

---

[9] For discussion of the notion of forcing the choice, see P. Montague, "Self-defence and choosing between lives", *Philosophical Studies*, Vol. 40, 1981. See also Seumas Miller "Self-defence and Forcing the Choice Between Lives", *Journal of Applied Philosophy*, Vol. 9, No. 2, 1992.

[10] See John Locke, *Second Treatise on Government* (any edition), Chapter 3.

to be killed by B is suspended, then B no longer has an obligation not to kill A. However, A still has a right not to be killed by C, and thus C's obligation not to kill A remains in force.

It must also be noted that these rights not to be killed can not only be suspended, they can also be overridden. So while A might still have a right not to be killed by (say) C, it might be the case that it is morally permissible for C to kill A. This would be the case if A's right not to be killed by C was overridden (but not suspended).

According to FIST, that a person stands to his attacker in a qualitatively different relation to the relation in which a third person stands to that attacker makes a crucial difference to the kind of moral justification available to the third person for killing the attacker.[11] The third person confronts a choice – if he can decisively intervene to save the defender's life, but only by killing the attacker – between two lives, one guilty and one innocent. From the point of view of the third person, both the defender and the attacker have a right not to be killed, and consequently the third person has a strong obligation not to kill the attacker (or the defender). However, the third person confronts a choice between killing a would-be murderer and allowing an innocent person to be killed. In that case, he ought to choose to preserve the life of the innocent person. Here the third person's obligation not to kill the attacker is not suspended; it is overridden. The duty of the third person to preserve an innocent life, coupled with the fact that the attacker is the guilty party, is sufficient to override the attacker's right not to be killed by the third person.

In FIST, the notion of a strong moral justification in the set of conditions for suspension is intended to embrace a fairly wide array of moral considerations. These would include considerations such as that the defender forced a choice upon the attacker in some "thick" sense of forcing the choice, e.g. intentionally or knowingly forcing the choice, and that the defender had seriously wronged the attacker. The conditions are incomplete, insofar as what is to count as a strong moral justification is not spelled out. But this incompleteness is unavoidable.

An important feature of FIST is that the attacker suspends his right not to be killed in cases in which the defender does not have to kill the attacker to save his life.[12] There are two general background intuitions here. Firstly, that whether or not a person has such a fundamental right as the right not to be killed must depend on properties of that person. It cannot depend on whether someone else, for example the defender, has or does not have a capacity to defend himself. Secondly, that if a person intentionally kills other people without any justification whatsoever, then that person has called into question their very entitlement to live; a person's right to live is not something that exists independently of the respect that that person has for the right to life of others. FIST, however, focuses in particular on the absence of any right of the attacker that he be spared by the defender – the one the attacker sought to kill. When the defender disarms the attacker, everything is not as it was

[11] Cheney Ryan ("Self-defence, Pacifism and the Possibility of Killing", *Ethics,* Vol. 93, 1983, p. 519) makes this kind of point in his discussion of "negative bonds".

[12] *ibid.*, p. 512.

before the attack. Before the attack, the presumption is that the attacker-to-be recognises the defender's right not to be killed. The attack reverses this presumption. The presumption must now be that the attacker does not recognise the existence of his obligation not to kill the defender.[13]

Notwithstanding our commitment to FIST, an account in terms of an attacker's suspension of his right not to be killed, we are still able to maintain, and do maintain, that the defender has, or might have, an obligation (of a different kind) not to kill the attacker in cases in which it is not necessary to kill the attacker to preserve his own life. If so, this obligation is not the obligation generated by the right that each agent has not to be killed. Rather, it would be one of a number of obligations. Some of these are generated by features of the attacker. For example, there is the obligation not to destroy what has value, and the life of the attacker still has, or may well have, value.[14] And there is the related obligation to be merciful to those who have wronged you. Other obligations involve considerations that are external to the attacker. For example, there may be dire consequences for the attacker's family if you kill him. Or perhaps there will be dire consequences for the community if defenders generally kill their attackers; hence the existence of laws to the effect that one must not kill in self-defence unless one has to. So our account is able to accommodate the intuition that one ought not to kill in self-defence unless one has to.

In FIST, the right not to be killed is relativised to single agents. Nevertheless, FIST can accommodate killers who seek not to kill victims *qua* individuals, but *qua* members of some group. Suppose some person, A, has a policy of killing people who belong to a certain category, e.g. a certain race group, or persons with a price on their head. Suppose also that B is a member of this category, and has reason to believe that, unbeknownst to the killer (namely A), he, B, is the next person belonging to that category that A will try to kill. Perhaps B's name is on the latest hit-list the killer is about to receive. In this kind of case, the killer has an intention to kill someone belonging to the category to which B belongs, and as a result will kill B unless B intervenes. In such cases, although the killer does not, strictly speaking, have an intention to kill B, nevertheless his right not to be killed by B is suspended.

Killing in Defence of Rights

As we have just seen, killing in order to defend one's own life or the life of another is morally justified on the grounds that each of us has a right to life. Moreover, we are entitled to defend that right to life by killing an attacker under three conditions. Firstly, the attacker is intentionally trying to kill someone – either oneself or another person – and will succeed if we do not intervene. We are not entitled to shoot dead an attacker whom we know is threatening us with a replica of a gun.

---

[13] I owe this way of putting the point to Kevin Presa.

[14] See D. Wasserman, "Justifying Self-defence", *Philosophy and Public Affairs*, Vol. 16, 1987, p. 359.

Secondly, we have no way of preserving our own or the other person's life other than by killing the attacker. For example, we are not able to flee to safety. Thirdly, and more problematically, our attacker does not have a morally justifiable reason for trying to kill. For example, it may be that a legally appointed executioner has a decisive morally justifiable reason for carrying out the death penalty in the case of a serial killer, but that the serial killer does not have a decisive morally justifiable reason for trying to kill the executioner in self-defence, supposing the opportunity arose.[15]

The killing of Mark Militano by Victorian police officers in 1986 is evidently a case of justified killing in self-defence, and/or of killing in defence of the lives of others. Police were following Militano and had evidence in the form of an overheard conversation, which was probably sufficient to charge him with conspiracy to commit armed robbery. Police cars converged on Militano, and one car swerved in front of Militano's vehicle, causing him to brake. Militano reached for his handgun and pointed it at one of the police. A number of police fired at Militano. Militano, apparently unharmed, ran from his car. A police officer fired a shot in the air, calling for him to stop. Militano turned, raised his pistol, and aimed at the police. Sergeant Ray Watson, the man who had overheard the conversation concerning the planned bank robbery, fired one shot from his .38 revolver. The bullet hit Militano in the head, and minutes later he died.[16] Clearly, at the point when Watson shot Militano, the above-mentioned three conditions for justifiable killing in self-defence – or defence of the lives of others – obtained. Firstly, Militano was intentionally trying to kill someone – either Watson or another officer – and would have probably succeeded if Watson did not intervene. Secondly, Watson had no way of preserving his own or the other police officers' lives other than by killing Militano. Thirdly, Militano did not have a morally justifiable reason for trying to kill Watson and/or the other police officers.

The case of Gary Abdallah illustrates the distinction between *justified* killing in self-defence and *excusable* killing in self-defence. Abdallah was suspected by Victorian police of involvement in the Walsh St. (Melbourne) killings of two police officers. However, there was insufficient evidence to prosecute him. There was however evidence of his attempted murder of a senior policeman's son. Detectives Clifton Lockwood and Dermot Avon were sent to arrest Abdallah. It was alleged that Abdallah produced a revolver, aimed it at Lockwood, was warned by Lockwood to put it down, and was shot dead by Lockwood when he failed to do so. The revolver turned out to be an imitation gun. The police officers were charged with murder, but found not guilty. While the gun was an imitation gun, it was *reasonably believed* to have been a real gun.[17] Accordingly, the first of the above-mentioned conditions for *justifiable* self-defence – that the attacker will *in*

---

[15] But see J. Teichman, "Self-defence", in her *Pacifism and the Unjust War* (Oxford: Blackwell, 1986).

[16] Tom Noble, *Untold Violence: Crime in Melbourne Today* (Melbourne: John Kerr, 1989), pp. 142-3.

[17] Hal Hallenstein, *Investigation into the Death of Gary John Abdallah: Coroner's Findings* (Melbourne: State Coroner's Office, 1994).

fact kill the defender unless the defender intervenes – can be weakened to generate a set of conditions for morally *excusable* self-defence. The relevant new condition is that the defender *reasonably believes* the attacker will kill him unless he intervenes.

Police have a right to kill in self-defence and to kill in defence of the lives of others. In this respect, they are no different from ordinary citizens. But a further point that needs to be stressed is that police on occasion have a legal and moral *duty* to kill to protect innocent lives. Indeed, they can be held legally liable if they fail to take the opportunity to shoot dead an armed and dangerous criminal who then goes on to (say) take the lives of innocent citizens. What of ordinary citizens? Do they have a moral – as opposed to legal – obligation to kill to protect others, at least in cases where the threat to life is immediate, certain and there is no alternative to using deadly force? The answer is a qualified affirmative. The qualifications are twofold. Firstly, the obligation of ordinary citizens to kill to protect others is only triggered in the absence of police; in the first instance, it is the duty of police to protect threatened lives. Secondly, not having been trained, and not having accepted a special responsibility, to protect the lives of others, ordinary citizens ought not to be expected to go to the same lengths or take the same risks as police officers are obliged to.

Having outlined the standard account of killing in self-defence or in defence of the lives of others, let us now consider a different, or at least an expanded, kind of moral justification for killing, namely what we will call "killing in defence of rights". Clearly the rights in question are rights above and beyond the right to life. However, in speaking of killing in defence of rights, one would obviously not want to include *all* moral rights, or at least *all violations* of all moral rights. For example, property rights are arguably moral rights, but for a police officer to kill someone to prevent them stealing a handbag would be morally unacceptable. So the question becomes: Are there any moral rights, apart from the right to life, the protection of which would justify police use of deadly force? Candidates for such rights might include a right not to be severely physically or psychologically damaged. Perhaps rape, serious child molestation and grievous bodily harm are actions the prevention of which might justify use of deadly force. Maybe police are justified in shooting a fleeing serial rapist if that is the only way to ensure his arrest.

If we go further afield, geographically and historically, we find other kinds of possible case. What do we want to say of the policy in Zimbabwe of police shooting rhino poachers on sight – given that rhinos are facing extinction and other methods have failed? Or what of the shooting on sight of cattle rustlers in the American West, in circumstances under which cattle rustling threatened ranchers' livelihoods? Again, what are we to say about shooting looters? The shooting of looters in disaster zones or in conditions of civil unrest has been an accepted policy in many parts of the world over a long period of time. And there are the (alleged) shootings on sight of armed robber-murderers in South Africa by police. There has been a frightening increase in the robbery of businesses in South Africa by heavily-armed gunmen, who sometimes shoot dead unarmed shopkeepers and others in the process of the robbery. On occasion, these gunmen will shoot to kill on sight police officers seeking to apprehend them. Such situations can escalate into quasi-military wars, with offenders and police treating each other as combatants. Finally, there are the de facto paramilitary confrontations in contexts such as Northern Ireland during the 1969-1994 period, in which police of the Royal Ulster Constabulary and Britain's armed forces, including the Special Air Service and the 14th Intelligence Company, conducted anti-Provisional Irish Republican Army operations. Having located an arms cache, security forces would stake out and attempt to arrest terrorist suspects who came to collect the weapons, knowing that in doing so they would provoke a fire-fight in which the suspects would be killed; in short, a military-style operation was being conducted.[18] The alternative strategy of confiscating the weapons, or rendering them inoperable and arresting the unarmed suspects, would normally be required of police operating under civilian rule. In short, the Northern Ireland context of the time was one in which offenders and security forces were engaged in a form of urban guerrilla warfare, notwithstanding the British government insistence that the IRA was essentially a criminal organisation, and the fact that members of the SAS could be convicted of murder for such acts.

Here we need to distinguish the question of the *types* of crime that might justify the use of deadly force, from the question of the *extent* of crime that might justify it. So there might be *widespread* crime within a society, e.g. murder, assaults, rape and armed robberies, and also large-scale fraud and theft; in addition, there might be a proliferation of *criminal organisations* that might be responsible for a good deal of serious and/or widespread crime. There are two points to be made here. First, a massive increase in certain crimes might conceivably justify the use or threatened use of deadly force; deadly force that would otherwise not be justified. Consider the case of widespread looting that threatens the economy in an impoverished society. Second, individual citizens acting on their own can do little to combat widespread crime or criminal organisations.

With the establishment of the nation state, and specifically of policing institutions, the responsibility for protecting and assisting those whose life, freedom or property is threatened from within a society has to a large extent devolved to the police. So the police have a special responsibility to protect and assist citizens when there are threats to their basic rights. Here we need to note the existence of pre-existing human rights and collective moral responsibilities. The members of a society have a collective moral responsibility to ensure that the human rights of the members of the society are protected. Thus, it is not simply a matter of an individual having an *individual* right and/or obligation to act in (say) self-defence or in defence of the life of another, when that individual is confronted with an immediate and possibly one-off opportunity to do so. Rather, the problem of widespread crime, especially human rights violations, and of organised crime, generates a *collective* moral responsibility on the part of members of the

[18] See Fionnuala Ni Aolain, *The Politics of Force: Conflict Management and State Violence in Northern Ireland* (Belfast: Blackstaff, 2000), p. 74.

community to act.[19] The reason that this moral responsibility is collective is in large part due to the inability of individuals acting alone to ensure the protection of moral rights under these conditions. Further, in complex societies this collective moral responsibility typically issues in the creation of an institution, viz. the police, whose members are trained, organised and authorised to discharge – on behalf of the members of the community – the collective moral responsibility of the members of the community to protect human and other moral rights. In so doing, the police do not *extinguish* the collective moral responsibilities of the members of the community to one another, much less the individual moral responsibilities to protect human and other rights, and upon which those collective moral responsibilities supervene.

We have been discussing the problem posed by widespread and organised violation of moral rights, and the consequent need for a police service. Let us now return to the question as to what specific *types* of crime might justify the use of deadly force by police. We have distinguished between the right to life and other rights, and suggested that police – and citizens – could be justified in killing to protect rights other than the right to life. But which of these rights? Let us draw a distinction between rights to things constitutive of the self and rights to things not constitutive of the self. What are some of the rights to things which are not constitutive of the self? We suggest that they include property rights, various freedoms – such as freedom of movement and freedom from unwanted sexual communications – and also many institutional rights, such as the right to a fair trial and the right to hold office.

We suggest that, at least in the first instance, police are justified in killing to protect rights to things constitutive of self-hood, including life, autonomy, and at least some additional elements of what we referred to in Chapter 1 as individual human identity. In particular, they are justified in killing in what is quite literally self-defence – the defence of the self – and they are justified in killing to protect other "selves", viz. other persons. We will shortly go on to argue that in some circumstances they are also justified in killing to protect certain other rights, which are rights to things not constitutive of self-hood.

Before doing so, we must briefly deal with the claim that there is no acceptable distinction to be made between rights to things constitutive of the self and rights to things not constitutive of the self.

Surely some such distinction is necessary. For we need to be able to distinguish between (say) a right to life and a right to property. If I defend myself against someone trying to kill me, it is defence of the self; it is literally the destruction of myself that is in question. Similarly, if I defend myself against someone trying to irreparably damage those parts of my brain in virtue of which I have the capacity to perform intellectual tasks, then it is defence of myself. Such capacities are constitutive of self-hood. However, if I defend my property – say, my car or an intrusion by an unarmed trespasser in my home – then I am not necessarily

---

[19] Seumas Miller, *Social Action: A Teleological Account* (New York: Cambridge University Press, 2001), Chapter 8.

defending myself. Neither my car nor my home are constitutive elements of myself. If my car is wrecked, or I sell my house, *I* am still intact.

Moreover, it is important not to assimilate the various rights to defend freedoms to the right to self-defence or the defence of others. For example, locking someone in a room is a violation of their freedom of movement. This freedom is essentially freedom of movement of one's body. Here we need to invoke a distinction between, on the one hand, the capacity of the agent *in him/herself* to freely move, and on the other, the existence of external impediments to his exercise of that capacity. The former but not the latter is constitutive (in part) of self-hood. To see this, consider first the resistance of a person, A, to an attempt by another person, B, to inject A with a drug that would permanently and irreversibly paralyse him. Here A's capacity to move is destroyed. Contrast this with the case where A is locked in a five-star hotel room for two days – with full service. Here no constitutive element of A's self-hood is destroyed. (This is not to say that prolonged imprisonment may not ultimately *cause* destruction of elements of the self. But this is a different matter. To cause *x* is not to be *x*.)

Finally, it is important to recognise that some rights to things not constitutive of self-hood have "violation thresholds", such that at points beyond the threshold, violations threaten things that are constitutive of self-hood. For example, if someone is incarcerated and suffers severe and longstanding limitations of their freedom of expression, privacy and freedom of movement, this may over time undermine that person's capacity to think and act independently. Such a loss of agency may come to constitute a partial destruction of self-hood. Again, an act of rape or assault may reach a threshold where it threatens to destroy aspects of self-hood, including the capacity to relate sexually or socially with other people.

We do not claim to have *precisely* drawn the distinction between elements of self-hood and other sorts of thing to which one has rights. We do not even claim that the distinction can be precisely drawn. We merely claim that it is evident that there is some such distinction to be drawn. This being so, we need to distinguish between killing in self-defence – or in the defence of other selves – and what we are calling killing in defence of rights.

Having distinguished between killing in defence of self and killing in defence of rights, let us now turn to the question whether the existence of such rights could provide a third justification for police use of deadly force – the first two justifications being self-defence and the defence of other selves.

Police Use of Deadly Force to Enforce the Law

The first point to be made here is that many of the above-mentioned moral rights – to things not constitutive of self-hood – are rights protected by the criminal law. Indeed, violations of many of these rights are regarded as serious crimes. The second point is that police forces exist (at least in part) to uphold the law, and especially laws against serious crimes. Accordingly, our question becomes: Are police officers morally entitled to use deadly force to protect citizens' moral rights, where the rights in question are not simply the right to life or rights to things constitutive of self-hood?

Let us take an example of a right which is protected by the law, and which is a right to something not constitutive of the self, namely the right to property. Are police morally entitled to use deadly force to defend citizens' property rights?

There are certainly some cases in which they are not. Consider an unarmed pickpocket who is fleeing a police officer. The officer is not morally entitled to shoot and kill for such a minor offence. Moreover, arguably the police officer is not morally entitled to shoot and kill an unarmed burglar, notwithstanding the fact that the burglar is making off with a million dollars-worth of someone else's goods, and that the only way to prevent his escape is by shooting him dead.

However, it appears that there are at least some cases in which the police are morally entitled to use deadly force in order to uphold the law, and specifically the laws protecting property rights. Consider the case of someone who has successfully robbed a bank and gotten away with millions of dollars of other people's savings. Let's say this person is hiding out, and is armed and prepared to shoot in order to avoid capture, though if left alone with his money, he will not shoot anyone. There are two moral questions here. Firstly, if an arrest attempt is to be made, how should it be done, and secondly, whether an arrest attempt should be made at all.

If an attempt is to be made, it will be a matter of deciding on the most effective method, ideally one that will minimise the risk to life. Perhaps the authorities should opt for a policy of containment and negotiation. Alternatively, the best option might be a surprise attack using forced entry. It may well be that in reality in situations of this kind, police have often pursued the wrong options, and the nature of their training may come into this. Moreover, if the methods of police in some jurisdiction are not best practice, and if they should have known this, then they may well have been professionally negligent. Obviously the negligence of a professional group in relation to situations where lives are at risk is completely morally unacceptable.

Further, professional negligence may be a by-product of the ethos or culture of an organisation. Perhaps members of a particular police service have developed an ethos of individual physical courage at the expense of reflection, and of "machismo" rather than concern for the consequences, and that this ethos has led to a tendency for early recourse to force rather than more considered methods such as negotiation. If so, then there would be cause for concern, and reason to reconsider the organisational structure and the education and training of the police service in question, including, in particular, education in the ethical principles underlying the legitimate and illegitimate use of force by police officers.

The Victorian coroner Hal Hallenstein has taken the view that in some of the police shootings and killings in Victoria in the 1980s and 1990s, the wrong options have been pursued. For example, Joshua Yap ended up in a wheel-chair after being shot by a police officer, Constable Steven Tynan, when Yap – armed with a hunting knife – attempted to rob a TAB agency with an accomplice, Chee Ming Tsen – who was "armed" with an imitation revolver. Tynan had fired only after: (a) he had called upon Yap and Tsen to surrender, and; (b) Yap had lunged at Tynan with the knife. However, Hallenstein concluded that Tynan and fellow officer

Constable Bodsworth ought not to have entered the TAB in the first place, but should have waited for assistance and opted for containment and negotiation. He said their actions were:

> ...arguably unnecessary, tactically unsound and in circumstances considered as acceptable breach of police force policy. A more satisfactory basis of acknowledgment would have been non-exposure by police members, an active seeking of non-firearms resolution of the situation and taking into account the foreseeable risks.[20]

An example where forced entry was used when containment and negotiation were arguably the best option was the shooting by Victorian police of Gerhard Alfred Sader. Four police officers led by Sergeant Watson raided Sader's Melbourne bungalow at dawn. Sader was wrongly suspected of illegal possession of arms and drugs. The police had been issued with search warrants on the basis of false information from an informer known to be unreliable. As it turned out, the police used a sledgehammer to break open an external gate prior to even getting to the door of the house. This would certainly have alerted Sader. When they finally broke open Sader's door, shouting "Police. Open up!", they stared at a figure in the darkness who later turned out to be Sader. Watson shot three times at the figure in the dark, on the grounds that he believed the person to be armed and about to shoot him. Sader was at most armed with a baseball bat.[21]

In the light of these kinds of cases, let us assume that the method most likely to minimise the risk to life is containment and negotiation. Let us also assume that in fact this is the one chosen. It remains true that the police are committed to apprehending the perpetrator. The police are typically institutionally required – whether or not they ought to be – not to simply let him go, and even in a situation of containment and negotiation, the use of deadly force may turn out to be necessary, albeit as a last resort. Consider, in this connection, a gunman who, having killed his wife in their home, refuses to give himself up to police negotiators, and is preparing to escape, notwithstanding the presence of police snipers. Should he be allowed to escape? Martin Bryant – the man who went on a shooting spree in Port Arthur, Tasmania, on April 28th, 1996, killing 35 innocent people with a semi-automatic rifle – should not have been allowed to escape, but what of the armed professional burglar seeking only to escape? In short, what is the moral justification for the use of deadly force in cases in which police confront a choice of either letting an offender go free or shooting him/her?

In these sorts of case, the police are not necessarily engaged in self-defence. In many of these cases, the best thing for police officers – if they were interested in self-defence – would be for them to get back into their patrol cars and return to the police station. Nor are they necessarily cases of killing in defence of others. The lives of ordinary citizens might not be at risk. For example, an offender – say, an

[20] Hal Hallenstein, *Investigation into the Death of Hai Foong Yap: Coroner's Findings* (Melbourne: State Coroner's Office, 1994), p. 164.

[21] Hal Hallenstein, *Investigation into the Death of Gerhard Alfred Paul Sader: Coroner's Findings* (Melbourne: State Coroner's Office, 1994).

armed burglar – might simply want to be left alone to spend his ill-gotten gains. Or the above-described husband who has killed his wife might cease to be a threat to anyone once he has killed his wife.

It might be argued against this that the police are engaged in self-defence since they are doing their moral duty in trying to apprehend the suspect, he ought not resist them, and if he does resist them, then their action of killing him is self-defence. After all, it might be claimed, he would have killed them if they had not killed him.

This response is flawed. It is simply false that he would have killed them if they had not killed him. The police had the option of not killing the suspect, or of retreating after they had begun the pursuit. What is true is that they have a duty to apprehend the suspect, and they cannot avoid shooting him on pain of failing to discharge this duty. But while the existence of this duty may render their killing of the suspect morally legitimate, it does not transform the killing into a case of self-defence, or of defence of others. Indeed, to claim that it does is to obscure the moral considerations in play here – to make it appear that the moral predicament of the police is simply one of choosing between their lives and the life of the suspect, as would be so in a genuine case of self-defence.

We have argued that in the kinds of case in question, the police are not simply engaged in self-defence or defence of others, either in the narrow sense of preservation of life, or the wider sense of preservation of self. Rather, there is some more complex set of moral considerations here. Let us pursue these further, initially by looking at the case of the police killing of Pavel Marinoff.

Marinoff was a psychopathic Bulgarian army deserter who had shot and wounded a number of police officers before being confronted by Sergeant John Kapetanovski and Senior Constable Rod Macdonald on the Hume Highway outside Melbourne.[22] They pulled a van over to the side of the road, rightly believing it to be driven by Marinoff. They ordered the driver to place his hands outside the car. The driver drew his pistol, fired several shots, and drove off. He had wounded both officers. However, Macdonald fired two shots from his shotgun through the rear window of the escaping car, killing Marinoff. Perhaps this was a case of killing a fleeing offender, rather than of killing in self-defence or in defence of the lives of others. After all, presumably Marinoff was at this stage simply seeking to make good his escape. Accordingly, neither the lives of the police nor the lives of others were under immediate threat. Even if this were so, it was nevertheless a morally justifiable killing of a fleeing offender. Marinoff's offences included attempted murder and grievous bodily harm. Further, Marinoff was armed and dangerous, and constituted a threat to the lives of others, and especially the lives of police officers. Arguably, it was the *duty* of Macdonald to shoot Marinoff.

There are various other cases of shootings of dangerous fleeing felons that can be drawn from other police services and used for illustrative purposes. For example, there are the shootings of fleeing suspected terrorists in Northern Ireland.

---

[22] See John Silvester, Andrew Rule and Owen Davies, *The Silent War: Behind the Police Killings that shook Australia* (Sydney: Floradale, 1995), p. 3.

And police have been held liable for not shooting at fleeing gunmen known to be terrorists.

Another case is that of Hussein Said, who attempted to assassinate the Israeli ambassador in England. He fired one shot which missed and then his gun jammed. He took flight. He was pursued by a bodyguard, who fired a warning shot and called upon Said to give himself up. When he continued to flee, he was shot and wounded. In the ensuing court case, the bodyguard's action was held by the judge to have been illegal, since Said no longer constituted an immediate threat to the life of anyone. Evidently, bodyguards and police can find themselves between a rock and a hard place. They might be held liable for murder if they shoot, and failure to discharge their duty if they do not.

Let us now consider the killing of Ian Turner by Constable Wayne Sherwell.[23] Sherwell stopped a car driven by Turner for speeding near St. Arnaud in country Victoria. Turner had no ID, and in the course of conversation aroused Sherwell's suspicions. Turner said he would look for ID in his bag, but instead pulled a sawn-off .22 on Sherwell. He then took Sherwell's police revolver. Sherwell grabbed Turner's hand and a struggle ensued. During the struggle, Turner called on Sherwell to give up and simply let him go free. Sherwell disarmed Turner and, now in possession of both weapons, ordered Turner to lie on the ground and allow himself to be handcuffed. He refused to do so, calling on Sherwell to let him go. When Sherwell refused his request and tried to radio for assistance, Turner blocked his way, calling on Sherwell to shoot him. Sherwell fired his gun in the air. Turner ran to his car while Sherwell called on his radio for assistance. Turner ran back to his car and produced a sawn-off shotgun which he pointed at Sherwell. Sherwell fired a couple of shots. Both men hid behind their respective cars. Further shots were fired by Sherwell. Turner did not fire any shots at any time. When other officers arrived at the scene, they found one of Sherwell's shots had killed Turner. Turner, it later emerged, was an armed robber.

At the point when Sherwell shot Turner he was acting in self-defence, and his killing of Turner was justifiable on grounds of self-defence. However, we would like to consider a further issue that the case raises.

It seems that throughout the whole episode, Turner had no desire to kill Sherwell, but rather acted in order to escape from Sherwell. Thus, initially Turner used the threat of deadly force pre-emptively in order to escape arrest, and subsequently he grabbed his shotgun because Sherwell was holding him prisoner and using the threat of deadly force to do so. So Turner essentially threatened, but never in fact used, deadly force in order to avoid arrest.

For his part, Sherwell, while prepared to *threaten* to use deadly force to prevent Turner's escape, only in fact seemed prepared to use deadly force in self-defence. In other words, if Turner had simply got into his car and driven off, Sherwell would quite possibly not have shot him. Moreover, if Turner had known that Sherwell would not have shot him other than in self-defence, Turner would not have pulled a gun on Sherwell in the first place, but would simply have driven off.

---

[23] Silvester, Rule and Davies, *op. cit.*, pp. 125-130.

The case is an example of an offender who uses the threat of deadly force to avoid arrest. It also illustrates the distinction between killing in self-defence and killing in order to prevent an offender escaping. Moreover, it illustrates this distinction notwithstanding the fact that the offender is armed and is prepared to use deadly force to escape arrest.

This distinction between killing in self-defence (or defence of others) and killing (or not killing) in order to prevent an offender escaping is further illustrated in the case of passive non-compliance discussed in Chapter 2; the case involving the dangerous criminal, David Martin, in an underground subway in England in 1982. Cornered in the underground subway by armed police, Martin was persistently ordered by police to give himself up, but refused to do so. However, he made no hostile movements against the police. The police were concerned that he might have a gun and might use it against them. Certainly his history indicated this might be so. Finally the police decided not to shoot him, but to rush and disarm him. He was found to be unarmed.

Three points need to be noted here. First, the police risked their lives in rushing Martin. He might have been armed, and if so, he may well have shot dead one or more of the police. Second, if Martin had been shot dead by the police, then the police may well have been found guilty of murder. Third, if Martin had been allowed to escape, he might have harmed, even killed, innocent people, and if so, the police would have been held liable for these consequences of their action of allowing him to escape.

Let us now consider the police killing of Graeme Jensen. Victorian police sought to arrest Jensen for murder. In fact he did not commit the murder. Nor did they have sufficient evidence to convict him of conspiring to rob a bank – the other matter for which he was under investigation. At most he could have been convicted of illegal possession of a firearm. Moreover, Jensen probably believed the police were out to kill him. At any rate, he tried to escape the police when they tried to arrest him. Jensen was armed and allegedly pointed his gun at officers who first warned him and then shot at him. It later turned out that Jensen's gun was not loaded. Jensen was escaping by car when the second shot went through the rear window and killed him. By one account, Jensen was killed in self-defence. By a second account, it was not a case of self-defence but of shooting a fleeing offender, the offence being illegal possession of an (unloaded) weapon.[24] On a third account, it was unlawful for police to even try to arrest him. If so, Jensen was murdered.[25]

At any rate, the Jensen killing raises at least two issues. In the case of Jensen, unlike Turner, the police initiated the threat of deadly force, and Jensen at most threatened deadly force for the purposes of making his escape. Moreover, the police used an extent of force that was disproportionate to the offence committed.

Let us now summarise the moral considerations that the above-described cases illustrate.

Firstly, there is the seriousness of the offence committed by the person shot dead by the police. In the case of a burglar, the crime is a violation of the right to

---

[24] Silvester, Rule and Davies, *op. cit.*, p. 37.

[25] Police were in fact charged with his murder but were not convicted.

property. While this is not a violation of a right to something constitutive of self-hood, it is a serious crime, and certainly far more serious than the petty theft involved in picking someone's pocket. In the case of Marinoff, the offence is a violation of the right to life, and far more serious still. This raises the issue of the proportionality of police use of deadly force.

Secondly, there is the question as to whether the offender is armed and prepared to kill in order to avoid imprisonment. Here we must distinguish between being prepared to avoid imprisonment, and being prepared to kill for other reasons, such as self-defence, revenge or to become rich.

So the following two considerations are evidently held in many western societies to be jointly sufficient to morally justify the police use of deadly force as a last resort.[26] First, the offence is serious in that it is a violation of a right to something constitutive of self-hood, or if not, it is a violation of some other right of an appropriately important kind. Second, the offender is prepared to use deadly force to avoid arrest. Some societies appear to take this view, while at the same time being opposed to capital punishment. There is no obvious inconsistency here. On the one hand, Australian society takes the view that killing is not justified as a punishment for criminals who are imprisoned and therefore no longer able to break its laws. On the other hand, society holds that police use of deadly force is justified if this is the only way to ensure that its laws against serious crimes are upheld, and in particular, if the perpetrators of serious crimes are themselves prepared to kill in order to avoid imprisonment. This last point is in need of further elaboration.

In the kinds of case under consideration, there are only *two* options confronting the police, letting the perpetrator escape or shooting him dead. However, what has been omitted from the argument thus far is that the fact that these are the only options is due to the perpetrator; he is responsible for this situation – he is forcing the choice between two evils.[27] The armed burglar mentioned earlier refuses to surrender himself and his stolen goods in the face of non-violent or non-lethal forms of pressure. He is ruling out a third option – the morally preferable option – namely, his peaceful surrender. In that case, the burglar is responsible for the choice between two evils confronting the police. That is, the burglar is not only responsible for violating people's property rights, he is also responsible for attempting to prevent the police from performing their duty, and indeed, he is responsible for forcing the police to choose between two evils. The two evils in question are allowing the perpetrator of a serious crime to escape, or shooting and killing that perpetrator.

This consideration may be enough to tip the scales in favour of police use of deadly force in this kind of case. If so, how would this tipping of the scales be achieved? Presumably the perpetrator would now be held to be *indirectly and in part* responsible for his own death. When a police officer shoots dead an armed

---

[26] However, this view is evidently controversial. It appears to be inconsistent with that advanced, for example, by Jerome Skolnick and J. Fyfe in *Above the Law: Police and the Excessive Use of Force* (NY: Free Press, 1993).

[27] For discussion of the notion of forcing the choice, see Montague, *op. cit.*

bank robber who is prepared to kill in order to prevent apprehension, the police officer's choice situation has been knowingly chosen by the burglar.

While police use of deadly force in these kinds of case may well be in principle morally justifiable, the justification is nevertheless problematic in a number of ways. Firstly, it places an enormous responsibility – and a corresponding opportunity for abuse – on individual members of the police force. For as we have seen, if police are entitled to kill in order to ensure that the law is upheld, then police may kill an armed bank robber even though he will not fire his gun if left alone. Moreover, in doing so they will kill this (alleged) bank robber prior to any considered judgement by a court of law that he has in fact broken the law. In such cases, it is the responsibility of the individual police officer, initially, to make the judgement that the person is an armed burglar who will kill in order to avoid apprehension, and then to go on to shoot this person dead in order that he not escape.

Secondly, it needs to be determined which crimes committed by *armed* perpetrators are sufficiently serious to warrant police use of deadly force. We have suggested that violations of rights to things constitutive of self-hood are sufficiently serious. It still remains to be determined what other rights violations are sufficiently serious. Here it is not simply a matter of determining which rights are sufficiently morally important to warrant protection by recourse to deadly force, but also the extent of the rights violations. Perhaps a single armed shoplifter is not a legitimate target, but what about an army of armed looters threatening the economic well-being of an impoverished community?

This latter problem raises perplexing questions concerning the moral balance to be struck between, on the one hand, the right to life of a suspect, and on the other, the rights of citizens to be protected by police from serious rights violations, which nevertheless stop short of threatening their lives or elements constitutive of self-hood. Here there are a number of considerations. How extensive are these rights violations? Are these rights violations likely – if they go unchecked – to have as a consequence the violations of citizens' rights to things which are constitutive of self-hood? What moral weight, if any, is to be attached to the threat posed by those who use arms to prevent their legitimate arrest, to the possession by the State of overriding coercive power to uphold its morally legitimate laws?

Finally, these kind of "forcing the choice" situations raises the question as to whether or not the police – and not the offender – knowingly created a situation in which they would have to kill the offender in self-defence, or at least failed to act when they knew that their inaction would lead to a situation in which they had to kill the offender in self-defence. These latter sorts of cases need to be distinguished from the ones here under consideration, namely ones in which an offender is forcing the choice upon the police of either using deadly force or allowing the offender to escape. Consider, in this connection, the following type of scenario involving the Special Investigation Section of the Los Angeles Police Department, who targeted armed robbers during the period 1965-1992: "The most controversial of the home-baked rules is the SIS practice of standing by and watching its surveillance subjects victimise innocent citizens, then confronting offenders as they leave the scene of their crime."[28] Here the SIS provided known offenders with the opportunity to commit very serious crimes by failing to arrest them for the less serious crimes they had already committed. The SIS did so in order to enable the offenders to commit the more serious crimes, and thereby either receive longer prison sentences, or be shot by the police attempting to flee the crime scene or resisting arrest.[29]

Let us conclude this chapter by outlining the main general conditions under which police use of deadly force might be morally justified, or at least might be morally justified if adequate police accountability can be ensured so as to prevent abuse of police powers. Note that the first two conditions – self-defence and defence of others – are in essence the same conditions under which ordinary citizens are entitled to use deadly force. The use of deadly force under conditions (i) and (ii) of (c) below is particular to the police, and also problematic in various ways, some already mentioned. At any rate, the use of deadly force under conditions (i) and (ii) make a number of implicit assumptions. One assumption is that the extent of reasonable suspicion is such as to justify making an arrest. However, killing an alleged offender to prevent his/her escape can presumably only be justified in situations in which there is certainty, or near certainty, that the alleged offender has in fact committed the offence. A higher standard of evidence than reasonable suspicion is required. Another assumption is that there *really are* no possible ways of preventing escape other than by using deadly force. So, for example, letting the suspected offender escape in the knowledge that there is a reasonable chance that he or she can be arrested at a later date is not an option.

(a) *Self-defence.* A police officer is morally entitled to kill another person if that person is trying to kill, maim, or otherwise threaten the self-hood of the officer, and will succeed unless the officer kills the person first.

(b) *Defence of Others.* A police officer is morally entitled – and may be morally obliged – to kill another person if that person is trying to kill, maim, or otherwise threaten the self-hood of some third person(s), and will succeed unless the officer kills the would-be offender first.

(c) *Uphold the Law:* (i) Fleeing felons. A police officer is, or might be, morally entitled – and may be morally obliged – to kill another person if that person (whether armed or unarmed) is rightly and reasonably suspected of the crimes of

---

[28] Jerome Skolnick and James Fyfe, *op. cit.*, p. 146.

[29] The police might argue that in some of these situations they would be unable to convict these offenders of any serious crimes, due to the difficulties of, for example, proving a conspiracy to commit an armed robbery, or even to prove attempted armed robbery. Accordingly – the argument might run – they had to choose between increasing the risk to life and limb (their chosen option), or allowing armed robbers to either get off scot-free (when they failed to be convicted of (say) conspiracy to conduct an armed robbery) or simply be convicted of minor offences, such as (say) car theft.

killing, maiming, or otherwise threatening the self-hood of some third person(s), is attempting to avoid arrest, and if the only way to prevent the suspected offender escaping is to kill him/her.

(ii) Armed suspects. A police officer is, or might be, morally entitled – and may be morally obliged – to kill another person if that person is rightly and reasonably suspected of the crimes of serious rights violations, is attempting to avoid arrest, is armed and using those arms to avoid arrest, and if the only way to prevent the suspected offender from escaping is to kill him/her.[30]

---

[30] An additional condition might be the following one, namely *Deterrence in States of Emergency*: A police officer is, or might be, morally entitled – and may be morally obliged – to kill another person if: (a) that person is rightly and reasonably suspected of a type of crime which is so widespread in an existing state of emergency as to constitute a serious threat to fundamental rights of citizens; (b) deadly force is the only available deterrence in the circumstances of this particular state of emergency; (c) that person is attempting to avoid arrest; (d) the only way to prevent the suspected offender escaping is to kill him/her; (e) perpetrators of the type of crime in question have been warned that they will be shot dead under conditions (a), (c) and (d), and; (f) the policy specified in conditions (a)-(e) has been adopted as a limited policy for a specific delimited period.

Chapter 4

Privacy, Confidentiality and Security in Policing

Thus far in this book, we have argued that: (a) normatively speaking, the central and most important purpose of police work is the protection of legally enshrined, justifiably enforceable, moral rights, and; (b) a distinctive feature of policing is its unavoidable and routine use of harmful methods, e.g. coercion and deception, that are considered to be morally unacceptable in ordinary circumstances. In the last chapter, our concern was with the right to life in policing contexts. Specifically, we examined the moral justification for police use of deadly force, and in effect argued that the justification for police use of deadly force was derived from, although somewhat wider than, the justification for an ordinary person's use of deadly force. In this chapter, our focus is on a less fundamental, but nevertheless important, moral right, namely the right to privacy. We consider a number of moral issues that arise as a result of the use by police of methods that infringe the right to privacy and also breach moral principles related to privacy, such as the moral requirement not to deceive.

Moral Right to Privacy

> Many people feel seriously diminished by the disclosure of personal information, even when it is accurate and they are not damaged professionally or socially. Small wonder that more then sixty years ago a prominent Boston lawyer who became one of our greatest jurists, Louis D. Brandeis, characterised the rights of privacy as "the most comprehensive of rights and the one most valued by civilised men." The thought was echoed by the late, great William O. Douglas, who said, "The right to be left alone is the beginning of all freedom."[1]

Brandeis *et al.* are surely correct in holding that privacy is an important moral value. However, the notion of privacy has proven to be a difficult one to explicate adequately. Nevertheless, there are a number of general points that can be made.[2]

First, privacy is a moral right that a person has in relation to other persons with respect to: (a) the possession of information about him/herself by other persons, or;

---

[1] Arthur Miller, *Miller's Court* (New York: Houghton Mifflin, 1982).

[2] An earlier version of the material in this section appeared in Seumas Miller, "Privacy and the Internet", *Australian Computer Journal*, Vol. 29, No. 1, 1997, pp. 12-16, and an earlier one still in Seumas Miller, *Issues in Police Ethics* (Keon, 1996).

(b) the observation/perceiving of him/herself – including tactile interference, such as body searches – by other persons. The range of matters regarded as private in this basic sense embraces much of what could be referred to as a person's "inner self". This inner self comprises a person's unexpressed thoughts, feelings, bodily sensations and imaginings. But it may also comprise elements or aspects of a person's body: roughly speaking, those elements or aspects that are not normally perceptually accessible to others in public spaces. This inner self is the core of the sphere that is subject to an individual person's autonomous decision-making. Here the inner self stands in contrast with the outer self; the self that is necessarily present to others or that a person chooses to make known or to present to others.[3] A person's autonomy with respect to this inner self is not primarily de facto autonomy, although a person does have a degree of de facto autonomy with respect to (say) what they are thinking. Rather, it is a moral right to autonomy in respect of their inner self.

Second, a person's moral right to autonomy in respect of their inner self – the right to privacy – derives from the fact that a person's inner self in large part comprises their personal identity; it is in large part who they are. (Naturally, a person's identity is also in part constituted by their outer or public self.) Moreover, a person's inner self is in part constituted by their autonomy with respect to their inner self; their ability, albeit limited, to decide what to think and feel – to decide, albeit within strict limits, who they are. More than anything else, it is the moral value of personal identity – including autonomy – that explains the moral repugnance of violations of privacy. The more intrusive and sustained these violations are, the more repugnant they are; and the more they involve an attempt to change – as opposed to merely passively observe – elements of one's personal identity, the more morally repugnant they are. Hence our deep moral aversion to thought control. Like unjustified attempts to restrict our movement, thought control is a violation of our autonomy, but at a deeper level it is an assault on our personal identity, including our autonomy – an assault on who we are.

Third, while closely related, the right to autonomy is not the same thing as the right to privacy. For one thing, a person has a right to autonomous decision-making in relation to a range of issues outside the sphere of the inner self; the right to autonomy embraces much of a person's decision-making in the public sphere. However, the right to autonomy and the right to privacy are conceptually connected. Roughly speaking, the notion of privacy delimits an area, viz. the inner self; however, the moral right to decide what to think and do is the right to autonomy, and the moral right to decide *who to exclude and who not to*, is an element of the right to autonomy. So the right to privacy consists of the right to exclude others (right to autonomy) from the inner self (the private sphere).

Fourth, a person's intimate relationship with another person gives rise to a zone of interpersonal privacy from which third parties are excluded. For example, a married couple has a right to engage in intimate sexual acts in their home unobserved by others. Such zones of interpersonal privacy or intimacy typically

---

[3] See Thomas Nagel, "Concealment and Exposure", in his *Concealment and Exposure and other Essays* (Oxford: Oxford University Press, 2002).

exist between members of families, e.g. parents and children, friends and lovers. Moreover, such intimacy is regarded as a moral good. Certainly the development of interpersonal relations with emotional depth requires, and is in part constituted by, intimacy. However, intimacy can be morally problematic. Consider the predatory intimacy that might obtain in an exploitative sexual relationship, or the betrayal of trust that results when an undercover operative finally "shops" an offender that he has "befriended".

Fifth, certain facts pertaining to objects a person owns, or monies a person earns, are held to be private simply in virtue of the right to ownership. Ownership appears to confer the right not to disclose, or have disclosed, information concerning the thing owned. Or at least there is a presumption in favour of non-disclosure, including non-disclosure to, or by, government departments; a presumption that can be overridden to a limited extent by, for example, the public interest in tax gathering, or in tracking the proceeds of a crime.

Sixth, certain facts pertaining to a person's various public roles and practices, including one's voting decisions, are regarded as private.[4] These kinds of facts are apparently regarded as private in part in virtue of the potential, should they be disclosed, of undermining the capacity of the person to autonomously function in these public roles, or to fairly compete in these practices. If others know how a person votes, the person's right to freely support a particular candidate might be undermined. If business competitors have access to a person's business plans, then they will gain an unfair advantage over the person. If a would-be employer knows a job applicant's sexual preferences, then the employer might unfairly discriminate against the job applicant by not hiring them because of their sexual preferences.

Seventh, and more generally, a measure of privacy is necessary simply in order for a person to pursue his or her projects, whatever those projects might be. For one thing, reflection is necessary for planning, and reflection requires a degree of freedom from the intrusions of others, i.e. a degree of privacy. For another, knowledge of someone else's plans can enable those plans to be thwarted. *Autonomy* – including the exercise of autonomy in the public sphere – requires a measure of privacy.

Eighth, the sphere of an individual's privacy can be widened to include other individuals who stand in a professional relationship to the first individual. Here part of the sphere of an individual's privacy, e.g. the bodily states of a sick person, is widened to include another person, e.g. the person's doctor, and the result is a *confidential* relationship. An analogous point can be made in relation to lawyers and their clients, and in relation to police and the victims of crimes who are also witnesses to those crimes.

Ninth, the data owned, and "actions" performed, by organisations and groups – including businesses and government agencies – or by individual persons in their capacity as members of organisations or groups, may also be regarded as private, or at least confidential. For example, a business company needs a measure of confidentiality in relation to its plans, if it is to be able to compete on equal terms

---

[4] See Stanley I. Benn, *A Theory of Freedom* (Cambridge: Cambridge University Press, 1988), p. 289.

in the marketplace. Again, law enforcement agencies must retain confidential information in relation to the activities of criminal organisations, if they are to successfully investigate those organisations.

Tenth, the notion that privacy is an absolute right that cannot be overridden under any circumstances is unsustainable. The rights to privacy of some individuals, and the right to confidentiality of members of some organisations, will in some cases be overridden by the rights of other individuals and other members of organisations to be protected by the law enforcement agencies from rights violations, including murder, rape, grievous bodily harm, paedophilia and armed robbery.

Let us now turn to some case studies that display some of the privacy and confidentiality issues that arise in policing.

Case Studies[5]

Case Study 4.1 Chook Fowler and "Crotch-Cam"

One can scarcely imagine the effect the videotape, played on June 5th, 1995, at the Royal Commission into New South Wales Police Corruption, had upon 30-year police veteran, Detective Inspector Graham "Chook" Fowler – though we are aware of the devastating effect it was subsequently to have on public confidence in the police. Fowler, who had headed the Kings Cross and the City of Sydney detectives, had been called as a witness, and was being questioned by Queen's Counsel Gary Crooke, assisting the Royal Commissioner Justice James Wood. 25 times, in the course of his examination, Fowler had denied being corrupt. Crooke then asked Fowler to watch the television monitor in front of him, saying, "One thing that I would ask you to consider is that this video is produced effectively for your consideration by the people of New South Wales and by all honest police." As the 22-minute video began showing scenes of Detective Inspector Fowler allegedly talking openly about protection rackets, he began to fidget and frown in the witness box. The video allegedly showed Fowler exchanging money with policeman Trevor Haken, who had been working undercover with the Commission for nine months.[6]

Filmed by a mini-video camera hidden under the dashboard in Haken's car, and later released to the media, excerpts were run on TV news broadcasts, establishing corruption as endemic amongst the state's detectives. The NSW Police Service suspended Fowler from duty that day. Detective Sergeant Trevor David Haken, who also appeared on the videotape, gave evidence before the Royal Commission against corrupt fellow officers and criminals. Haken's evidence was the touchstone, the critical turning point in the Commission's investigations, and

---

[5] Case Studies 4.1 and 4.2 are in part taken from Seumas Miller, John Blackler and Andrew Alexandra's *Police Ethics* (Sydney: Allen and Unwin, 1997), pp. 99-101 and pp. 187-189 respectively.

[6] *Daily Telegraph-Mirror* (Sydney newspaper), June 6th, 1995, p. 1.

revealed he had been a corrupt officer who had been "turned". Of the beginnings of his involvement with the Royal Commission, Haken's wife said, "There was nothing unusual about the two plain-clothes police officers who came to the door that Saturday morning, August 20th, 1994. They said they had a summons for him [Haken], so I got him and they went out the front… He came in and said he had to go to court. I've never seen anyone look so grey."

Haken had finally been caught out. The NSW Crime Commission had enough evidence to put him in jail for years... Shortly afterwards the Crime Commission evidence was handed over to the recently formed Police Royal Commission.[7]

The *Herald* subsequently learned that it was the State Crime Commission which held the key which the Royal Commission used to unlock the door to police corruption. The Crime Commission handed over material about Trevor Haken which apparently allowed the Royal Commission to force him to "roll over" and become a "supergrass" for the State.[8]

Perhaps it was professional pride after being exposed as a fraud, but Haken took to the role of undercover investigator with relish, taking ever-greater risks and gathering valuable information for the Royal Commission.[9]

The existence of 80 taped conversations such as those involving Fowler was revealed; Haken indicated he had collected and distributed $AU26,180 in bribes during this period. By August 22nd, Haken had named 24 persons as corrupt,[10] newspapers suggesting he might name as many as 200.[11] The toll of police named – or "stung" – by Haken soon included acting Chief of Staff, Chief Superintendent Bob Lysaught, and acting Commander of the Fraud Enforcement Agency, Detective Superintendent Brian Meredith.

It is clear that not merely Haken's confession of past wrongdoings, but his ongoing and active collaboration with the Royal Commission, had provided the major break the Commission needed to penetrate the solidaristic detective cohort. Contradicting suggestions Haken's cooperation with the Royal Commission had been coerced, on August 24th, 1995, counsel assisting the Royal Commission made things plain:

> Mr. Agius was at pains yesterday to point out that Haken was not threatened, and Haken agreed with him that he had never asked what the Royal Commission might have on him. From that day [September 2nd, 1994], Haken, armed with his secret recording device and the mobile recording studio in his car, was extraordinarily busy... On June 5th [1995], Haken's undercover role ended when he stepped into the witness box for the first time. Only the day before, in a military-style operation, his family had been taken from their home at Mt. Kuring-gai to parts unknown.[12]

[7] *Sydney Morning Herald*, "Spectrum", March 8th, 1997, p. 6.
[8] *Sydney Morning Herald*, July 15th, 1995, p. 5.
[9] *Sydney Morning Herald*, "Spectrum", March 8th, 1997, p. 6.
[10] *Sydney Morning Herald*, August 22nd, 1995, p. 1.
[11] *Sydney Morning Herald*, August 19th, 1995, pp. 25-6.
[12] *Sydney Morning Herald*, August 25th, 1995, p. 1.

Haken, with his wife and children, disappeared from their home of 20 years into the witness protection scheme; it would seem Witsec, the Australian Federal Police program, moved the separated Jayne Haken and her children to the US – the Hakens' marriage had not survived the stresses his activities imposed upon it. Although his police career was finished, Haken remained an asset of NSW's Director of Public Prosecutions, and he was involved as a principal witness in a number of further criminal prosecutions arising from the Royal Commission.

Case Study 4.2 Chinese Walls

Detective Blank, a state police officer, was organisationally pressured to "produce" – to bring matters he and others were investigating to a speedy conclusion. The information Detective Blank sought to enable him to pursue those inquiries was often statutorily denied him; Blank, no legalist, was not awed – as one learned in the law might be – by law's mystique. As a "craftsman" of the law, Blank sought therefore to find his way around this legal obstacle.

Detective Blank's endeavours brought him eventually to "the bourse", which, since we are speaking hypothetically, we will locate in (say) the Non-Commissioned Officers' mess of the plain-clothes branch of an Australian Armed Forces' Service Police. People it on Friday evenings with guests from Customs, Special Branch, Federal and State Police, and the Independent Commission Against Corruption – an alphabet soup of enforcement agencies; investigators from departments of government whose twain was never supposed to meet. Social isolation, common interests, and the need for a discreet and protected venue in which to socialise, drew them together; the conversational topic was invariably "shop", the bourse an inevitable outcome.

That's how Detective Blank thought of this venue; a place of exchange, in which information was the currency, a commodity to be traded. He knew of several similar venues.

State and Federal Drug Task Forces, joint Police and Government Insurance Office fraud investigations, State and Federal Police inquiries into Workcover and other workers' compensation fraud; all built sanctioned connections that were gainfully continued, extending far beyond regular "networking". Contact between (say) insurance company Loss Assessors and the Arson and Fraud Squads were relationships made in law-enforcement heaven. Blank suspected information was making its way not only between sequestered organs of government, but between government and the private sector.

Blank sought out a Telecom investigator, and indicating scribbled particulars on a Post-It tag said, "I am interested in this girl's de facto; we want to interview him about a bunch of break-and-enters. According to the Australia Post and Social Services' investigators, they have left their address and there's no forwarding address, but she had a telephone connected in her name. Can you find out where she asked the Telecom rebate cheque for her deposit to be forwarded?" Post-It tags, and notes on drink coasters and paper napkins, were being exchanged throughout the bar; Blank already had several in his pocket.

Blank was approached by an investigator from a small Federal agency. Blank greeted him, saying, "I think I have a way around your problem, Dave; your suspect won't come in for an interview, you can't arrest him, because the Acts you administer don't specify an arrest power, but you need to speak with him, right?"

"I ran a check on our Computerised Warrant System and he owes us over two grand in unpaid traffic warrants. The Warrant Constable from the local station will arrest him for you, executing the warrants on him Monday morning, about 06.00 at the address you gave me – you can interview him at the police station whilst he's in custody on the warrants and charge him before the local court, okay?" The Federal investigator said, "Knew we could depend on you, Blanky, but how about the future? What about the next time some suspect jacks-up on us? We have to be able to operate."

"Blanky, I've got a biggie to ask you; can you get our investigators made Special Constables in this state?" Blank mulled the request over; a convincing body of judicial decision and *dicta* held that Special Constables in New South Wales enjoy much of the authority of the state police, empowering them to arrest under most State and Federal Acts. The charter of this small Federal agency extended to only a handful of Federal Acts, none of which specified an arrest power: as Special Constables in New South Wales, they would be able to sidestep this difficulty.

Blank said, "So you're looking for a way to exceed the powers granted to you by the Federal Acts you enforce?" The investigator said, "Blanky, the Senate hearings on our mandate at the moment obliges us to put our proposed amendment to the Acts giving us arrest powers on the back burner for a while. Do you think you can help us with our problem, at least as far as this state is concerned?"

Blank temporised; "What does your Minister say?" "Officially, nothing; privately, our Department Head gave us a wink and a nudge. I have a letter here from our branch, requesting Special Constable status for our investigators." When Blank hesitated, the investigator said, "Our department is very small, but we have access …*to everything*; we would be extremely grateful."

Detective Blank, accepting the official communication, thought to himself, "The *ex officio* status of the bourse is reaching another plateau of reality altogether."

The Right to Privacy and Law Enforcement

As we saw above, privacy is an important moral right. However, the right to privacy is not absolute; the right to privacy can be overridden under certain circumstances. In relation to accessing of data and/or intercepting of communications by law enforcement agencies, a balance has to be struck between the rights of citizens – including suspects – to privacy and confidentiality on the one hand, and the rights of actual and potential victims to protection from serious crime on the other. Moreover, the state of technology at a given point in time to some extent determines the possibility of striking the appropriate balance at that time. For example, the current availability to the general public of very secure computer systems and of high-level encryption products makes accessing of data and/or intercepting of communications on the Internet by law enforcement agencies extremely difficult and expensive.

In striking this balance, whether it is in relation to communications by telephone or by some other means, a number of principles need to be kept in mind.[13]

First, because such accessing and/or intercepting are by definition an infringement of the right to privacy, the presumption must be against their use. This presumption can be overridden by other very weighty moral considerations – especially the need to protect other moral rights – or by exceptional circumstances, such as might obtain in wartime. But the presumption cannot be overridden by a blanket appeal to the common good or to the general need for security.

Second, the benefits of such accessing and/or intercepting must offset the likely costs, including the costs in terms of the erosion in public trust.

Third, the accessing and/or interception in question must be in relation to serious crimes.

Fourth, there must be at least a reasonable suspicion[14] that the person whose privacy is to be infringed has committed, or intends to commit, a serious crime – or is implicated in a serious crime – and that the resulting information is likely to substantially further the investigation under way in relation to that crime. (See Case Study 4.1.)

Fifth, there must be no feasible alternative method of gathering the information that does not involve an infringement of privacy.

Sixth, the law enforcement officials must be subject to stringent accountability requirements, including the issuing of warrants in circumstances in which the justification provided is independently adjudicated.

Seventh, those whose privacy has been infringed must be informed that it has been infringed at the earliest time consistent with not compromising the investigation, or connected investigations.

It is sometimes suggested that infringements of privacy are not morally wrong if the person whose privacy is invaded does not know about it, and if there are no harmful consequences. However, we have argued that persons have a *moral right* to privacy. Therefore, an unauthorised invasion of that privacy is a prima facie moral wrong, irrespective of whether the person knows his/her privacy has been invaded, and irrespective of the harmful consequences. The point is simply that the "invader" is in possession of information, or has made observations, which he or she does not have a right to possess or to make; indeed, he or she has acquired that information, or made those observations, in violation of the privacy rights of another person. If a person steals someone else's property, then the thief has committed a wrong, notwithstanding the fact that the victim might never notice

[13] An earlier version of the material in this section appeared in Miller, "Privacy and the Internet", *op. cit.*

[14] The more intrusive and sustained the infringement of the right to privacy, the higher the standard of evidence that ought to be required in relation to reasonable suspicion, e.g. probable cause, or even good and decisive reasons.

that the item has gone missing; there is a perpetrator and a victim, even though the victim is unaware that they are a victim.

An increasingly important issue in relation to privacy is the integration and sharing of different sets of information available to different government – including law enforcement – agencies. This kind of situation is evidenced in Case Study 4.2. This is morally problematic in that, as we have seen, there is a presumption against the gathering of information on citizens by government officials, including law enforcement personnel. This presumption can be overridden in relation to specific kinds of information required for specific legitimate purposes, such as tax gathering or the investigation of someone reasonably suspected of engaging in serious criminal activity. But information gathered for one purpose should not be made available for another purpose, unless a specific case can be made out for doing so. The problem with the "bourse" in Case Study 4.2 is that there are no such strictures in place. It is an unregulated information exchange.

Nor is the bourse simply a problem for isolated individuals whose rights might be infringed; the problem is potentially a societal one. One of the purposes of privacy law is to deny, as far as possible, the formation of linkages between statutory bodies, and thereby to prevent such linkages enabling the coming into being of a "Big Brother" system of invasive inquiry and social control of the kind that existed in Eastern Europe under communism.[15] Accordingly, organisational "Chinese walls" are supposed to separate the investigators employed by one of the several different organs of government from the investigators employed by another of these organs. Limited contact across the statutory barriers might only be made – or denied – at the highest level, and for good reason; and done so in a parsimoniously sanctioned and limited manner following stringent protocols.

Another issue here is the relationship between public-sector investigators and private-sector investigators. What, for instance, would be the status of Telecom's investigators after the privatisation – or part-privatisation – of Telecom, the former monopolistic and wholly Australian government-owned telecommunications provider? Did the Australian Commonwealth Bank investigators' status change with the privatisation of the bank? Is the erasing of the line between police investigations and investigations in the private sector problematic? The problem here is the possibly disparate and conflicting commitments of investigators in the two spheres.[16] The ends of police investigators ought clearly to be driven by the public interest in law enforcement and protection of the individual rights of citizens. By contrast, private investigators must aim at the organisational interests of the corporation that employs them, possibly to the exclusion of the interests of the public at large. And there is the very real question of the independence of investigators operating under the control of the management of an organisation in the private sphere.

---

[15] See, for instance, Stanley Cohen, *Visions of Social Control: Crime, Punishment and Classification* (Cambridge: Polity Press, 1985).

[16] See, for instance, Les Johnston, *The Rebirth of Private Policing* (London: Routledge, 1992).

Privacy, Law Enforcement and Encryption

Notwithstanding the above discussion of the status of the right to privacy and the need to protect that right from unjustified infringements, there is a perception among many operational detectives that legal rules have gone too far in preserving the rights of suspects, to the extent that they have become a major impediment to effective investigation. One of the alleged reasons for this is the advent of new technologies – including the new information and communication technologies – and their exploitation by criminals.

Nor are these complaints without their theoretical backers. Amitai Etzioni argues that the prevailing concern to protect individual privacy in relation to the Internet, in particular, is misguided, and that public safety and public health are being put at risk by policies driven by strong commitments to individual privacy.[17] As always, there is a need to balance individual rights against the public good, and according to Etzioni the balance has shifted too much in favour of individual rights. Given the sustained theoretical nature of Etzioni's discussion of these matters, we will consider his view in some detail.

Our concern here is with encryption. In the course of examining this issue, we will offer a critique and adjustment to the general communitarian conception of the right to privacy that he offers. It should be said at the outset that we are by no means completely at odds with Etzioni. Nevertheless, in our view his position is seriously deficient in a number of respects.

In essence, encryption is a complex code that protects the secrecy of electronic communications. Moreover, some of these codes (hyper-encryption) are very difficult, if not impossible, to crack. There has been an enormous increase in the use of encryption technologies, including the use of hyper-encryption.

There are obviously considerable benefits that accrue to business, government and individuals from the use of encryption, including the safeguarding of confidentiality and privacy. Unfortunately, hyper-encryption also affords opportunities for criminals to protect their communications, and thereby thwart the efforts of law enforcement agencies to apprehend criminals and protect ordinary citizens.

Accordingly, the question becomes: Should public authorities have the capability to decipher encrypted messages?[18]

Etzioni argues that they should, on the grounds that the threats to public safety posed by the new encryption technologies outweigh the right to privacy of those

---

[17] Amitai Etzioni, *The Limits of Privacy* (New York: Basic Books, 1999). An earlier version of the material in this section appeared in Seumas Miller, "Privacy, Encryption and the Internet", in A. D'Atri, A. Marturano, S. Rogerson and T. Ward Bynum (eds.), *Proceedings of the 4th ETHICOMP International Conference on the Social and Ethical Impacts of Information and Communication Technologies* (CD format) (Rome, 1999), pp. 1-11.

[18] Etzioni, *op. cit.*, p. 77.

using encryption. Citing D. E. Denning and W. E. Baugh,[19] Etzioni lists threats posed by encryption to law enforcement, public safety and national security.[20] The items on this list can be classified into three relevant categories of threat: (a) encryption can make it impossible to obtain necessary *evidence*; (b) encryption can frustrate communications intercepts in relation to the *known or suspected criminal activity* of individuals and organisations, and; (c) encryption can hinder *intelligence-gathering*. Etzioni also mentions that encryption can lead to *greater infringements of privacy* than would otherwise have occurred, as when, for example, investigators opt for intrusive audio and visual surveillance when they are unable to intercept e-mail messages. However, even if true, this does not of itself justify infringements of privacy, but only lesser, rather than greater, infringements of privacy. For this reason we will disregard it in our discussion below.

By Etzioni's lights, privacy ought to be infringed only if there is "a well documented and macroscopic threat to the common good, not merely a hypothetical danger".[21] Notwithstanding the low probability (and indeed hypothetical nature) of some macroscopic dangers posed by encryption, Etzioni judges the capability to decipher is warranted by virtue of the high disutility of the macroscopic dangers, were they to occur. For example, biological terrorism is perhaps improbable, but it has a very high disutility. Moreover, privacy ought to be infringed only by a given method if this method is likely to secure the end for which it is being used, and if there is no other non-intrusive, or less intrusive, method.

In the case of encryption, public key recovery is the means to avert macroscopic dangers: "A key recovery system is a backup system for encryption keys that enables the encrypted data to be deciphered, even if the primary keys are destroyed. Public key recovery involves placing a key with public authorities."[22] In this connection, Etzioni discusses the practical question as to whether or not strong encryption products might be available from sources outside the jurisdiction of the public authority in question. He points out that such outside sources might themselves have a backup key, and even if they did not, the consumer might not be aware whether or not the sources have such a backup key. Moreover, as Etzioni notes,[23] even if criminals could use their own specialised systems, the use of such systems would point law enforcement agencies towards where the criminals were concentrated. (And such use would restrict the lines of criminal communication in relation to other non-secure systems.) At any rate, we are going to accept Etzioni's claim that public key recovery, if introduced, would be of considerable assistance to law enforcement agencies in particular, and that there is no alternative (and less intrusive) means. Accordingly, the question of whether or not to introduce a public

---

[19] D. E. Denning and W. E. Baugh, "Encryption and Evolving Technologies as Tools of Organised Crime and Terrorism" (US Working Group on Organised Crime, National Strategy Information Centre, 1997).

[20] Etzioni, *op. cit.*, pp. 78-80.

[21] *ibid.*, p. 12.

[22] *ibid.*, p. 81.

[23] *ibid.*, p. 86.

key recovery system resolves itself into a theoretical question concerning the balance to be struck between the individual right to privacy on the one hand, and the need for public safety on the other.

Etzioni concludes that public safety overrides individual privacy, and does so by virtue of the necessity for the use of a public key recovery system to deal with the significant macroscopic public safety problem posed by hyper-encryption. Moreover, Etzioni suggests that the introduction of a public key recovery system is simply an extension to computer technology of prevailing accepted law enforcement powers in relation to older technologies, e.g. telephone interception.[24]

There are a number of problems with Etzioni's arguments and his overall conception. Let us now turn to these.

Etzioni tends to run together a variety of different public agencies under the umbrella term "public authorities". This is potentially confusing, since different public agencies have very different responsibilities, and presumably, therefore, very different needs in terms of access to information. Accordingly, we will be concerned in what follows only with law enforcement agencies.

We have already argued that law enforcement powers in contemporary liberal democracies in relation to telephone interception are acceptable if they are constrained by the principles that we set out above, e.g. the interception in question is in relation to a serious crime, there is reasonable suspicion that the person whose privacy is to be infringed is implicated in the crime, and it is probable that the resulting information is likely to substantially further the investigation in relation to that crime. Moreover, we accept that these (suitably constrained) law enforcement powers in relation to telephone interception are analogous to possession on the part of law enforcement agencies of the ability to decipher encrypted messages. It follows that if a public key recovery system is necessary for law enforcement agencies to have the ability to decipher encrypted messages, then – other things being equal – a public key recovery system ought to be established. However, it also follows that the exercise of the resulting ability to decipher encrypted messages ought to be constrained by the same principles that constrain telephone interception.

In fact, Etzioni seems to accept something like the above set of principles or conditions.[25] At any rate, let us now return to the above-mentioned three categories of threat that according to Etzioni justify the possession on the part of law enforcement agencies of the ability to decipher encrypted messages. The first category consists of encrypted messages that are needed for evidence. Assume that the evidence pertains to serious crimes, and that there are reasonable grounds for thinking that this is so. There is still a problem, namely that the person whose privacy is to be infringed might be someone other than a suspect, and other than a person seeking to aid or protect a suspect; the person might be a complete innocent, and be known by the investigators to be such. Naturally, such an innocent person might be prevailed upon to consent to furnish the necessary evidence. But in that case there would be no infringement of privacy. At any rate, the general

---

[24] *ibid.*, pp. 91-94.
[25] *ibid.*, p. 92.

point is that the first category of threats does not conform to the above-mentioned conditions, and Etzioni has not made out an adequate case for their inclusion.

The second category, namely encrypted messages sent by persons known or reasonably suspected to be involved in criminal activity, are of a kind that comply with the above six requirements, or could be made to do so. Accordingly, they do not present a problem for Etzioni. What of the third category?

These are encrypted messages that might facilitate intelligence-gathering purposes. Obviously this category of threats does not necessarily conform to all, or indeed any, of the above six requirements. In particular, this category does not conform to the requirement that the person about whom the intelligence is being gathered, and whose privacy is being infringed, is reasonably suspected of some serious crime. Moreover, intelligence-gathering is by definition at times speculative and hunch-driven, rather than strongly evidence-based. Accordingly, Etzioni has not made out an adequate case for the inclusion of this third category.

We conclude that Etzioni has made out a case for law enforcement agencies having the capability to decipher encrypted messages under very restricted conditions; roughly speaking, the conditions under which they currently have the capability to access or intercept messages that are not encrypted. However, these conditions would not justify the interception or accessing of at least two of the general categories of encrypted messages that Etzioni believes ought to be able to be accessed by law enforcement agencies.

It might be argued that Etzioni has presented more powerful arguments than we have allowed. In particular, he has the general argument of the need to ensure public safety. While this is one of the main general justifications offered by Etzioni for infringement of individual privacy, it is in our view unacceptable.

First, the benefits of such general practices must offset the costs, including the costs in terms of the erosion in public trust. As the East European experience under communism has taught us, high levels of surveillance, intelligence-gathering and detailed record-keeping are inconsistent with an open, free society based on trust between public bodies and private citizens. Etzioni has not in our view offered convincing support for the proposition that the level of infringement of privacy that he advocates would not ultimately have too high a cost, but since in principle he might be able to, let us set this argument aside.

Second – and most important – since accessing and/or intercepting are by definition an infringement of privacy, the presumption must be against their use. That presumption can be overridden in particular cases or by exceptional circumstances, such as in wartime, but not by a *blanket* appeal to the common good or to the general need for public safety. Here we come to the nub of what is problematic about Etzioni's communitarianism. Let us deal with this issue in greater detail.

We are in full agreement with Etzioni that privacy is not an absolute right that cannot be overridden under any circumstances, whether it is privacy on the Internet or on any other communication or information system. The rights to privacy of some individuals, and the rights to confidentiality of members of some organisations, will in some cases be overridden by other moral considerations. For example, the rights to privacy of some individuals and/or confidentiality rights of members of organisations can *in some instances* be overridden by certain moral rights of other individuals, such as the right to life or the right to autonomy. Consider, in this connection, the communications of drug-dealers, pederasts, saboteurs and terrorists. Consider also programmers who devise and release destructive viruses and worms that infiltrate strategic government and economic computer systems via the Internet. All these communicators have an interest in sophisticated forms of encryption. Accordingly, law enforcement agencies have a legitimate need of access to "plain text" versions of encrypted communications for the purposes of tracking down such persons.

Further, we agree with Etzioni – and Miller has argued as much elsewhere[26] – that in relation to accessing of data and/or intercepting of communications on the Internet by law enforcement agencies, a balance has to be struck between rights to privacy and confidentiality on the one hand, and the rights to protection from serious crime on the other. Moreover, the state of technology at any point in time to some extent determines the possibility of striking a balance. Perhaps the current availability to the general public of very secure computer systems and of high-level encryption products has shifted the balance too much in favour of rights to privacy and confidentiality. If so, then arguably recourse to public key recovery systems is needed to redress this imbalance.

However, the crucial question in the striking of this balance concerns what is to be put on the scales. Etzioni opts for public safety as against individual moral rights. *Contra* Etzioni, we suggest that public safety is too general and amorphous a notion. What is called for in its place is a more precise and differentiated notion. In the first place, we need to specify a set of individual moral rights that override the individual right to privacy. These would include the right to life, and the right not to suffer grievous bodily harm. Accordingly – in the first place – we have individual moral rights being put in the balance against individual moral rights, and not – as Etzioni holds – a public good being put in the balance against an individual moral right.

In the second place, there is a restricted range of specific public goods, such as the integrity of government computer systems, which might under certain circumstances tip the scales against the individual right to privacy. However, two points are important to note here. First, there is a presumption in favour of the individual right to privacy in such cases. Second, the crucial consideration that might offset this presumption is the direct, or indirect, infringement of individual moral rights (albeit in some cases jointly-held rights) that might result from threats to these public goods. For example, individual citizens have a right to be protected from (say) terrorism. But in that case, the communications of those who break into government computer systems, and do so for the ultimate purpose of putting the lives of citizens at risk to terrorists, are no longer protected by the moral right to privacy.

We have been arguing against Etzioni's communitarian account of the balance to be struck between the right of individuals to privacy and the need for public

---

[26] Miller, "Privacy and the Internet", *op. cit.*

safety. We have proffered instead an individualist rights-based account, and suggested in effect that individual rights to privacy can be infringed, but only by virtue of threats to other more important individual moral rights. But there is a further dimension of Etzioni's account that is deficient in our view, namely his account of the right to privacy. Let us now turn to this issue.

Etzioni distinguishes between two sorts of privacy, informational privacy and decisional privacy (the right to control one's own acts).[27] In fact, as he himself points out, the latter seems to be a species of autonomy, rather than privacy. At any rate, our concern is with his account of privacy, not autonomy.

According to Etzioni, privacy is a contingent notion, dependent on socio-historical context, yet in our time in need of re-conceptualisation. In so far as this does not constitute a rejection of the notion of a residual common core element of privacy that exists in all socio-historical contexts, this is innocuous enough. If Etzioni means to reject any such common core element, then his account becomes incoherent; if there is no common core, then he cannot literally be speaking of the same thing from one context to another.

In fact, most of Etzioni's arguments are not really to do with re-conceptualising the notion of privacy, but rather with shifting, indeed increasing, restrictions on individual privacy in the light of his concerns about public health and public safety. However, Etzioni does make some communitarian claims about the concept of privacy. The main one of these is: "Privacy thus is a societal license that exempts a category of acts (including thoughts and emotions) from communal, public and governmental scrutiny".[28] As a corollary to this, Etzioni claims:

> ...privacy encompasses behaviours that members of a particular social entity are positively expected, by prevailing social mores or laws, to carry out so as not to be readily scrutinizable. For instance, defecating is expected or required to take place out of sight in many societies.[29]

In all this, Etzioni confuses two very different kinds of claim. The first kind of claim concerns the various socio-historical conditions which gave rise to the concept or concepts of privacy, and which currently sustain a conception of privacy in (say) contemporary American society. The second kind of claim concerns the (moral) normative nature and morally acceptable restrictions on privacy. If we interpret Etzioni's above-quoted statements as making the first kind of claim, then they are more or less acceptable. They are more or less plausible accounts of the socio-historical character of the concept(s) of privacy. However, if we interpret the statements as making the second kind of claim, then they are unacceptable. For thus interpreted, Etzioni is suggesting that an individual's moral right to privacy is somehow conferred on the individual by the society to which he or she belongs. That is, the individual only has a particular right in so far as the *society decides* that the individual has that right; today you can have a right to life,

---

[27] Etzioni, *op. cit.*, p. 15.
[28] *ibid.*, p. 196.
[29] *ibid.*

but tomorrow perhaps you cannot. This is an incoherent conception of moral rights, and one that opens the door to totalitarianism.

Elsewhere, Etzioni claims that his conception of the right to privacy rests squarely on the legal conception contained in the Fourth Amendment.[30] Once again, this is an unacceptable and dangerous move. Moral notions, including privacy, ground legal conceptions, and not vice versa. Once we accept the proposition that moral notions ought to be grounded in legal ones, then the way is clear to simply change the law, and thereby claim to have changed morality. But this is absurd; lawyers, judges and politicians cannot make morality up. Rather we can – if we are lucky – cause them to reflect morality in the laws that they make and apply.

Professional Confidentiality

Thus far, our concern has been with privacy *per se*. Let us now examine the closely related notion of confidentiality. Specifically, what is professional confidentiality, and what is the relation between privacy and professional confidentiality?

As noted above, privacy is an important moral right, and there is a close relationship between privacy and professional confidentiality. Indeed, there is at least one central kind of case in which confidentiality derives from the right to privacy.

There are circumstances under which a professional's knowledge concerning a client's inner self or intimate relations is in the client's interest. A doctor or psychologist should know about a patient's bodily sensations or mental states, in so far as this is necessary for successful treatment, and in so far as the patient has consented to be treated. Similarly, a police investigator might need to know various personal and private details about a victim of (say) child abuse, if the crime is to be established, and the offender apprehended and successfully prosecuted. This need to know for the benefit of the client is one ground for a principle of confidentiality. Such information, while available to the doctor or psychologist, social worker or police officer, would still be unavailable to others. Moreover, the need for professional confidentiality might be given additional moral weight by being: (a) the subject of a promise on the part of the professional to the client not to disclose the sort of information in question to others, and; (b) enshrined in the law so that the professional has a legal duty not to disclose this information to others. Accordingly, for the occupant of the professional role to disclose this information concerning their client to unauthorised third parties would constitute a moral and legal breach of confidentiality.

Although clients have a (derived) right to confidentiality, there are circumstances under which a psychologist or police officer or other professional may disclose confidential information concerning their client, notwithstanding the fact that it is not in the client's interest, or at least notwithstanding the fact that the

[30] *ibid.*, p. 203.

client has not given his or her informed consent. Such cases include ones in which the client is seriously harming, or is likely to seriously harm, some third party, and cases in which the client is seriously harming or is likely to seriously harm him/herself, and is not able to give informed consent. Consider an unconvicted serial murderer who discloses his past crimes, and an intention to commit a further murder, to his psychologist. Evidently the murderer's right to professional confidentiality – a right in turn based on a right to privacy – is overridden by greater moral considerations, viz. the right to life of the person the murderer intends to kill.[31]

A further point here concerns breaches of confidentiality. As far as possible, any breach of confidentiality should be contained. Such containment amounts to a requirement of confidentiality. In the above-described murderer/psychologist scenario, the psychologist is morally obliged to breach the confidentiality of her relationship with the murderer by going to the police. However, the information provided to the police ought now be the object of a further confidentiality requirement, at least until the investigation has been completed.

So the right to professional confidentiality, like the right to privacy, is a non-absolute right. The principle of confidentiality can be overridden under certain circumstances by other moral considerations, including ones that are enshrined in the law. These include the rights of third parties at risk from clients.

Thus far, we have been concerned with a species of professional confidentiality that derives from the right to privacy of clients, victims and others. However, there are grounds other than privacy for the professional confidentiality. In policing, there is an imperative not to compromise investigations by disclosing confidential information. The duty to keep confidences so as not to compromise investigations is based on a number of different considerations. It is in part based on the need to ensure that offenders do not escape justice, e.g. a tip-off to an offender can undermine a police investigation. It is also in part based on the need to ensure that witnesses and/or informants are protected. However, the ultimate and central moral basis for the principle of confidentiality in the context of police investigations is the moral rights of victims, or potential victims. If confidentiality in criminal investigations is breached, then citizens can have no guarantee that their rights – their legally enshrined, justifiably enforceable, moral rights – will be protected; rather, offenders will be able to offend with impunity.

So much for our general characterisation of confidentiality. We have suggested that the notions of privacy and confidentiality need to be kept separate. We claim that professional confidentiality sometimes derives from the more fundamental right to privacy, and sometimes derives from other moral rights, especially rights that directly or indirectly protect persons from various forms of criminal activity. Let us now look at two specific areas of policing in which confidentiality is of the utmost importance, namely internal witnesses and informants.

---

[31] Alternatively, the client's right to confidentiality is not breached in this case; rather, the right never extended so far as to include non-disclosure of serious criminal offences.

Internal Witnesses

To help focus our discussion, we will provide an account of a particular witness support program, viz. that of the New South Wales Police. The development in the 1990's of the NSW Police Service's Internal Witness Support Program, and the establishment of the Internal Witness Support Unit (IWSU), is reflective of a professionalising police management's acknowledgment not only of the importance of ensuring witnesses are able to give evidence without fear of the consequences, but also of the strength of the police culture – and management's increasing capacity to come to terms with the aberrant aspects of that culture. (See Case Study 4.1.)

A thumbnail sketch of police culture suggests it is based on: (a) police officers' social isolation within society, and; (b) their apprehension of physical danger. The product of that culture is; (c) a solidaristic mindset anchored by the expectation of mutual support in time of danger. The group loyalty this engenders, less "mateship" than survival instinct, anathematises those failing to support the mutuality of the occupational ethic.

The punitive instinct of many a police service's paramilitary command structure, and resultant worker distrust in management, has long since added police management to the felt dangers against which the workforce has sought to protect itself. Corruption may parasitically flourish in a setting in which a perceived need for group integrity, and a situationally apathetic, sometimes complicit police management, militates against malfeasance being denounced; a situation in which police accusing other police of corruption may be victimised by their peers for "breaking ranks", and/or by police management for "making trouble".

Management's ill-advised response has been at times the denunciation of all aspects of police culture, a reaction as invalid as denouncing parenthood on the basis of the incidence of incest. This counter-productive approach served only to reinforce unthinking worker-solidarity behind which corruption sheltered. That finally becoming clear, management changed tack; the problem was not that of invoking good men and women to denounce corruption, the problem was worker-empowerment – making it *possible* for the police workforce to denounce corruption.

In 1995, in the context of the Royal Commission into Corruption in the NSW Police Service, an Internal Witness Support Program was set up by the Police Service. The Royal Commission, in its final report, expressed itself satisfied with the 1995 Internal Witness Support Program, whose operations it described in the following terms:

> 6.13 In broad summary, where a person now qualifies as an internal witness, the procedures applicable and the support available involve the following:
>
> - the commander of the IWSU is notified of each internal police complaint. Once a complainant is assessed as being an internal witness, the file is allocated to a case officer within the Unit;

- the case officer seeks further information so that a full assessment can be made of the complainant's suitability for assistance under the program;
- the commander of the IWSU sends a report to the Executive Director, Human Resources, notifying the complainant's status under the program. Staff are not placed in the program without their consent;
- the case officer asks the witness to nominate a mentor and a support officer. The mentor is a senior officer available to provide support and positive reinforcement to the witness. The support officer provides support to the witness at the work location. In cases where the witness desires support to be provided solely by the IWSU, a case officer within the Unit assumes the role;
- the proposed mentor and support officer are briefed about the program and provided with briefing notes by the IWSU case officer. They are encouraged to make an informed choice about whether they are willing to take on the role;
- support officers and mentors submit 'command line file notes' directly to the IWSU case officer;
- the IWSU maintains a computer file on all registrants. The computer system used within the IWSU is secure and confidential;
- each file is reviewed periodically, at which time the case officer makes personal contact with the witness; and
- there are also regular reviews to ensure that the Unit is tailoring its response on a needs basis.[32]

Notwithstanding the progress that has been made in this area, and the good report card provided by the Royal Commission, we are entitled to harbour a degree of scepticism in relation to the success of witness support programs. The basis for such scepticism is located in the continued strength of the dysfunctional aspects of police culture, and the poor track record of police organisations in their duty to protect police who report their corrupt colleagues. No matter how well-designed institutional arrangements such as the IWSP might be, they rely on the integrity of those who comprise them – the members of a sub-organisation within a police service organisation – and also on the willingness to trust the members of the IWSP, or other like sub-organisation, on the part of those who might have reason to seek their assistance. But it is precisely the lack of a sufficiency of integrity and trust that has undermined anti-corruption programs in police organisations in the past.

Informants

We have been discussing the importance of protecting confidentiality, and therefore the necessity for a degree of secrecy, in policing. However, there are contexts in policing in which high levels of secrecy are morally problematic. One such kind of case involves informants. (See Case Study 4.1.)

The use of informants by police has always been considered something of a two-edged sword. Typically, informants are members or associates of the criminal

[32] *Final Report of the Royal Commission into the NSW Police Service, Vol. II: Reform*, May, 1997, pp. 400-1.

element. And they inform on other criminals, or provide information to police, for a multiplicity of reasons; though primarily for their own advantage. Such advantages might be thought – at least by the informant – to include the police refraining from investigating offences already committed by the informant, or even turning a blind eye to present and future offences of the informant. Sometimes the informant, in effect, might be coerced by the police officer; non-cooperation might lead to arrest and conviction for past offences hitherto ignored. This is morally undesirable from the perspective of the moral rights of the informant. At other times, the relationship between (say) a detective and his informant can become one in which the detective is manipulated by the informant. If this relationship is secretive – the police organisation has no knowledge of it – then the problem is unlikely to be resolved, and the relationship likely to be very damaging, not only to the detective, but to police operations.

Some informants might not be prepared to provide information unless confidentiality is guaranteed. On one view, the relationship between police officers and their informants is one of trust on a par with that between professionals and their clients. Even if this is so, the requirements for confidentiality between police and police informants are obviously different. For one thing, the reason for confidentiality in the case of informants might have more to do with the possible harm that might come to the informant from those he or she is informing about, rather than from the informant's basic right to privacy.

As a result, in part, of the findings of commissions into police corruption in various jurisdictions in Australia and elsewhere, e.g. the Royal Commission into the NSW Police Service, the use and handling of informants has been tightened. There are requirements that the informant be named in documentation, that a police officer with an informant has a supervisor who meets with the officer and the informant, and that the supervisor monitors the officer's dealings with the informant. Some police would argue that it is now virtually impossible to "run gigs" effectively. Yet in times of increasing police workloads, informants have also been recognised as one of the most cost-effective ways of solving crime. It has been suggested by some authorities that police, *both* uniformed police and detectives, should make more use of informants.

Entrapment

In the final section of this chapter, we will examine some of the ethical issues, including privacy issues, raised by police use of entrapment.[33] Many undercover operations might be considered to be entrapment in the ordinary common sense meaning of that term, i.e. to *trap* someone. (This sense of entrapment is to be

---

[33] For a useful overview of the legal and ethical issues raised by current forms of entrapment, and the application of contemporary republican normative theory to these issues, see Simon Bronitt and Declan Roche, "Between rhetoric and reality: socio-legal and republican perspectives on entrapment", *International Journal of Evidence and Proof*, No. 4, 2000.

distinguished from various legal definitions of the term.) Consider Case Study 4.1, in which Trevor Haken traps or entraps Chook Fowler.

Clearly the infringement of the right to privacy is a central feature of undercover operations in which a police officer establishes a relationship and gains the trust of an offender. Indeed, important questions arise here as to the morally admissible nature and extent of such relationships. It is one thing to establish friendly relations, it is another to establish a sexual relationship.

In some undercover operations, police in effect act as observers, albeit *inside*-observers. The offenders commit the offences that they commit independently of the actions of the undercover operatives. However, often undercover operatives interact with offenders in such a way as to make a difference to whether or not, or when, where or how, an offence is committed. This was the case with Chook Fowler in Case Study 4.1; Haken was not simply an observer, he was also an active participant. This is entrapment in our target sense of the term. Consider the following scenario.[34]

Detective James McLaughlin of Keene, New Hampshire, USA, poses as a young boy in chat-rooms on the Internet. He looks for adults who are seeking sex with underage boys. He does so for the purpose of providing evidence to secure criminal convictions. In one case, Detective McLaughlin arrested a 47-year-old British marine insurance expert named Philip Simon Rankin. After a long series of e-mail communications, during which a "relationship" was established, McLaughlin and Rankin agreed to meet in a restaurant in Keene, Rankin doing so in the belief that he was going to be meeting a 14-year-old boy.

We are using the term "entrapment" to refer to a pro-active law enforcement strategy used in many jurisdictions in preference to reactive strategies, such as complaints investigations. Entrapment makes use of undercover operatives posing as drug buyers, prostitutes or criminals. It can involve the building of lengthy interpersonal relationships. The most important consideration in favour of entrapment is evidenced in Case Study 4.1. Corruption in the NSW Police was systemic, and evidently the only way to bring corrupt police to justice was by way of entrapment involving "turned" corrupt police officers operating undercover. Only such officers would be trusted by corrupt fellow officers, and only a managed entrapment scenario would enable reliable evidence, such as videotapes, to be obtained.

Entrapment can be random or targeted. Targeted entrapment focuses on a specific person (or persons) who is/are reasonably believed to be involved in crime. Random entrapment is not directed at any specific person. For example, a police officer posing as a prostitute on a street corner in order to entrap clients is engaged in random entrapment.

Entrapment raises a number of ethical issues, including: (a) deception; (b) the infringement of privacy; (c) uncertainty in relation to the moral culpability of the offender, i.e. the offender was "tricked" into doing what he or she otherwise would

---

[34] This is taken from Walter Sinnott-Armstrong, "Entrapment in the Net?", *Ethics and Information Technology*, No. 1, 1999, p. 95.

not have done, and; (d) impropriety of law enforcement agents, since they might be creating crimes that otherwise would not exist.

Accordingly, questions arise as to the moral and legal limits that ought to be placed on entrapment. The options here range from banning all forms of entrapment, to allowing certain kinds of entrapment in relation to a narrowly circumscribed set of crimes. Here there are at least two relevant preliminary considerations. First, many serious crimes, such as murder, rape, and grievous bodily harm, do not lend themselves to entrapment. After all, entrapment must involve the actual commission of a crime, and presumably allowing someone to be murdered in order to convict the murderer is morally unacceptable. On the other hand, some related crimes, such as conspiracy to commit murder, might be suitable for entrapment. Second, given the morally problematic nature of entrapment, it should only be used sparingly, and presumably only in relation to serious crimes. So random or targeted entrapment of petty thieves is morally problematic. On the other hand, targeted entrapment of paedophiles is morally justified.

Let us briefly consider deception in relation to entrapment. If a suspect is to be entrapped, he or she will need to be deceived. However, such deception will occur at the investigatory stage of police work. Evidently, when deception occurs at the investigatory stage – as opposed to the testimonial stage – it may well be morally justifiable.[35] Thus lying to a murderer to enable an arrest is morally justified, whereas lying in court is not morally justified.

Let us now turn to privacy issues. Infringement of privacy in entrapment scenarios is morally justifiable under certain conditions. As we have argued above, privacy is not an absolute right, whether privacy on the telephone, the car phone, the Internet or on any other communication or information system. The rights to privacy of some individuals, and the right to confidentiality of members of some organisations, will in some cases be overridden by the rights of other individuals and other members of organisations to be protected by the law enforcement agencies from the perpetrators of serious crimes such as murder, child pornography, armed robbery and fraud.

As we have already argued, infringements of privacy by law enforcement officials are morally justifiable if certain conditions are met. These conditions include the following ones: (a) there is reasonable suspicion that the person whose privacy is to be infringed intends to commit a serious crime; (b) the methods in question are effective, and; (c) there is no alternative non-intrusive, or less intrusive, method of investigation.

Arguably, entrapment is required – or is far more effective than reactive methods, such as investigating complaints – in relation to certain crimes. The crimes in question include ones that do not involve a complainant, e.g. drug-dealing, or areas such as organised crime, where offences might be difficult to prove because offenders are well-organised, well-funded and/or highly secretive. But in relation to certain kinds of offence and offender, arguably entrapment does

---

[35] Jerome Skolnick, "Deception by Police", *Criminal Justice Ethics*, Vol. 1, No. 2, Summer/Fall, 1982.

better on a cost/benefit analysis than reliance on informers, or on undercover operatives who observe but do not entrap. Informers often provide unreliable information, and often fail to provide evidence of the guilt of those they implicate in crimes. Undercover operations are resource intensive and their outcomes uncertain. This is especially so when undercover operatives simply wait for a suspect to create the opportunity to commit a crime, and then hope to gather evidence in relation to the crime when it does happen. By contrast, entrapment involves stage-managing a crime at a time and place chosen by police; so there is an assurance that the crime will be recorded and the offender convicted. (See Case Study 4.1.)

If persons who have been entrapped are justifiably to be convicted, then they must have committed a crime. However, even if they have performed a criminal act, there might be important reasons not to convict them. Specifically, they might have been the victims of morally unjustified entrapment. What tests ought to be applied to determine whether someone was the victim of morally unjustified entrapment? In the USA, two legal tests to determine whether someone has been entrapped have been proposed; the subjective test and the objective test. However, only the subjective test is actually in use.[36] Note that in the sense of "entrapment" in question in the legal environment of the USA, entrapment is necessarily unlawful; in the USA, entrapment, by definition, involves pro-active policing practices that fail (in particular) the subjective test.

The subjective test asks whether the suspect has a disposition to commit crimes of the kind in question. Theoretically, but not necessarily, or indeed actually, in law, we might establish the existence of a disposition on the basis of his/her past behaviour, e.g. past criminal convictions. Evidently the point of this test is to ensure that the person entrapped has the requisite degree of culpability; an important motivating reason for using this test is the concern that without it, the police might induce an intention or inclination to commit a crime that was otherwise absent.[37]

The objective test asks whether or not the State has acted improperly by virtue of instigating the crime. This resolves itself into two issues. The first issue is whether or not the contribution of the police to the creation of the opportunity to commit the crime is excessive. For example, suppose an undercover police officer supplies a person with the raw materials and the equipment to manufacture heroin, and suppose that the raw materials and equipment is not available to the person from any other source(s). The second issue is whether or not the inducement offered to commit the crime was unreasonable (too strong), e.g. offering someone a million dollars to engage in illicit sex.[38]

---

[36] For useful discussions of these tests and the issues that they raise, see Gerald Dworkin, *The Theory and Practice of Autonomy* (Cambridge: Cambridge University Press, 1988), Chapter 9, and John Kleinig, *Ethics in Policing* (Cambridge: Cambridge University Press, 1996), Chapter 8.

[37] Dworkin, *op. cit.*, p. 134, and Kleinig, *op. cit.*, p. 153.

[38] Dworkin, *op. cit.*, p. 135, and Kleing, *op. cit.*, p. 154.

One problem for the subjective test is how to provide evidence of a disposition. This problem is heightened in legal contexts in which knowledge of past crimes and convictions is not normally allowed to be used in determining guilt in relation to a current crime. A further possible problem for the subjective test is that it does not rule out strong inducements. Police officers might abuse the system by offering inducements that are too strong, and yet conviction would follow if the suspects had strong dispositions to commit the crime.[39] A related problem arises from the fact that a disposition to commit a crime is not equivalent to an intention to commit that crime. Suppose someone has a disposition to commit a crime. However, knowing that he has this disposition, he puts himself in a context in which there is no opportunity to commit the crime. Consider a heroin addict who wants to avoid taking heroin and decides to live in a heroin-free area, or a paedophile who wants to avoid the crime of paedophilia by ensuring that he is never in the company of children. Now assume a police officer presents the heroin addict with heroin, or the paedophile with what he (the paedophile) believes is an opportunity to engage in sex with a child. These examples show that the mere presence of a disposition is not sufficient for morally justified entrapment; so the subjective test – at least as described above – would have to be strengthened.

A possible problem for the objective test is that it protects some people who should be found guilty.[40] Suppose strong inducements are used in cases of suspects with strong dispositions to commit the crime, and suppose these suspects are in fact guilty of this kind of crime. Such inducements will be ruled out by the objective test, and yet the guilty persons in question will go free. On the other hand, it is far more preferable that some of the guilty go free than that some of the innocent are convicted. So this objection is relatively weak. A stronger objection is that the objective test – in so far as it involves random testing – amounts to the government engaging in integrity testing of its citizens. This is surely unacceptable; governments have no right to convict a citizen merely because the citizen fails to resist an inducement to commit a crime, even if it is an inducement that they ought to have resisted. As Dworkin points out, "To encourage the commission of a crime in the absence of any reason to believe the individual is already engaged in a course of action is to be a tester of virtue, not a detector of crime".[41] Moreover, the objective test is not a particularly effective test of virtue. For someone who lacked the disposition to commit that kind of crime, or indeed crimes in general, might nevertheless fail the objective test on a single occasion.

What might be acceptable is targeted integrity testing of individuals reasonably suspected of committing the crime that is the subject of the test. Moreover, random integrity testing of certain categories of public servants, such as police or politicians, in relation to a circumscribed set of crimes might be acceptable under certain conditions. For example, suppose bribe-taking is rife in a specific government department, and all other measures have failed to curtail it; perhaps random integrity testing is now warranted. The general moral justification for this

---

[39] Sinnott-Armstrong, *op. cit.*, p. 99.
[40] *ibid.*
[41] Dworkin, *op. cit.*, p. 144.

is that such public servants need to have a certain standard of integrity in relation to specific kinds of inducement, and they voluntarily accept a public office on the basis that they meet that standard. Accordingly, their integrity might reasonably be open to testing, especially if it is made clear to them before they accept the public office that their integrity might be subjected to a test.

There is a general objection to entrapment, and this objection apparently stands irrespective of whether the subjective test or the objective test is applied. This is the objection that entrapment involves the creation of crime, rather than the detecting or preventing of crime that would have existed independently of entrapment.[42] If this objection is sustained, it is decisive; entrapment should be abandoned. But is this objection sustained?

In order to assist our deliberations, consider the following.[43] Suppose a person, A, forms an intention to commit the one-off crime of stealing $5,000 of drug money. Person A believes the money was abandoned by his drug-dealing neighbour, B, in the garden outside B's house when B was arrested by the police, and that his crime will go undetected. Suppose that, unknown to A, this money was in fact confiscated by the police. However, the police decide not to remove the money, but rather to leave it with the purpose of entrapping A, who they suspect might be tempted by the prospect of such "easy money", notwithstanding his general compliance with the law. A goes to steal the money and is caught red-handed.

Notice that if the objective test is applied, the police are entitled to engage in this kind of entrapment. In the first place, the inducement, viz. $5,000, is of a kind that the normal citizen could reasonably be expected to resist. In the second place, it was the drug-dealer who created the opportunity for theft; all the police did was fail to remove this opportunity. On the other hand, this kind of entrapment is ruled out by the subjective test; for A does not have a disposition to steal.

Given the nature of this one-off opportunity, and A's general disposition to comply with the law, A would not have committed any crime if the police had not entrapped him. The reason is that he would never have been afforded the opportunity to commit the only sort of opportunistic crime that he is capable of committing. Yet given that he believed that the opportunity had arisen, he formed the intention to commit the crime. We suggest that the mere possession of an intention – in a context of police provision of opportunity – is not sufficient to justify entrapment. The reason is not that A is not culpable; clearly A is guilty of an act of theft. Rather, the reason is that entrapment under these conditions involves the creation of crime, rather than the detecting or preventing of crime that would have existed independently of entrapment.

Let us take another look at our scenario, but this time let us assume that, unbeknown to the police, A has a disposition to commit opportunistic acts of theft of large amounts of money, if they are left lying around and A believes he will escape detection. But let us further assume that there are no such opportunities. While A hopes for such opportunities, and tells his friends he is waiting for such

---

[42] *ibid.*, p. 136.

[43] See Dworkin, *op. cit.*, p. 140, for a contrary view.

opportunities, none have been or are ever likely to be forthcoming. As it happens, a one-off opportunity does come, and A is entrapped. As before, the objective test does not rule out this kind of entrapment. Moreover, the subjective test does not rule out this kind of entrapment either; for A has a disposition to engage in opportunistic theft of large amounts of money.

Notwithstanding the existence of A's disposition to engage in opportunistic theft of large amounts of money, it still remains the case that A would not have committed any crime if the police had not entrapped him. The reason is that he would never have been afforded the opportunity to commit the only sort of opportunistic crime that he is disposed to commit. Accordingly, we suggest that the possession of a disposition and an intention – in a context of police provision of opportunity – is not sufficient to justify entrapment. The reason is that entrapment under these conditions involves the creation of crime, rather than the detecting or preventing of crime that would have existed independently of entrapment.

As a corollary to the above, we conclude that neither passing the subjective test nor passing the objective test (nor passing both tests) is sufficient to justify entrapment. Needless to say, this does not show that entrapment is not justified under certain circumstances.

Walter Sinnott Armstrong[44] argues that entrapment on the Internet is dissimilar to other forms of entrapment by virtue of being: (a) less intrusive, since there are not so many innocent people involved as (say) posing as a drug-dealer at a university campus; (b) less dangerous to police, and; (c) less abuse-prone, since the evidence is there for all to see.

However, the general problems with entrapment also afflict entrapment on the Internet. Entrapment, whether on the Internet or not, faces the general objection that it involves the creation of crime. Moreover, the above-mentioned objections to the objective and the subjective tests remain. On the other hand, specific forms of entrapment, e.g. targeted entrapment and random entrapment of certain categories of public officer, might well be justifiable.

Let us bring this chapter to a close by attempting to detail the general conditions under which entrapment of ordinary citizens might be morally permissible.[45] In so doing, we will try to accommodate the various objections made above to entrapment, and to the subjective and objective tests.

First, there are a number of such general conditions, such as the condition that the method of entrapment is the only feasible method available to law enforcement agencies in relation to a certain type of offence, and that the offence type is a serious one. This condition reflects the general presumption against entrapment.

Second, the entrapment should be the targeted entrapment of a person (or group) who is/are reasonably suspected of engaging in crimes of the relevant kind. This condition rules out testing the virtue of citizens.

---

[44] Sinnott-Armstrong, *op. cit.*

[45] See Dworkin, *op. cit.*, p. 144, for a reasonably similar set of conditions to this. See also Kleinig, *op. cit.*, p. 158.

Third, the suspect is ordinarily presented with, or typically creates, the kind of opportunity that they are to be afforded in the entrapment scenario. This condition in large part rules out police creation of crime.

Fourth, the inducement offered to the suspect is: (a) of a kind that is typically available to the suspect, and; (b) such that an ordinary citizen would reasonably be expected to resist it.[46] This condition rules out excessive inducements, and therefore one way in which crime might be created by the police.

Fifth, the person not only has a disposition[47] to commit the type of crime in relation to which they are to be entrapped, but also a standing intention to commit that type of crime. This condition not only protects those with inoperative inclinations to crime, but also those with a fleeting intention to commit a one-off crime – an intention not underpinned by any disposition to criminal activity. Evidence of a disposition to commit a type of crime might consist of an uninterrupted pattern of past crimes of that type, and no evidence of any change in attitude or circumstance. Evidence of a standing intention to commit that type of crime might be verbal and/or evidence of current detailed planning activities, and/or attempts to provide the means to commit such crimes.

---

[46] Or – in the case of tests for personnel in high-risk occupations – "such that a person in that role would reasonably be expected to resist it."

[47] The existence of such a disposition might be established by recourse to evidence such as an uninterrupted pattern of past crimes, and no evidence of a change in attitude or circumstances.

Chapter 5

Corruption and Anti-Corruption in Policing

In this chapter, we discuss corruption in policing and strategies for combating police corruption. In the first section, we discuss the concept of corruption; in the second section, the nature and causes of police corruption, in particular; in the third section, so-called "noble cause" corruption in policing; and in the fourth section, we look at strategies for combating police corruption.[1]

Concept of Corruption

The nature of corruption, the causes and effects of corruption, and how to combat corruption, are issues that are increasingly on the national and international agendas of politicians and other policy-makers. For example, the World Bank has relatively recently come around to the view that economic development is closely linked to corruption reduction.[2] By contrast, the theoretical notion of corruption has not received much attention.[3] Existing conceptual work on corruption consists in little more than the presentation of brief definitions of corruption as a preliminary to extended accounts of the causes and effects of corruption and the ways to combat it.[4] Moreover, most of these definitions of corruption are unsatisfactory in fairly obvious ways.

---

[1] A much earlier and abridged version of this chapter appeared in Seumas Miller, *Issues in Police Ethics* (Keon, 1996).

[2] See World Bank's *Helping countries combat corruption: The role of the World Bank* (Washington DC: World Bank, 1997).

[3] An earlier version of the material in this section, entitled "Corruption: Some Theoretical Issues", appeared in the *Proceedings of the National Conference of the Australian Association for Professional and Applied Ethics* (Melbourne, 2003). Another version is to appear in Seumas Miller, Peter Roberts and Ed Spence, *Corruption and Anti-corruption: An Applied Philosophical Approach* (Prentice Hall, 2004), Chapter 1.

[4] For example, Robert Klitgaard, Ronald Maclean-Abaroa and H. Lindsey Parris in their *Corrupt Cities: A Practical Guide to Cure and Prevention* (Oakland, Calif.: ICS Press, 2000), p. 2, define corruption as "misuse of office for personal gain". For a recent review of the general literature on corruption, see Jonathan Hopkins, "States, markets and corruption: A review of some recent literature", *Review of International Political Economy*, 2002.

Consider one of the most popular of these definitions, namely "Corruption is the abuse of power by a public official for private gain".[5] No doubt the abuse of public offices for private gain is paradigmatic of corruption. But when police fabricate evidence out of a misplaced sense of justice, this is corruption of a public office, but not for private gain. And when a punter bribes a boxer to "throw" a fight, this is corruption for private gain, but it does not necessarily involve any public office-holder; the roles of boxer and punter are not necessarily public offices. Indeed, there is a whole range of different forms of corruption outside the public sphere. Consider corruption in relation to the role of father. Suppose a father persuades his naïve, but nubile, 13-year-old daughter to provide sexual favours to middle-aged businessmen in exchange for payments to him and gifts for her; this is corruption, but it is not abuse of a public office.

In the light of the failure of such analytical-style definitions, it is tempting to try to sidestep the problem of providing a theoretical account of the concept of corruption by simply identifying corruption with specific legal and/or moral offences.

However, attempts to identify corruption with specific legal/moral offences are unlikely to succeed. Perhaps the most plausible candidate is bribery; bribery is regarded by some as the quintessential form of corruption.[6] However, ccorruption is exemplified by a very wide and diverse array of phenomena, of which bribery is only one kind. Paradigm cases of corruption include the following. A national leader channels public monies into his personal bank account. A political party secures a majority vote by arranging for ballot boxes to be stuffed with false voting papers. A respected researcher's success relies on plagiarising the work of others. A police officer fabricates evidence in order to secure convictions. A number of police officers close ranks and refuse to testify against a colleague that they know to be corrupt. The government minister for law and order directs the Police Commissioner to have police aggressively confront and disrupt lawful street demonstrations, in order to create a manageable level of public disorder from which the government will derive political benefit in a forthcoming election. It is self-evident that none of these corrupt practices are instances of bribery.

Further, it is far from obvious that the way forward at this point is simply to add a few additional offences to the initial "list" consisting of the single offence of bribery. Candidates for being added to the list of offences would include fraud, nepotism, fabricating evidence, perverting the course of justice, and so on. However, there is bound to be disagreement in relation to any such list. For example, law enforcement practitioners in Australia and elsewhere often distinguish between fraud on the one hand, and corruption on the other. Most important, any such list needs to be justified by recourse to some principle or principles. Ultimately, naming a set of offences that might be regarded as instances

---

[5] For one of the most influential statements of the abuse of public office for private gain definitions, see Joseph Nye, "Corruption and Political Development: A Cost-benefit Analysis", *American Political Science Review*, Vol. 61, No. 2, 1967, pp. 417-27.

[6] The definitive account of bribery is John T. Noonan's *Bribes* (New York: Macmillan, 1984).

of corruption does not obviate the need for a theoretical, or quasi-theoretical, account of the concept of corruption.

As it happens, there is at least one further salient strategy for demarcating the boundaries of corrupt acts. Implicit in much of the literature on corruption is the view that corruption is essentially a legal offence, and essentially a legal offence in the economic sphere.[7] Accordingly, one could seek to identify corruption with economic crimes, such as bribery, fraud and insider trading. To some extent, this kind of view reflects the dominance of economically-focused material in the corpus of academic literature on corruption. It also reflects the preponderance of proposed economic solutions to the problem of corruption. After all, if corruption is essentially an economic phenomenon, is it not plausible that the remedies for corruption will be economic ones?[8]

The first point to be made here concerns the proposition that corruption is necessarily a legal offence. Many examples of corruption are not necessarily unlawful. That paradigm of corruption, bribery, is a case in point. Prior to 1977, it was not unlawful for US companies to offer bribes to secure foreign contracts.[9] So corruption is not necessarily unlawful. This is because corruption is not at bottom simply a matter of law; rather it is fundamentally a matter of morality.

The second point concerns the (allegedly) necessarily economic character of corruption. An academic who plagiarises the work of others is not committing an economic crime or misdemeanour, and might be committing plagiarism simply in order to increase his academic status; there may not be any financial benefit sought or gained. As is well-known, academics are more strongly motivated by status than by wealth. A police officer who fabricates evidence against a person he believes to be guilty of paedophilia is not committing an economic crime, and may do so because he believes the accused to be guilty, and does not want him to go unpunished; economics is not necessarily involved as an element of the officer's crime or as a motivation. As is well-known, when police do wrong they are often motivated by a misplaced sense of justice, rather than by financial reward. Again, a person in authority who abuses his power by meting out cruel and unjust treatment to those subject to his authority, and who does so out of sadistic pleasure, is not engaging in an economic crime, and is not motivated by economic considerations. As is well-known, many of those who occupy positions of authority are motivated by a desire to exercise power, rather than by a desire for financial reward.

Economic corruption is an important form of corruption; however, it not the only form of corruption. There are non-economic forms of corruption, including many types of police corruption, judicial corruption, political corruption, academic

---

[7] This is implicit in much of Susan Rose-Ackerman's influential work on corruption. See her *Corruption and Government: Causes, Consequences and Reform* (Cambridge: Cambridge University Press, 1999).

[8] See Rose-Ackerman, *op. cit.*, for this kind of view. See Barry Hindess, "Good Government and Corruption", in Peter Larmour and Nick Wolanin (eds.), *Corruption and Anti-Corruption* (Canberra: Asia Pacific Press, 2001), for this kind of critique.

[9] See the *Foreign Corrupt Practices Act* of 1977, Public Law 95-213 (5305), December 19th, 1977, United States Code 78a, Section 103.

corruption, and so on. Indeed, there are as many forms of corruption as there are human practices and institutions that might become corrupted. Further, economic gain is not the only motivation for corruption. There are a variety of different kinds of attractions that motivate corruption. These include status, power, addiction to drugs or gambling, and sexual gratification, as well as economic gain. Contrary to what Gordon Gekko said in the film *Wall Street*, greed is not good; it is bad. But greed is not the only vice.

Thus far, we have argued that the various currently influential definitions of corruption, and the recent attempts to circumscribe corruption by listing paradigmatic offences, have failed, and failed in large part because the class of corrupt actions comprises an extremely diverse array of types of moral and legal offences.

That said, we have made *some* progress in this section of the chapter. At the very least, we have identified corruption as fundamentally a moral, or at least immoral, phenomenon – as opposed to a legal, or at least illegal, phenomenon. While many corrupt acts are unlawful – or ought to be unlawful – this is not necessarily the case. Moreover, it is evident that not all acts of immorality are acts of corruption; corruption is only one species of immorality. Consider an otherwise gentle husband who in a fit of anger strikes his adulterous wife and kills her. The husband has committed an act that is morally wrong; he has committed murder, or perhaps culpable homicide, or at least manslaughter. But his action is not necessarily an act of corruption. Obviously the person who is killed (the wife) is not corrupted in the process of being killed. Moreover, the act of killing does not necessarily corrupt the perpetrator (the husband). Perhaps the person who commits a wrongful killing (the husband) does so just once and in mitigating circumstances, and also suffers remorse. Revulsion at his act of killing might cause such a person to embark thereafter on a life of moral rectitude. If so, the person has not been corrupted as a result of his wrongful act.

An important distinction in this regard is that between human rights violations and corruption. Genocide is a profound moral wrong; but it is not corruption. This is not to say that there is not an important relationship between human rights violations and corruption; on the contrary, there is often a close and mutually reinforcing nexus between corruption and human rights violations.[10] Consider the endemic corruption and large-scale human rights abuse that have taken place in authoritarian regimes such as that of Idi Amin and Suharto. And there is increasing empirical evidence of an admittedly complex causal connection between corruption and the infringement of subsistence rights; there is evidence, that is, of a causal relation between corruption and poverty. Most important, often actions that are human rights violations – and especially actions that are violations of moral rights more generally – are also acts of corruption. Thus, wrongfully and unlawfully incarcerating one's political opponent is a human rights violation, but it is also corrupting the political process. This is especially the case in an area such as policing, in which issues of moral rights are so central. Consider corrupt actions

---

[10] See Zoe Pearson, "An International Human Rights Approach to Corruption", in Larmour and Wolanin (eds.), *op. cit.*

such as fabricating evidence, "testilying", "using the third degree", and so on. All these actions violate the moral rights of suspects, and in particular their moral *institutional* rights within the institutions of the criminal justice system. But they are also actions that corrupt some of the most important constitutive institutional processes of that system.

The important general point to be made here is that, on pain of losing the concept of corruption entirely, we need to find a way of distinguishing between corrupt actions, and immoral actions more generally. The latter, very wide class comprises actions that infringe moral principles, violate moral rights, defeat moral ends, and so on. To this task of defining corrupt actions we now turn.

If we are to provide a serviceable definition of the concept of a corrupt action – and specifically, one that does not collapse into the more general notion of an immoral action – we need firstly to focus our attention on the moral *effects* that some actions have on persons and institutions. If an action is corrupt, then it corrupts something or someone – so in our view, corruption is not only a moral concept, it is a *causal* concept. We take it that an action is corrupt only if it has a *corrupting effect* on a person's moral character, or a corrupting effect on an institution. If an action has a corrupting effect on a person's character, it will typically be corrosive of one or more of a person's virtues. These virtues might be virtues that attach to the person *qua* human being, e.g. the virtues of compassion and fairness in one's dealings with other human beings. Alternatively – or perhaps, additionally – these virtues might attach to persons *qua* occupants of specific institutional roles, e.g. impartiality in a police officer. If an action has a corrupting effect on an institution, then it has a corrupting effect on institutional processes and purposes, and/or on persons *qua* occupants of institutional roles. Our concern in this chapter is with the corruption of institutions. Accordingly, we are only interested in the corruption of persons in so far as they are occupants of institutional roles, and specifically the role of police officer.

In relation to the concept of *institutional* corruption, our first claim or presupposition is that an action is corrupt only if it has a corrupting effect on an institutional process, role or purpose. Note here that an infringement of a specific law or institutional rule does not in and of itself constitute an act of corruption. In order to do so, any such infringement needs to have an institutional *effect*, e.g. to defeat the institutional purpose of the rule, to subvert the institutional process governed by the rule, or to contribute to the despoiling of the moral character of the role occupant.

Our second claim is that if an action is corrupt, then the person who performed it either did so intentionally, or he or she performed it knowing the institutional harm it would cause – or, at the very least, the person could and should have foreseen the harm it would cause. So in general, persons who perform corrupt actions are blameworthy for so doing. Nevertheless, we use the term "in general" because there are cases in which someone knowingly performs a corrupt action but is (say) coerced into so doing, and is therefore not blameworthy. So on our account it is possible to perform an act of corruption and yet remain blameless.

Our third claim concerns persons – in the sense of institutional role occupants – who are corrupted. The contrast here is twofold. In the first place, persons are being contrasted with *institutional processes and purposes* that might be corrupted. In the second place, those who are *corrupted* are being contrasted with those who *corrupt* (the corruptors).

Those who are corrupted have to some extent, or in some sense, allowed themselves to be corrupted; they are *participants* in the process of their corruption. Specifically, they have *chosen* to perform, or to refrain from performing, the actions, or omissions, which ultimately had the corrupting effects in question on them, and they could have chosen otherwise.[11] In this respect, the corrupted are no different from the corruptors. Nevertheless, those who are corrupted and those who corrupt are different in respect of their intentions and beliefs concerning the corrupting effect of their actions. Specifically, those who become corrupted did not necessarily intend their actions to have the effect of corrupting them, and nor did they necessarily foresee that they would be corrupted by their actions. Indeed, it might be the case that they could not reasonably have been expected to foresee that they would become corrupted. This is especially the case with young children who allow themselves to be corrupted, but cannot be expected to realise that their actions, or more likely omissions, would have this consequence. Nevertheless – absent special conditions, e.g. coercion – morally responsible adults who have become corrupted are at least to some degree blameworthy for not resisting the process of their corruption.[12]

Notice that a corruptor of other persons or things can in performing these corrupt actions also and simultaneously be producing corrupting effects on him or herself. That is, acts of corruption can have, and typically do have, a side effect in relation to the corruptor. They not only corrupt the person and/or institutional process that they are intended to corrupt; they also corrupt the corruptor, albeit usually unintentionally. Consider bribery in relation to a tendering process. The bribe corrupts the tendering process; and it will probably have a corrupting effect on the moral character of the bribe-*taker*. However, in addition, it might well have a corrupting effect on the moral character of the bribe-*giver*.

Here we need to distinguish between a corrupt action that has no external effect on an institutional process or on another person, but which contributes to the corruption of the character of the would-be corruptor; and a *non-corrupt* action which is a mere *expression* of a corrupt moral character, but which has no corrupting effect, either on an external institutional process or other person, or on the would-be corruptor himself. In this connection, consider two sorts of would-be

---

[11] We are assuming here that in at least many cases of coercion, the coerced have a choice, i.e. they could have chosen not to perform the action that they were coerced into doing. On the other hand, if the action they performed was (say) drug-induced or otherwise not under their control, then they cannot be said to have chosen to perform it in our sense.

[12] Nevertheless, since it is possible to be corrupted without intending or foreseeing this – indeed, without the existence of any reasonable expectation that one would foresee it – one can be blameless for being corrupted in a way that one cannot be blameless for an act of corruption. This is because a putative act of corruption would not be – according to our account – an act of corruption if the putative corruptor did not intend, foresee, and could not reasonably have been expected to foresee the corrupting effect of his actions.

bribe-givers whose bribes are rejected. Assume that in both cases their action has no external corrupting effect on an institutional process or other person. Now assume that in the first case, the bribe-giver's action of offering the bribe weakens his disposition not to offer bribes; so the offer has a corrupting effect on his character. However, assume that in the case of the second bribe-giver, his failed attempt to bribe generates in him a feeling of shame and strengthens his disposition not to offer bribes. So his action has no corrupting effect, either on himself or externally on an institutional process or other person. In both cases, the action is the expression of a partially corrupt moral character. However, in the first, but not the second, case, the bribe-giver's action is corrupt by virtue of having a corrupt effect on himself.

On the assumption that our above-stated three claims or presuppositions are correct, let us now elaborate the resulting theoretical account of actions that corrupt institutions.

The notion of such a corrupt action presupposes two prior notions: (a) the notion of an uncorrupted, and morally legitimate, institution, or institutional process, role or purpose, and; (b) the notion of an uncorrupted, morally worthy person who is the occupant of an institutional role. That is, the act of corruption brings about, or contributes to bringing about, a corrupt condition of some person and/or some institution. But this condition of corruption exists only relative to: (i) an uncorrupted condition, which condition is; (ii) the condition of being a morally legitimate institution or sub-element thereof, or the condition of being a morally worthy person, or at least of being a person possessed of some worthy character trait. Consider the uncorrupted judicial process. It consists of the presentation of objective evidence that has been gathered lawfully, of testimony in court being presented truthfully, of the rights of the accused being respected, and so on. This otherwise morally legitimate judicial process is corrupted if one or more of its constitutive actions are not performed in accordance with the process as it is rightly intended to be. Thus, to present fabricated evidence, to lie on oath and so on, are all potentially corrupt actions. In relation to moral character, consider a hitherto honest cop who begins to take bribes for turning a blind eye to the illegal activities of his corrupt colleagues, and does so under the twin pressures of a dysfunctional police culture, and the financial pressures he is under as the only bread-winner in a large family. By engaging in such a practice, he initially compromises his moral principles, and then risks the erosion of his moral character; he is undermining his disposition to act honestly.

On the view we are putting forward, actions are acts of corruption because they corrupt a person (or element of moral character) and/or an institution (or sub-element thereof). Moreover, the corrupt condition of the person or institution corrupted exists only relative to some moral standards, which are definitional of the uncorrupted condition of that institution, or of the moral character of persons in institutional roles. The moral standards in question might be minimum moral standards, or they might be moral ideals. Corruption in relation to a tendering process is a matter of a failure in relation to minimum moral standards enshrined in laws or regulations. On the other hand, gradual loss of innocence might be regarded as a process of corruption in relation to an ideal moral state.

If the process of corruption proceeds far enough, then we no longer have a corrupt official or corruption of an institutional process or institution; we cease to have a person who can properly be described as (say) a judge, or a process that can properly be described as (say) a judicial process – as opposed to proceedings in a kangaroo court. A coin that has been bent and defaced beyond recognition is no longer a coin; rather, it is a piece of scrap metal that can no longer be exchanged for goods.

By our lights, an institutionally corrupt action is an action, or an element of a pattern of actions, that contributes to the despoiling of the moral character of a person *qua* role occupant, or to the undermining of a morally legitimate institutional process, role or purpose.[13] Further, a corrupt person is a person whose moral character has been despoiled by his or her actions, and/or by interactions with others; and a corrupt institution is a morally legitimate institution, the constitutive roles, processes or purposes of which have been undermined by the actions of members of that institution, and/or by virtue of interactions with persons outside the institution.

In this connection, we need to make the following four points.

First, we reiterate that (in general) – and notwithstanding the above-stated differences between corruptors and the corrupted – morally responsible persons who perform corrupt actions, and morally responsible persons who are corrupted by such actions, are to some degree blameworthy for so acting or so being effected. So, in the paradigm case, a person who corrupts others does so intentionally and without a good and decisive reason for so doing; and – again in the paradigm case – a corrupted person knowingly allows himself to be corrupted, and does so without adequate justification or excuse. Consider, in this connection, a police officer who routinely accepts bribes from offenders in return for not investigating or arresting these offenders.

Moreover, among such instances of corruption, there are ones in which corruptors and the corrupted are culpably *negligent*; they do, or allow to be done, what they reasonably ought to have known should not be done, or should not have allowed to be done. For example, a safety inspector within an industrial plant, who is negligent with respect to his duty to ensure that safety protocols are being complied with, might be guilty of corruption by virtue of contributing to the undermining of those safety protocols.[14]

There are complexities in relation to corruption involving culpable negligence that are not necessarily to be found in other forms of corruption. Consider a company official who has a habit of allowing industrial waste products to be discharged into a river because this is the cheapest way to be rid of the unwanted products. But now assume that the official does so prior to the availability of any relevant scientific knowledge concerning the pollution that results from such discharges, and prior to the existence of any institutional arrangement for

---

[13] This kind of definition has ancient origins. See Hindess, *op. cit.*, for a recent discussion.

[14] And there is a further and related point to be made here. In general, corruptors corrupt and the corrupted allow themselves to be corrupted, without adequate moral justification for so doing or allowing to be done.

monitoring and controlling pollution. By our lights, the official is not necessarily acting in a corrupt manner. However, the same action might well be a case of corporate corruption in a contemporary setting, in which this sort of pollution is well and widely understood, and anti-pollution arrangements are known to be in place in many organisations. While those who actively corrupt institutional processes, roles and purposes are not necessarily themselves the occupants of institutional roles, those who are culpably negligent tend to be the occupants of institutional roles who have failed to discharge their institutional obligations.

Second, the corruption of an institution – as opposed to a person – does not assume that the institution in fact existed at some past time in a pristine or uncorrupted condition. Rather an action, or set of actions, is corruptive of an institution in so far as the action, or actions, has a negative moral effect on the institution. This notion of a negative moral effect is determined by recourse to the moral standards constitutive of the processes, roles and purposes of the institution, as that institution morally ought to be in the socio-historical context in question. Consider a police officer who fabricates evidence, but who is a member of a police service whose members have always fabricated evidence. It remains true that the officer is performing a corrupt action. His action is corrupt by virtue of the negative moral effect it has on the institutional process of evidence-gathering and evidence presentation. To be sure, this process is not what it ought to be, given the corrupt actions of the other police in that particular police force. But the point is that his action contributes to the further undermining of the institutional process; it has a negative moral effect as judged by the yardstick of what that process ought to be in that institution at that time.

Third, the despoiling of the moral character of a role occupant, or the undermining of institutional processes and purposes, would typically require a pattern of actions – and not merely a single, one-off action. So a single free hamburger provided to a police officer on one occasion does not corrupt, and is not therefore an act of corruption. Nevertheless, a series of such gifts to a number of police officers might corrupt. They might corrupt, for example, if the hamburger joint in question ended up with (in effect) exclusive, round-the-clock police protection, and if the owner intended that this be the case.

Note here the pivotal role of habits. We have just seen that the corruption of persons and institutions typically requires a pattern of corrupt actions. More specifically, corrupt actions are typically habitual. Yet, as noted by Aristotle, one's habits are in large part constitutive of one's moral character; habits "maketh the man" (and the woman). The coward is someone who habitually takes flight in the face of danger; by contrast, the courageous person has a habit of standing his or her ground. Accordingly, morally bad *habits* – including corrupt actions – are extremely corrosive of moral character, and therefore of institutional roles and ultimately institutions.

However, there are some cases in which a single, one-off action would be sufficient to corrupt an instance of an institutional process. Consider a specific act of "testilying" in court by a police officer that has the consequence that a person is convicted of a crime he did not commit. Suppose the police officer does this once and only once. Nevertheless, that particular testimony is false, and the court process has been undermined. Is this one-off act of testilying an instance of corruption? Surely, it is, since it corrupted that particular instance of the institutional process of giving testimony.

Fourth, note that in relation to institutions, and institutional processes and roles, we have insisted that if they are to have the potential to be corrupted, then they must be *morally* legitimate, and not merely legitimate in some weaker sense, e.g. lawful. Perhaps there are non-moral senses of the term "corruption". For example, it is sometimes said that some term in use in a linguistic community is a corrupted form of a given word, or that some modern art is a corruption of traditional aesthetic forms. However, the central meaning of the term "corruption" has a strong moral connotation; to describe someone as a corrupt person or an action as corrupt is to ascribe a moral deficiency and to express moral disapproval. Accordingly, if an institutional process is to be corrupted, it must suffer some form of moral diminution, and therefore in its uncorrupted state, it must be at least morally legitimate. So although marriage across the colour bar was unlawful in apartheid South Africa, a police officer, Officer A, who refused to arrest a black man who married a white woman was not engaged in an act of corruption. On the other hand, if another police officer, Officer B, did arrest and charge black men who married white women, the officer may well be engaged in an act of corruption. Officer A's act was not corrupt because a legally required, but morally unacceptable, institutional procedure – arresting and charging mixed-race married couples – cannot be corrupted. It cannot be corrupted because it was not morally legitimate to start with. Indeed, the legal prohibition on marriage across the colour bar is in itself a corruption of the institution of marriage. And so Officer A's act of refraining from arresting and charging the black man and the white woman was not only not corrupt; it was a refusal to engage in corruption. By contrast, Officer B's practice of arresting and charging mixed-race marital couples was corrupt; it was undermining the institution of marriage as it ought to be.

In the light of the diverse range of corrupt actions, and the generic nature of the concept of corruption, it is unlikely that any precise definition of corruption is possible; nor is it likely that the field of corrupt actions can be neatly circumscribed by recourse to a set of self-evident criteria. It seems that we should content ourselves with the somewhat vague and highly generic definition of corruption that we have provided above, and then proceed in a relatively informal and piecemeal manner to try to identify a range of moral and/or legal offences that are known to contribute under certain conditions to the despoiling of the moral character of persons, and/or to the undermining of morally legitimate institutions. Such offences obviously include bribery, fraud, nepotism, and the like. But under certain circumstances, they might also include breaches of confidentiality that compromise investigations, the making of false statements that undermines court proceedings or selection committee processes or the earned reputations of public figures, the selective enforcement of laws or rules by those in authority, and so on and so forth.

The wide diversity of corrupt actions has at least two further implications. Firstly, it implies that acts of corruption have a correspondingly large set of moral deficiencies. Certainly all corrupt actions will be morally wrong, and morally wrong at least in part because they despoil moral character or undermine morally legitimate institutions. However, since there are many and diverse offences at the core of corrupt actions – offences such as bribery, fraud, nepotism, making false statements, breaching confidentiality, and so on – there will also be many and diverse moral deficiencies associated with different forms of corruption. Some acts of corruption will have the moral deficiency of deception, others of theft, still others of not being impartial, and so on.

Secondly, the wide diversity of corrupt actions implies that there may well need to be a correspondingly wide and diverse range of anti-corruption measures to combat corruption in its different forms, and indeed in its possibly very different contexts.

Nature and Causes of Police Corruption

Case Studies

Case Study 5.1 The Birmingham Six[15]

On 21st November, 1974, two public houses in Birmingham were bombed by the IRA. 21 people were killed. Six men were charged with the largest number of murders in British history, and in June 1976, they were tried in Lancaster. The trial lasted 45 days. The evidence against the six men consisted of forensic evidence and the written confessions of four of the men. There was also circumstantial evidence about associations with known IRA people. The admissibility of the confessions was disputed by the defence on the basis that they had been beaten out of the defendants. The judge allowed the confessions to go before the jury. All six defendants were convicted.

On Thursday, 14th March, 1991, the "Birmingham Six" won their freedom. In March 1990, the Home Secretary had ordered a new inquiry into the case, after representations from the men's solicitors in which the forensic police evidence was challenged. Following the inquiry of Sir John May into the wrongful conviction in the Maguire case (May, 1990), which was closely linked to the Guildford Four case, the credibility of the forensic science techniques used in the Birmingham Six case was totally demolished. In August 1990, the Home Secretary referred the case back to the Court of Appeal after the policy inquiry had, quite independently, found discrepancies in the police interview record of one of the men. It seemed that the police had fabricated documentary evidence against the six men. The Director of Public Prosecutions could no longer rely on either the forensic or the police evidence that convicted the six men in 1975. The Court of Appeal heard the case at the beginning of 1991, and quashed the convictions of the six men.

---

15 This case study is from Seumas Miller, John Blackler and Andrew Alexander, *Police Ethics* (Keon, 1995), p. 114. See also Seumas Miller, John Blackler and Andrew Alexandra, *Police Ethics* (Sydney: Allen and Unwin, 1997), p. 182.

Case Study 5.2 Robert Leuci

Detective Robert Leuci was a member of NYPD Narcotics Division's Special Investigative Unit. SIU Detectives, although junior grade, were acknowledged the force's most expert drug investigators. In an addicted city, increasingly victimised by drug-related crime, their headline-grabbing, multi-million dollar drug busts, turning in suitcases, a steamer trunk – once a whole closet full of drugs – earned universal approbation; the city fathers tagged them "Princes of the City".

There was elitism and a positive *esprit de corps* in the SIU which, together with a solidaristic tendency that defeated supervision, meant that the NYPD didn't look too closely at the unit's MO. This policy was apparently justified by a stream of high-profile arrests that reflected credit on the remainder of a department, otherwise not enjoying a good press. Working with a patently corrupt legal system, amongst suspects, lost to the moral pressures of normal society, the SIU's autonomous four-man teams pursued their investigations in an ecology of moral ambiguity – a place where values collide. Beyond the ethical command of even their own tainted force, their methods descended into the same order of criminality they sought to suppress.

Leuci was undergoing a personal crisis: a younger brother's previously undetected narcotics habit; his father's recognition of his and his workmates' corruption. He began to unburden himself to Nicholas Scoppetta, a prosecutor from the Commission to investigate Alleged Police Corruption, the "Knapp Commission". Part of the text of an initial contact, including Leuci's *apologia pro vita sua*, is reproduced here:

"You people of the Knapp Commission," he said, "are focusing on the Police Department. You tell cops that you are out to catch them taking meals, taking Christmas presents, giving drugs to junkies. It's absolutely incredible. Cops are looking at you and saying, 'You bastards. It's you guys – the assistant district attorneys, lawyers, judges who run the system – and the whole fucking thing from top to bottom is corrupt. We know how you become a judge. You pay $50,000 and you become a judge. We see stores open on Sunday on Fifth Avenue, but they can't be open in Little Italy. The only people that know us, care for us, love us, are other cops. You people are just looking to hurt us. You want to lay on us the responsibility for fucking up the system.'"

"Do you know what it's like to be a narcotics detective?" Leuci continued. "Do you have any conception? Do you know what it's like on a February night in South Brooklyn a block from the piers, with two addict informants in the back of the car, both of them crying, begging you for a bag of heroin? Do you know what it's like going home 50 miles away, and getting a phone call five minutes after you're home saying, 'I blew the shot, please come back and give me another bag.' And driving 50 miles back in and watching him tie up and walking out of the room. Then working with him the next morning and locking up some dope-pusher that's just as sick as he is. It's an insanity. And going into the office and the lieutenant says you have to make five arrests this month. Do you know what it's like working six, seven days a week? You have to be one of the best, otherwise you go back to swinging a stick."

Scoppetta's every nerve was attuned to Leuci's mood. But his mind was racing, looking for the key word, each time Leuci paused, to keep him talking.

"You're in Westbury, or West End Avenue," Leuci ranted on. "We're in El Barrio, we're on 15th Street. You want us to keep everybody inside the barricades so you can stay outside. I'm on Pleasant Avenue and 116th Street at three o'clock in the morning, just me and my partner and Tony-somebody that we have been following for three weeks, and he's going to offer me money, and me and my partner are going to decide whether we'll take it or not. You don't care about me, and some black revolutionary is going to whack me out if he gets a chance, some newspaper is going to call me a thief whether I do it or I don't do it. The only one who cares about me is my partner. It's me and him and this guy we caught. We're going to take him to jail and lock him up. We're going to take his money. Fuck him, fuck you, fuck them."

Scoppetta listened, waiting... "I see what kind of man you are, and I see what kind of man my partner is, and there's no comparison, see? I'm going to side with him. He tells me, 'It's okay, Bobby; hey Bobby, it's you and me against the rest of the world.' You guys are eating in the Copa six nights a week. We try to get 40 dollars expense money and the department won't even give us that." Leuci swallowed painfully. "You're winning in the end anyway. We're selling ourselves, our families. These people we take money from own us. Our family's future rests on the fact that some dope-pusher is not going to give us up, or some killer, some total piece of shit, is not going to give us up."[16]

Case Study 5.3 Corrupting the Democratic Process

Bjelke-Petersen was planning a sharp restriction on the right to assemble and the right to dissent. At the time, as the National Party later accepted, "…there had been no illegal street marches of any consequence." On 4th September [1977], Bjelke-Petersen announced a change to the law on street marches. Hitherto, if police refused a permit, applicants could appeal to a magistrate. He now stated that appeals could only be made to Police Chief Lewis. Protest marches, he said, will be "…a thing of the past. Nobody, including the Communist Party or anybody else, is going to turn the streets of Brisbane into a forum. Protest groups need not bother to apply for permits to stage marches because they won't be granted. That's government policy now."

The right of appeal was thus no appeal at all; it may appear that the function of the legislation was not to stop demonstrations, but to incite them for propaganda purposes in the hinterland... Lewis' police force was now functioning as virtually a private army of the regime. Constable Michael Egan confirmed 18 months later that Special Branch police provoked violence at demonstrations. He said undercover police were "running through the crowd and stirring them up, pushing people over and going hysterical."

---

[16] This case study is from Robert Daley, *Prince of the City* (London: Granada, 1979), pp. 19-20.

An anti-uranium rally was held in Brisbane on Saturday, 22nd October. Mayhem ensued: 400 people were flung into police wagons; a Melbourne newspaper called it "Joh's War". Bjelke-Petersen asked the Australian Broadcasting Tribunal to permit television stations to cover an election-eve demonstration on Friday, 11th November. Labor leader Tom Burns appealed to demonstrators not to march.[17]

Causes of Police Corruption

Recent commissions of inquiry into police corruption, including the Mollen Commission into the New York Police Department and the Royal Commission into the NSW Police Service, have uncovered corruption of a profoundly disturbing kind. Police officers have been involved in perjury, fabricating evidence, protecting pederast rings, taking drug money and selling drugs. In South Africa, police have been involved in murder, armed robbery and rape, as well as theft, fraud, fabrication of evidence, and the like. High levels of police corruption have been a persistent historical tendency in police services throughout the world. Corruption in policing is neither new nor especially surprising. Indeed, a number of causes of police corruption have been identified.

As discussed in previous chapters, in order to do their job effectively, police have been given a number of rights and powers – such as the right to use coercive force in ways forbidden to others, and the power to do so – and wide discretion in the exercise of these rights and powers. Police have many opportunities to abuse these powers; to harass the innocent with threats or trivial charges, to turn a blind eye to serious crime, and so on.

They also face considerable temptations to avail themselves of these opportunities. They may be offered material inducements, such as the offer of money or favours in return for protection, or dropping of charges, for example. They may be tempted by the opportunity to express some personal prejudice, against (say) a particular racial group. Or they may be influenced by the chance to avoid what we could think of as the costs of police work. After all, a lot of conscientious police work is unpleasant – dangerous, or tedious, or time-consuming. The temptation to take short-cuts to avoid these costs, or to seek benefits to offset these costs, is considerable. (See Case Studies 5.1 and 5.2 above.)

A further contributing factor to police corruption is the inescapable use by police officers of what in normal circumstances would be regarded as morally unacceptable activity. The use of coercive force, including in the last analysis deadly force, is in itself harmful. Accordingly, in normal circumstances it is morally unacceptable. So it would be morally wrong, for example, for a private citizen to forcibly take someone to his house for questioning. Similarly, locking someone up deprives them of their liberty, and is therefore considered in itself

[17] Evan Whitton, *The Hillbilly Dictator; Australia's Police State* (Sydney: ABC Enterprises, 1988), pp. 45-6.

morally wrong. Again, deception, including telling lies, is under normal circumstances morally wrong. Intrusive surveillance is in itself morally wrong – it is an infringement of privacy. And the same can be said of various other methods used in policing.

Coercion, depriving someone of their liberty, deception and so on, are harmful methods; they are activities which considered in themselves and under normal circumstances are morally wrong. Therefore they stand in need of special justification. As we have argued in Chapter 1, in relation to policing there is a special justification. These harmful and normally immoral methods are on occasion necessary in order to realise the fundamental end of policing, namely the protection of moral rights. However, the fundamental point that needs to be made here is that the use of these harmful methods by police officers – albeit methods which in the right circumstances are morally justifiable – can have a corrupting influence on police officers. A police officer can begin by engaging in the morally justifiable activity of telling lies to criminals, and engaging in elaborate schemes of deception as an undercover agent, and end up engaging in the morally unjustifiable activity of telling lies and deceiving innocent members of the public or his fellow officers. A police officer can begin by engaging in the morally justifiable activity of deploying coercive force to arrest violent offenders resisting arrest, and end up engaging in the morally unjustified activity of beating up suspects to secure a conviction.

It might be suggested that such methods could be wholly abandoned in favour of the morally unproblematic methods already heavily relied upon, such as rational discourse, appeal to moral sentiment, reliance on upright citizens for information, and so on. Doubtless in many instances morally problematic methods could be replaced. And certainly overuse of these methods is a sign of bad police work, and perhaps of the partial breakdown of police-community trust so necessary to police work. However, the point is that the morally problematic methods could not be replaced in *all* instances. For one thing, the violations of moral rights which the police exist to protect are sometimes violations perpetrated by persons who are unmoved by rationality, appeal to moral sentiment, and so on. Indeed, such persons, far from being moved by well-intentioned police overtures, may seek to influence or corrupt police officers for the purpose of preventing them from doing their moral and lawful duty. For another thing, the relevant members of the community may for one reason or another be unwilling, or unable, to provide the necessary information or evidence, and police may need to rely on persons of bad character, or methods such as intrusive surveillance.

So unfortunately, harmful methods which are in normal circumstances considered to be immoral are on occasion necessary in order to realise the fundamental end of policing, namely the protection of moral rights.

The paradox whereby police necessarily use methods which are normally morally wrong to secure morally worthy ends sets up a dangerous moral dynamic. The danger is that police will come to think that the ends always justify the means; to come to accept the inevitability and the desirability of so-called "noble cause corruption". From noble cause corruption, they can in turn graduate to straightforward corruption; corruption motivated by greed and personal gain.

Further, as a matter of sociological fact, police display a high degree of group identification and solidarity. In many ways, such solidarity is a good thing: without it, effective policing would be impossible. But it can also contribute to police corruption. Police who refrain from acting against their corrupt colleagues out of a sense of loyalty are often compromised by this failure, and ripe for more active involvement in corrupt schemes. (See Case Study 5.2 above.)

A particularly significant contributing factor to police corruption is the widespread use in contemporary societies of illegal drugs such as heroin, cocaine and Ecstasy. (Again, see Case Study 5.2 above.) Police officers, especially detectives, are called on to enforce anti-drug laws in circumstances having the following features: (a) there are large amounts of money, and a willingness on the part of drug-users, and especially drug-dealers, to bribe police; (b) there are no complainants – the "victims" are not persons who would come to the police and report that they have been the victim of a criminal act; (c) corrupt police officers can accept bribes or steal drugs or drug money with relative impunity, given (b); (d) there is a feeling in some sectors of the community that drug addiction is not so much a crime as a medical condition, and that therefore drug-taking should not be regarded as a crime; (e) young police officers typically share the attitudes of their peers outside policing, and thus may regard the use of illegal drugs as a relatively minor offence, and; (f) police officers who are especially vulnerable, such as young police officers or those working in drug investigations, may out of fear turn a blind eye to drugs, or even succumb to drug-taking themselves, and thereby enter the spiral of corruption which moves from moral vulnerability to moral compromise, and thence to corrupt activities.

Let us now list some of the general conditions which contribute to police corruption. These conditions include: (a) the necessity at times for police officers to deploy harmful methods, such as coercion and deception, which are normally regarded as immoral; (b) the high levels of discretionary authority and power exercised by police officers in circumstances in which close supervision is not possible; (c) the ongoing interaction between police officers and corrupt persons who have an interest in compromising and corrupting police; (d) the necessity for police officers to make discretionary ethical judgements in morally ambiguous situations, and; (e) the operation of police officers in an environment in which there is widespread use of illegal drugs and large amounts of drug money.

In addition to these causes of police corruption, there are some less obvious ones.

Firstly, lack of competence can be a contributor to, and even a species of, corruption. Normally we do not think that incompetence is morally blameworthy, even where it contributes to a bad outcome, since someone cannot be blamed for not bringing about what they did not have the capacity to bring about. However, we can blame people for failing to act to equip themselves with necessary skills or knowledge when they have been provided with the opportunity. For example, a police officer who out of laziness or indifference fails to acquaint himself sufficiently with certain aspects of the law, and then through ignorance of the law proceeds to make unlawful arrests, is engaging in a form of corrupt activity. His actions are wrongful, and the reason that he is performing those actions is self-interest, or at least self-indulgence.

We can also blame people for continuing on in a job when they know they do not possess, and cannot acquire, the necessary skills or aptitude for the job. This kind of moral failure is illustrated by a police officer who continues on in the job knowing that he is too fearful to make arrests which he should have been making. Weakness is a moral failing, and he is weak. But weakness is not in itself corruption. What makes such a police officer corrupt is that even though he knows he is weak, and therefore lacking in the ability to adequately function as a police officer, he continues in the job for reasons of self-interest.

Secondly, police can count as corrupt even where they use their expertise for the achievement of the right ends, when they do so by making use of bad means. The officer who "verbals" someone he knows to be guilty of violent crime, in order to secure the conviction which would otherwise be impossible, achieves such good ends as the punishment of the guilty, as well as the protection and reassurance of the public. These are ends which police should try to achieve, indeed ends which are partially constitutive of their role. As we have already said, this kind of corruption is known as "noble cause" corruption. We turn now to a discussion of noble cause corruption.

Noble Cause Corruption

The notion of noble cause corruption receives classic expression in the film *Dirty Harry*.[18] Detective Harry Callaghan is trying to achieve a morally good end. He is trying to find a kidnapped girl whose life is in imminent danger. In the circumstances, the only way he can determine where the girl is in order to save her is by inflicting significant pain on the kidnapper, who is otherwise refusing to reveal her whereabouts.

The image of Harry Callaghan inflicting non-lethal pain on a murderous psychopath is emotionally, and indeed ethically, compelling. However, the question that needs to be asked is whether fabricating evidence, beating up suspects, "verballing" suspects, committing perjury and so on, to obtain convictions is in the same moral category as Harry's action. The answer is in the negative.

For one thing, Harry Callaghan's predicament is a romantic fiction, or at best a highly unusual combination of circumstances. Most instances of police fabrication of evidence, and even excessive use of force, have not been used to save the life of someone in imminent danger, nor have they been the only means available to secure a conviction. For another thing, the ongoing recourse to such methods not only violates the rights of suspects, it tends to have the effect of corrupting police officers. To this extent, the moral harm that results from such methods not only

---

[18] See Carl B. Klockars, "The Dirty Harry Problem", reprinted in A. S. Blumberg and E. Niederhoffer (eds.), *The Ambivalent Force: Perspectives on the Police* (New York: Holt, Rinehart and Winston, 1976).

harms suspects, it can eventually destroy the moral character of those police officers deploying these methods.

The dangers attendant upon noble cause corruption demand that we provide a principled account of the difference between justifiable use of normally immoral methods and noble cause corruption. In Chapter 1 we did so, in effect. There we argued that when police officers act in accordance with the legally enshrined moral principles governing the use of harmful methods, they achieve three things at one and the same time. They do what is morally right; their actions are lawful; and they act in accordance with the will of the community.

It might be argued – and seems to have been argued by Andrew Alexandra[19] – that recourse to the notion of the use of harmful methods in accordance with communally-sanctioned objective moral principles does not remove the theoretical problem posed by noble cause corruption, and specifically the alleged (by Alexandra) immorality of even the lawful use of harmful methods by police. To be sure, a suspect who is guilty of a serious crime has not been treated immorally if he is lawfully – and not unreasonably – harmed by being coerced, deceived or surveilled.[20] But Alexandra asks: What if he is innocent? In *that* case, harmful methods have been lawfully used, but their use is immoral – suggests Alexandra. Let us respond to this argument. Firstly, the person harmed needs to be a suspect, i.e. there is, or should be, some form of evidence that he is guilty. Nevertheless, sometimes persons reasonably suspected of committing crimes are in fact innocent. However, innocent persons wrongly suspected of crimes are not harmed by the police *in the knowledge* that they are innocent. So we do not have intentional harming of persons known to be innocent. Rather, we have intentional harming of persons thought likely to be guilty; and we have unintended harming of the innocent as a by-product of police work. Troublesome as this is, it does not put immorality at the core of the police function, as Alexandra seems to suggest. If there are some police methods that do involve intentional harming of those known to be innocent, e.g. intrusive surveillance of a criminal engaged in sexual activity with a woman known not to be a criminal, then perhaps these methods ought not to be deployed.

The moral problem of noble cause corruption arises in policing when moral considerations pull in two different directions, and especially when the law thwarts, rather than facilitates, morally desirable outcomes. But here we need to distinguish types of case.

Assume that a police officer breaks a morally unacceptable law, but acts in accordance with the law as it ought to be. For example, suppose a police officer refuses to arrest a black person who is infringing the infamous "pass laws" in apartheid South Africa. Such a police officer is not engaged in noble cause corruption; for breaking a morally unacceptable law is not engaging in corruption, and therefore not engaging in noble cause corruption.

---

[19] Andrew Alexandra, "Dirty Harry and Dirty Hands", in Tony Coady, Steve James, Seumas Miller and Michael O'Keefe (eds.), *Violence and Police Culture* (Melbourne: Melbourne University Press, 2000).

[20] We are assuming here that the law appropriately tracks reason-based ethical principles.

A second kind of case involves a police officer breaking a law which, although not morally unacceptable, is nevertheless flawed, in that it does not adequately reflect the ethical balance that needs to be struck between the rights of suspects and the rights of victims. For example, assume that a law only allows a suspect to be detained for questioning for a limited period of time; a period which is wholly inadequate for certain kinds of criminal investigation. The law is not necessarily immoral, but it ought to be changed. A police officer who detains a suspect for slightly longer than this period has technically breached the law; but the officer has not violated a suspect's rights in any profound sense. Once again, the term "corruption" is too strong. This is not a case of noble cause corruption; though it is a case of unlawful, and perhaps unethical, conduct.

A third kind of case involves a police officer violating a suspect's legally enshrined moral rights by, for example, using the third degree or fabricating evidence or committing perjury. The point about these kinds of case is that the police officer has not only acted illegally, but also immorally. If a police officer engages in this kind of corrupt activity, and does so in order to achieve morally desirable outcomes, such as the conviction of known perpetrators of serious crimes, then the officer is engaged in noble cause corruption. Let us examine this kind of case further.

Noble cause corruption is obviously not morally justified if there is some lawful means to achieve the morally desirable outcome. But are there cases in which the only way to achieve a morally obligatory outcome is to act immorally?

In order to enable us to explore the philosophical issues associated with noble cause corruption further, and to focus our discussion, let us consider the following case study.[21]

Case Study 5.4 Noble Cause Corruption

A young officer, Joe, seeks advice from the police chaplain. Joe is working with an experienced detective, Mick, who is also Joe's brother-in-law, and looked up to by Joe as a good detective who gets results. Joe and Mick are working on a case involving a known drug-dealer and paedophile. Joe describes his problem as follows:

"Father – he has got a mile of form, including getting kids hooked on drugs, physical and sexual assault on minors, and more. Anyway, surveillance informed Mick that the drug-dealer had just made a buy. As me and Mick approached the drug-dealer's penthouse flat, we noticed a parcel come flying out the window of the flat onto the street. It was full of heroin. The drug-dealer was in the house, but we found no drugs inside. Mick thought it would be more of a sure thing if we found the evidence in the flat rather than on the street – especially given the

[21] The discussion in this section relies heavily on Seumas Miller's "Corruption and Anti-Corruption in the Profession of Policing", *Professional Ethics*, Vol. 6, Nos. 3 & 4, 1998, pp. 83-107. Another version of this material appeared in Seumas Miller, "Noble Cause Corruption in Policing Revisited", in Robert Adlam and Peter Villiers (eds.), *A Safe, Just and Tolerant Society: Police Virtue Rediscovered* (Waterside Press, 2004).

number of windows in the building. The defence would find it more difficult to deny possession. Last night, Mick tells me that he was interviewed and signed a statement that we both found the parcel of heroin under the sink in the flat. He said all I had to do was to go along with the story in court and everything will be sweet, no worries. What should I do Father? – perjury is a serious criminal offence."[22]

In this scenario, there are two putative instances of noble cause corruption. The first one is Mick intentionally unlawfully loading up the evidence and committing perjury in order to secure a conviction. As it is described above, this instance of noble cause corruption is not morally sustainable. For there is a presumption against breaking communally-sanctioned ethical principles enshrined in the law, and this presumption has not been offset by the moral considerations in play here. Indeed, it is by no means clear that in this situation, Mick's unlawful acts are even necessary in order for the drug-dealer to be convicted. Moreover, achieving the good end of securing the conviction of the drug-dealer is outweighed by the damage being done by undermining other important moral ends, namely due process of law and respect for a suspect's moral rights.[23]

Nor is there anything to suggest that this is a one-off unlawful act by Mick, and that he had provided himself with what he took to be a specific and overriding moral justification for committing it on this particular occasion. Indeed, the impression is that Mick loads up suspects and commits perjury as a matter of routine practice. Further, there is nothing to suggest that police powers in this area – at least in Australia – are hopelessly inadequate, that police and others have failed in their endeavours to reform the law, and that therefore police officers have no option but to violate due process law, if they are to uphold so-called "substantive" law. Of course, it is a different matter whether or not current Australian anti-drug policies are adequate to the task. Evidently they are not. But this in itself does not justify an increase in police powers in particular. For if anything is clear, it is that a policy of criminalisation is by itself inadequate. Accordingly, Mick, and like-minded detectives do not have available to them the argument that noble cause corruption is justifiable because there is a discrepancy between what police powers ought to be, by the lights of objective ethical principles, and what they in fact are. In the first place, there is no such discrepancy; although arguably current anti-drug policies are failing. In the second place, loading up suspects, perjury and the like, could never be lawful procedures grounded in objective ethical principles. Lastly, if in fact an increase in police powers were morally justified, then the appropriate response of the police ought to be to argue and lobby for this increase, not engage in unlawful conduct. It might be the case that an irredeemably obstructionist political system, that consistently failed to provide police with adequate powers in spite of sustained and well-put arguments and lobbying by police and others, might justify police exercise of

[22] The above case study was provided in a suitably disguised form by Father Jim Boland, Chaplain to the NSW Police.

[23] Howard Cohen, "Overstepping Police Authority", *Criminal Justice Ethics*, Summer/Fall, 1987, p. 57.

unlawful powers of a kind that ought to be lawful, e.g. detaining a suspect for a period longer than was lawful.

There is a second possible example of noble cause corruption in our scenario which is more morally troublesome. This is Joe committing perjury in order to prevent a host of harmful consequences to Mick, Joe and their families. If Joe does not commit perjury, Mick will be convicted of a criminal act, and their careers will be ruined. Moreover, the friendship of Mick and Joe will be at an end, and their respective families will suffer great unhappiness. The second example is a candidate for justified, or at least excusable, unlawful behaviour on the grounds of extenuating circumstances. Let us assume that were Joe to commit perjury, his action would be morally justified, or at least morally excusable. The question to be asked now is whether it is an act of noble cause corruption.

Certainly, such an act of perjury is unlawful. But here we need to distinguish a number of different categories. Some acts are unlawful, but their commission does not harm any innocent person. Arguably, such unlawful acts are not necessarily immoral. The drug-dealer will be harmed in that he will go to prison, but he is not innocent; he is a known drug-dealer and paedophile who deserves to go to prison.

But the fact that the drug-dealer is guilty of serious crimes does not settle the issue. Consider Joe's actions. Some acts are unlawful, but their commission does not infringe anyone's moral rights. Joe's act will certainly infringe the drug-dealer's moral rights, including the right to a fair trial based on admissible evidence. Moreover, perjury undermines a central plank of due process law: without truthful testimony, the whole system of criminal justice would founder; perjury is a species of institutional corruption. Considered in itself, the act of perjury is a serious moral wrong, and an act of corruption.

Unfortunately, as we have already seen, the moral costs of Joe not committing perjury are also very high – perhaps higher than those involved in perjury.

We can conclude that Joe faces a genuine moral dilemma; he will do moral harm whatever he does. Does it follow that we have found an instance in which noble cause corruption is justified? Here there are really two questions. Firstly, is Joe's action an instance of noble cause corruption? Secondly, is his action morally justified? The distinction between corruption – including noble cause corruption – on the one hand, and immorality on the other, is a fine distinction in this context; but it is no less real for that.

As we have seen in earlier chapters, corruption is a species of immorality, and corrupt actions are a species of immoral actions; nevertheless, not all immorality is corruption, and not all immoral actions are corrupt ones.

Most corrupt actions have a number of properties that other immoral actions do not necessarily possess. First, corrupt actions are typically not one-off actions. For an action to be properly labelled as corrupt, it has to in fact corrupt, and therefore is typically a manifestation of a disposition or habit on the part of the agent to commit that kind of action. Indeed, one of the reasons most acts of noble cause corruption are so problematic in policing is that they typically involve a disposition to commit a certain kind of action. Acts of noble cause corruption are typically not simply one-off actions; they are habitual.

Now Joe's action is not habitual. However, as we saw in Chapter 1, some acts of corruption are one-off. So the fact that Joe's action is a one-off, non-habitual action does not settle the question as to whether it is corrupt or not.

Secondly, most corrupt actions – involving as they do a habit to act in a certain way – are not performed because of a specific non-recurring eventuality. Rather, they are performed because of an ongoing condition or recurring situation. In the case of noble cause corruption in policing, the ostensible ongoing condition is the belief that the law is hopelessly and irredeemably inadequate, not only because it fails to provide police with sufficient powers to enable offenders to be apprehended and convicted, but also because it fails to provide sufficiently harsh punishments for offenders. Accordingly, so the argument runs, police need to engage in noble cause corruption; that is, they need to develop a habit of bending and breaking the law in the service of the greater moral good of justice, given the irremediable features of the criminal justice system.

Now although Joe is motivated to do wrong to achieve good, or at least to avoid evil, he is responding to a highly specific – indeed extraordinary – circumstance he finds himself in, and one which is highly unlikely to recur.[24] He has not developed a disposition or habit in response to a felt ongoing condition or recurring situation. However, again the point has to be made that some corrupt actions are one-off, non-habitual actions that are responses to a highly specific, non-recurring circumstance. Accordingly, we cannot conclude from the non-recurring nature of these circumstances that Joe's action is not a corrupt act.

Third, corrupt actions are typically motivated at least in part by individual or narrow collective self-interest. In the case of policing, the interest can be individual self-interest, such as personal financial gain or career advancement. Or it can be the narrow collective self-interest of the group, such as in the case of a clique of corrupt detectives.

Certainly Joe's action is not motivated by self-interest. However, it is a defining feature of acts of noble cause corruption that they are not motivated by self-interest (or narrow collective self-interest), and so this feature of Joe's action does not prevent it being an act of corruption – and specifically, an act of noble cause corruption.

Given that Joe's act of perjury undermines a legitimate institutional process, and given the possibility of one-off acts of noble cause corruption, it might seem that Joe's act is corrupt. But this move is a little too quick. Certainly Joe's action undermines a legitimate institutional process. However, as noted in Chapter 1, for his act to be corrupt, Joe has to be morally culpable in some degree. Now Joe is aware that his act of perjury will undermine a legitimate institutional process; it is not as if he is ignorant of the institutional damage that he is doing. On the other hand, he is well-motivated; he is aiming at the good, albeit by doing what is *prima facie* morally wrong.

---

[24] See Edwin Delattre, *Character and Cops*, 2nd Edition (Washington, DC: AEI Press, 1994), Chapter 11, for a discussion of such extraordinary situations, and the need – as he sees it – for consultation with senior experienced police officers.

It might be thought that his action is an instance of noble cause corruption. In order for his action to be an act of noble cause corruption it has to be corrupt, and in order for it to be corrupt it must fulfil the following two conditions: firstly, it must corrupt something or someone – in the case of Joe, a legitimate institutional process, viz. testimony is corrupted – and; secondly, the agent must be morally responsible for the act, i.e. he must have performed an act which has a corrupting effect, and one which he knew would have this effect, or which he ought to have known would have this effect. If these two conditions are not met, then the action is not an act of corruption. In the case of Joe's action, both these conditions are met. So Joe performs an act of corruption, albeit – given his motivation – an act of noble cause corruption. Note that it is possible for the action to be corrupt, and yet for the agent not to be culpable, for example in the circumstance that although the action was corrupt in itself, it was not morally wrong, all things considered.

So Joe's action was corrupt, but the question remains as to whether Joe's action was morally wrong from an "all things considered" standpoint.

It seems to us that Joe faces a genuine moral dilemma. Perhaps it would be morally wrong for him to commit perjury. However, even if this is so, we do not believe that he would be morally culpable if he committed perjury in these circumstances. For the dilemma is such that we cannot confidently claim that Joe ought to have known that committing perjury *in these circumstances* would be morally wrong. We conclude that whether or not Joe's act of perjury in these circumstances would be morally wrong, Joe would not be morally culpable in performing it.

We have seen that corrupt actions, including acts of noble cause corruption, are typically – but not necessarily or invariably – habitual actions; typically, they are not one-off actions performed in accordance with moral principles that have been applied to a particular non-recurring situation. So in most cases of noble cause corruption, the motivating force is in part that of habit, and there is no attempt to perform a rational calculation of the morality of means and ends on a case-by-case basis. Accordingly, there is an inherent possibility, and perhaps tendency, for such acts of noble cause corruption not to be morally justified when individually considered. After all, the police officer who has performed such an individual act of noble cause corruption has simply acted from habit, and has not taken the time to consider whether or not the means really do justify the ends in the particular case. Moreover, given a presumption against infringing communally sanctioned and legally enshrined ethical principles, this failure to engage in moral decision-making on a case-by-case basis is surely morally culpable by virtue of being – at the very least – morally negligent.

What we have said thus far points to the morally problematic nature of doing wrong to achieve good as a matter of unthinking routine. This does not show that noble cause corruption is after all motivated by individual (or narrow collective) *self-interest*. Rather, noble cause corruption remains noble in the sense that it is motivated by the desire to do good. However, there is a weaker claim to be made here, namely that most acts of noble cause corruption are motivated, or at least in part sustained, by a degree of moral negligence.

The officer who habitually performs acts of noble cause corruption does not feel the need to examine the rights and wrongs of his (allegedly) ends-justified immoral actions on a case-by-case basis. Yet given the presumption against infringing communally-sanctioned ethical principles enshrined in the law, surely decision-making on a case-by-case basis is typically morally required. Moreover – as we saw above – acts of noble cause corruption have not been communally sanctioned; they are actions justified – if they are justified at all – only by some set of moral principles held to by the individual police officer or group of officers. Further, this set of alleged ethical principles is typically not objectively valid; it is not a set that ought to be enshrined in the law. Rather, these allegedly ethical principles are in fact typically spurious; they are the kind of principle used to justify actions of the sort that Mick commits, viz. loading up suspects and perjury.

Accordingly, there is a strong possibility of, and perhaps tendency to, moral arrogance, moral insularity, and the application of unethical principles inherent in noble cause corruption. Accordingly, noble cause corruption is both dangerous in its own right, and likely to be at least in part self-serving.

In short, while acts of noble cause corruption are by definition not motivated by individual (or narrow collective) self-interest, in so far as they are habitual actions, they are likely to be indirectly linked to, and in part sustained by, self-interest. Indeed, this conceptual claim of an indirect connection between noble cause corruption and self-interest seems to be supported by empirical studies. It appears to be an empirical fact that police who start off engaging in noble cause corruption often end up engaging in common or garden, out-and-out corruption.[25]

Combating Police Corruption

In this final section, we turn to the question of combating police corruption. We do so in the context of: (a) our assumption that policing ought to be conceived as an emerging profession, and one having the (teleologically understood) moral foundations outlined in the first section of this chapter, and; (b) our claim that moral vulnerability is a fundamental defining feature of police work, and that in the case of the profession of policing, the tendency to corruption ought to be regarded as a basic occupational hazard and treated accordingly.[26]

There are four basic areas which can be looked at in relation to corruption reduction in policing, namely recruitment, reduction of opportunities for corruption, detection and deterrence of corruption, and reinforcing the motivation to do what is right.

It is obvious that if there is a tendency to corruption in policing, it is crucial that those who are recruited have the highest moral character. If there is a good chance

---

[25] See Justice James Wood, *Final Report: Royal Commission into Corruption in the New South Wales Police Service* (Sydney: NSW Government, 1998).

[26] Much of the material in this section is part of Miller's paper, "Creating Good Policing", presented in July 1995 at the Ethics/Professional Standards Seminar, Masonic Centre, Sydney, as part of NSW Police Service Development Program.

that even those of good character can be corrupted, there is obviously no chance of those of bad character being reformed by undertaking police work. It is also important to recruit those who are capable of becoming competent. For the incompetent will find it difficult to identify strongly with the ends of the profession, and they can easily become disaffected and cynical. They are therefore susceptible to corruption. Consider, in this connection, the recruitment of South African *Kitskonstabels* in the 1980s, and the attendant corruption, indeed mayhem, that followed.

While it is important to try to reduce the opportunities for corruption – by, for example, regular rotation of personnel in high-risk areas – the very nature of police work militates against massive reduction in the opportunities for corruption. Probably the greatest reduction in the opportunities for police corruption have occurred not as a result of policies directed at police, but rather as a result of legislative and other policies directed at offences and offenders. For example, decriminalisation, including the decriminalisation of abortion and of homosexuality, had the effect of reducing the opportunities for police corruption. Again, diversionary schemes for juvenile offenders may have the effect of reducing the number of criminals, and thus ultimately reducing the opportunities for police corruption.

The third area is detection and deterrence of police corruption. Detection and deterrence of police corruption is achieved in large part by institutional mechanisms of accountability, both internal and external, and by policing techniques such as complaints investigation, use of informants, auditing, surveillance and testing.[27] Here the above-described constitutive tendency to corruption in police work can be used to justify an extensive system of accountability mechanisms – a system more extensive than may be necessary in other professions – and used also to justify the deployment of techniques of detection and deterrence that might not be acceptable in some other professions.

In most police services, there is an array of accountability mechanisms, including internal accountability on the part of individual members of police services to their superiors and to departments of internal affairs. Indeed the existence of departments of internal affairs – some of which function as internal spy agencies – implies that police services realise that the tendency to corruption is a constitutive feature of policing. Typically, there are also mechanisms to ensure external accountability of a police service to government and the community.

Sometimes these mechanisms of internal accountability are less successful than they might be, due in part to the tendency for such mechanisms of accountability to come to embody and to reinforce the "us-them" mentality that sometimes exists between lower-echelon police officers and the police hierarchy on the one hand, and between police officers and departments of internal affairs on the other. Part of the solution to this problem may lie in the introduction of mechanisms of peer accountability to supplement existing mechanisms. Accountability mechanisms

[27] Seumas Miller, "Authority, Discretion and Accountability: The Case of Policing", in Charles Sampford, Noel Preston and C. Bois (eds.), *Public Sector Ethics: Finding and Implementing Values* (London: Routledge, 1998).

whose members include lower-echelon police officers may be more successful because peers may have a more precise knowledge of what is actually going on at street-level in a particular place at a particular time, but, more generally, because such mechanisms may be more acceptable to lower-echelon officers due to the fact that they are "owned" by them. This is especially the case in the context of our assumption that policing ought to be conceived as an emerging profession functioning in terms of collegial systems of accountability, rather than in terms of top-down hierarchical systems.

Mechanisms of accountability ought to include joint police/community institutional structures. Such structures allow communities to make known problems and to hold police to account – say, via ministers of police – in relation to police responsiveness to these problems. It is a platitude that police/community cooperation is necessary for successful policing. An ambivalent community will shield law-breakers, contribute to an us-them mentality, and lead to a secretive police force in which police corruption is more likely to flourish.

Techniques of detection and deterrence that may be appropriate for a profession with a constitutive tendency for corruption include not only routine procedures such as complaints investigation, but also techniques such as granting indemnity to corrupt officers in order to get them to implicate others, testing for drug use, and elaborate testing for corruption. If corruption is an occupational hazard in policing, then extraordinary methods may have to be used to combat it. Some of these methods raise important ethical and other problems. For example, it is not unknown for criminals who have been granted indemnity to provide evidence which turns out to be false.

The final area that can be looked at in relation to reducing corruption is that of the motivation to do what is morally right. Obviously it is important to reduce where possible the opportunities for corrupt practices. Equally obviously, there will always be police officers who desire to do what is illegal or otherwise immoral, and so there will always be a need for mechanisms and techniques of detection and deterrence.

However, it is not enough to try to reduce opportunities for corruption, and to introduce an elaborate system of detection and deterrence.

For one thing, systems of detection and deterrence have significant costs, and not only in terms of resources, but also in terms of the autonomy of individual police officers and the institutional independence of the police service. For while accountability is not the same thing as commandability, the logical endpoint of increasing accountability is a huge corpus of regulations, and ongoing and intrusive investigative and regulatory activity, all of which stands in some tension with individual professional autonomy and institutional independence.

Most important, reliance on detection and deterrence alone bypasses the issue of moral responsibility which lies at the heart of corruption. In the last analysis, the only force strong enough to resist corruption is the moral sense – the desire to do what is right and avoid doing what is wrong. In what remains of this chapter, we want to briefly explore this notion of moral responsibility in policing.

If most police officers, including members of departments of internal affairs and of the police hierarchy – the ones who investigate corruption – do not for the most part know what is right and what is wrong, and do not have a desire to do what it right, then no system of detection and deterrence, no matter how extensive and elaborate, can possibly suffice to control corruption.

Knowledge of right and wrong, and the desire amongst police officers to do what is right, is importantly connected to issues of professionalisation in policing.

We have claimed that professions typically exist to secure some fundamental end which is a human good or goods. For doctors the end or goal is health, for lawyers justice, for academics knowledge, and for police protecting the moral rights of citizens. The achievement of this fundamental end (or ends) requires specialised skills, knowledge and individual – and especially discretionary ethical – judgement. Ideally, members of professions internalise the fundamental ends which define their particular profession.

The paradigm of a corrupt professional is one who not only abandons the fundamental end or goal of his or her profession, but also uses this professional position – or the skills and knowledge associated with it – for self-interested or immoral ends. The corrupt professional thereby undermines the ends of the profession. For example, the academic Cyril Burtt fabricated evidence to support his psychological theories and thereby achieve academic fame.

The paradigm of a corrupt professional organisation, or section of an organisation, is not simply one in which individual practitioners exploit their position or skills for self-interested or immoral ends and ultimately suffer no loss of self-esteem. It is not simply one in which, on an individual basis, the ends of the institution have been abandoned in favour of the attractions of the corrupt life. Rather, in such institutions, or sections of such institutions, corrupt individuals engage in interdependent corrupt activity – and do so quite often at senior levels. Moreover, in a corrupt institution, or section of an institution, the fact that corrupt individuals cooperate enables them to powerfully influence those who are not corrupt; the corrupt compromise and intimidate those who desire to avoid becoming corrupt themselves, and especially those who seek to expose corruption. Corruption has become an institutional phenomenon; there is systemic corruption.

There is an important relationship between systemic corruption and social norms, in the sense of regularities in action which embody moral attitudes and principles.[28] Corruption is a species of moral wrongdoing, and therefore typically infringes social norms. So all corruption is moral wrongdoing, but not all moral wrongdoing is corruption. For example, murdering one's spouse out of revenge is a morally wrongful action, but it is not necessarily corrupt. One feature of corrupt actions that distinguishes them from many other species of immorality is that corrupt actions are typically motivated by felt self-interest. Another feature is that corrupt actions are not one-off actions, as is the above-mentioned act of murder. Rather, a corrupt action typically results from a disposition to perform that kind of action; corrupt actions are typically habitual actions.

---

[28] Seumas Miller, "Social Norms", in G. Holmstrom-Hintikka and R. Tuomela (eds.), *Contemporary Action Theory* (*Volume 2 – Social Action*), Synthese Library Series (Boston: Kluwer, 1997).

Systemic corruption involves a large number of (typically institutional) actors engaging in cooperative corruption. So systemic corruption typically consists of a large number of individuals cooperatively and habitually engaging in wrongful actions that infringe social norms, and doing so out of believed collective self-interest.

Given this relationship between corruption and social norms, it is not surprising that systemic corruption flourishes in contexts in which social norms are not robust; and systemic corruption is corrosive of social norms.

Systemic corruption also undermines mechanisms of detection and deterrence. Effective systems of detection and deterrence rely in part on transparency. But transparency works as an anti-corruption measure only if those to whom corruption is made transparent are themselves committed to morally upright conduct, and have a clear grasp of what morally upright conduct consists in. Ultimately then, control of corruption relies on robust social norms. Since systemic corruption undermines social norms, it undermines the possibility of controlling corruption.

Given the importance of the desire to do what is morally right, and given this connection between corruption and social norms, what impact, if any, can professionalisation have on police corruption?

Arguably – other things being equal – members of the professions are potentially less open to corruption than some other occupational groups, by virtue of the (well-founded) self-image many of the professions have that the fundamental end of professional work is a human good realised by the exercise of creative expertise, and that true professionals possess creative expertise and internalise this good. On the other hand, the elitism, and strong and closed cultures of many professions, in conjunction with the need to develop specific virtues and apply moral principles in specific professional settings, is fertile ground for corruption. Lawyers can end up with an addiction to legalistic procedures and winning in the adversarial system at the expense of substantive justice, police can end up routinely breaking the law in the service of noble ends, and doctors clubbing together to avoid one of their number from being successfully sued for malpractice. And minor corrupt actions can, over time, turn into major corruptions of character.

Professional expertise, individual autonomy, and internalisation of the moral ends of policing are important in terms of developing and sustaining the desire on the part of police to do what is right. However, focusing on police officers as individuals is not enough. The desire to do what is right needs to be reinforced by utilising the intrinsically collective nature of policing, and in particular, by stressing that police officers are collectively responsible for controlling corruption. It is a mistake to simply undermine police solidarity and loyalty, leaving only isolated individuals who are responsible only for their own actions and who do what is right only because they fear to do what is wrong. It is equally a mistake to rely wholly on the individual heroism of the likes of Frank Serpico, Philip Arantz and Michael Drury. Serpico was a New York police officer who refused to be corrupted in 1966 and indeed reported corruption to reluctant superiors. He finally went to the *New York Times*. Subsequently, the Knapp Commission into corruption into the NYPD was established. Arantz and Drury were New South Wales police officers who blew the whistle on corruption. In the case of Arantz, in 1971 he disclosed NSW crime figures to the press – they contrasted sharply with the official ones. An attempt was then made to discredit him; the Police Commissioner ordered he be taken to a psychiatric ward. In the case of Drury, in 1982 he was approached by a corrupt detective to change his evidence in a forthcoming trial. When he refused to do so, he was seriously wounded by a "hitman".

It is obvious that police officers are collectively responsible for ensuring that the moral ends of policing are realised. Law enforcement, maintenance of order and so on, cannot possibly be achieved by individual police officers acting on their own. Policing is a cooperative enterprise. However, police corruption undermines the proper ends of policing. Moreover, police corruption depends in part on the complicity or tacit consent of the fellow officers of the corrupt. So controlling police corruption is a collective responsibility. It follows that not only is loyalty to corrupt officers misplaced, it is an abrogation of duty. Collective responsibility entails selective loyalty – loyalty to police officers who do what is right, but not to those who do what is wrong. The loyalty of police officers is only warranted by those who embody the ideals of policing, and in particular by those who are not corrupt. Indeed, collective responsibility also entails such actions as whistleblowing, and support for, rather than opposition to, well-intentioned whistleblowers.

The collective effort to ensure that the fundamental ends of policing are pursued will contribute to the internalisation by police officers of those ends, and of the morally appropriate means for their realisation. More importantly, such a collective effort will ensure that police officers identify with those ends, so that self-respect, as well as the respect of others, depends on the pursuit of those ends in accordance with acceptable shared moral principles, and on the collective opposition to corruption. In short, successful combating of corruption in policing crucially depends on the establishment and maintenance of an objectively morally-desirable structure of robust social norms. Such a structure includes norms prescribing the pursuit of the moral ends of policing, as well as norms prescribing the methods of policing. What specific policies could contribute to a robust structure of social norms in policing that resists, and indeed combats, corruption?

A structure of objectively morally-desirable social norms can be reinforced by ensuring a just system of rewards and penalties within the police organisation. Unjust systems of promotion, unreasonably harsh disciplinary procedures for minor errors, unfair workloads and so on, are all deeply corrosive of the desire to do one's job well and to resist inducements to do what is illegal or otherwise immoral.

Morally-desirable social norms can further be reinforced by ensuring an appropriate system of command and control, including for the purposes of accountability; appropriate, that is, to the kinds of responsibilities that attach to the role of police officer. It may be that very hierarchical militaristic/bureaucratic systems of command and control are inappropriate in most areas of modern policing, given the nature of the role of police officer. Police officers have considerable powers – including the power to take away people's liberty – and they exercise those powers in situations of moral complexity. It is inconsistent to give someone a position of substantial responsibility involving a high level of discretionary ethical judgement, and then expect them to mechanically and unthinkingly do what they are told. Moreover, mechanisms of peer accountability are more appropriate to autonomous professional practitioners than top-down hierarchical mechanisms.

The desire and ability to do what is right do not exist independently of the habit of reflection and judgement on particular pressing ethical issues. This is so not only for individual reflective practitioners, but also when it comes to developing reflective organisations or groups. Moreover, the nexus between the desire and ability to do what is right, and the habit of ethical reflection, is especially important in policing. This is because of the moral vulnerability of police. Police confront a variety of temptations, they typically operate in unsupervised settings, they deploy harmful and normally immoral methods in the service of morally worthy ends, and they necessarily confront morally charged situations requiring the exercise of discretionary ethical judgement. Accordingly, the desire and ability to do what is right needs to be continuously reinforced by ensuring that ethical issues in police work, including the ethical ends of policing itself, are matters of ongoing discussion and reflection in initial training programs, further education programs, supervision, ethics committees and in relation to ethical codes. Since a desire to do what is morally right, and the attendant capacity for ethical reflection and judgement, are in fact important in policing – far more important than in many other professions – ethical discussion and deliberation ought to have a central place in policing.

Chapter 6

Restorative Justice in Policing

In this book, we have argued that the central and most important purpose of the institution of the police is the protection of moral rights. We have further argued that the use of harmful methods is both routine and inescapable in police work. In relation to harmful methods, we have thus far discussed in detail police use of deadly force (Chapter 3) and police use of surveillance and related methods that infringe individual privacy (Chapter 4). However, the most obvious harmful method deployed by police is arrest and imprisonment; the infringement of individual freedom or autonomy. Of course, for the most part imprisonment is not something that is a matter for the police to decide; rather the courts determine whether or not an offender will be imprisoned, and if so, for how long. Nevertheless, imprisonment is in some sense a goal of much police work; many offenders are investigated, arrested and charged by police in the context of a criminal justice process which has as its endpoint that these offenders are imprisoned, albeit as a consequence of conviction and sentencing by the courts. So the goal of much – but admittedly not most – police work is imprisonment. However, there is a growing sense that imprisonment is not the answer to criminality, or at best only a small part of the answer. This is in part because imprisonment may not be an appropriate form of punishment for many offenders, and in part because it does not necessarily deal with the needs of victims. More generally, we have argued that criminality essentially consists of the violation of moral rights, and therefore of a rupture in the moral relationship between the offender and the victim. Accordingly, one thing that is called for is a restoring of that moral relationship; hence the importance of restorative justice. However, arguably, the restoration of a moral relationship depends on the preservation of the moral autonomy of both the offender and the victim. If this is so, and if imprisonment undermines individual autonomy, then to this extent imprisonment is a problematic response to criminality in so far as the response to criminality ought to be the restoration of moral relationships. Naturally, it must be accepted that the restoration of moral relationships is not, and cannot be, the only societal response to criminality. At any rate, since our concern in this chapter is with restorative justice, and since restorative justice implies individual moral autonomy, we begin with a brief discussion of the relation between individual autonomy and imprisonment.[1]

---

[1] An earlier version of the material in this chapter appeared as Seumas Miller and John Blackler's "Restorative Justice", in Heather Strang and John Braithwaite (eds.), *Restorative Justice: Philosophy to Practice* (Aldershot: Dartmouth Press, 2000).

Imprisonment

The most obvious feature of prisons is that they restrict freedom; to be a prisoner is to have lost one's freedom. However, being imprisoned is not the only way to lose one's freedom, or at least one's autonomy. This is in part because there are different kinds of freedom. There is freedom of movement, freedom to buy and sell, freedom of association, freedom of thought and speech, and so on. Obviously prison restricts some of these freedoms more than others. And techniques such as, for example, the use of handcuffs, or psychological techniques such as brainwashing, impact on one's freedom or autonomy; prison is not the only way to lose or reduce one's freedom.

Let us then briefly consider the notion of autonomy.

Here we assume that an autonomous agent is a rational agent – an agent capable of reasoning – and also a moral agent in the sense of a morally sentient agent. We also assume that autonomy is principally a property of persisting agents, rather than of discrete actions. In this respect, there is a contrast with at least some notions of freedom, e.g. the notion involved in expressions such as "a freely performed action". It does not make much sense to say that John was an autonomous agent for ten seconds of his life, or that some action was autonomously performed, even though the agent who performed it lacked autonomy. Prison restricts both freedom in the sense of freely performed actions, as well as autonomy.

A rational agent is not necessarily a moral agent. Roughly speaking, a human moral agent is a rational agent who is disposed to make true judgments and valid inferences in relation to the moral worth of human actions, attitudes, motivations, emotions, agents, and so on. Here the actions, attitudes and so on, in question include those of others, as well as one's own. For human moral agents, at least, operate in an interpersonal and social world.

Let us now turn directly to the notion of autonomy. Given the distinction between rational agents and moral agents, there might be a distinction between autonomous rational agents and autonomous (rational) *moral* agents. Certainly, there is a distinction between exercises of *freedom* in the sense of freely-chosen actions of rational agents, and *autonomy* in the sense of autonomous (rational) moral agents; and between exercises of *freedom* in the sense of freely-chosen actions of (rational) moral agents, and *autonomy* in the sense of autonomous (rational) moral agents. For there are freely-chosen actions that have no moral significance, and there are moral and immoral agents who freely choose to perform actions that they know to be morally wrong.

From the fact that an agent is rational and moral (in the above-described senses), it does not follow that the agent is an autonomous moral agent. To see this, imagine a moral agent who always acts on true moral judgments derived from correct moral principles, but nevertheless the agent's beliefs in the correctness of these moral principles is entirely dependent on the hypnotic power of some arch-manipulator.

So being rational and moral (in the above-described senses) are necessary, but not sufficient, conditions for being autonomous. There is at least one further condition that is necessary for autonomy, or at least necessary for the autonomy of moral, including human, agents. This condition is the non-existence of a certain kind of state of affairs *external* to the putatively autonomous human agent. These states of affairs are ones in which the decisions or actions of an external agent or agents is a sufficient condition for the agent in question performing the action that he performs, or believing in the moral principle that he believes in and acts on. Autonomy involves a degree of independence. Self-evidently, prisons and prison officers limit the independent actions of prison inmates, and to that extent prison inmates lack autonomy.

There are further necessary *internal* conditions for being autonomous, e.g. self-mastery of the sort undermined by drug addiction.

Autonomy is intrinsically good; it is good in itself. But autonomy is also a means to other goods. For example, the freedom to pursue a career is a means to making money, and ultimately a means to well-being.

It is no accident that prisons have come to be seen as the paradigmatic form of anti-freedom or anti-autonomy.

Prisons separate people from the outside world, force them into close proximity, and control much of their day to day existence. Irving Goffman has coined the term "total institutions" to describe such environments,[2] where there is a social division between the world of the keepers and the world of the kept (prisoners). The keepers tend to regard the environment as theirs, whilst the kept are subject to it.

Goffman suggests that total-institutions not only undermine autonomy by providing external barriers to the freedom of inmates, e.g. prison walls, they also tend to create clients who permit themselves to be managed; prisons undermine self-mastery. A dependent frame of mind may be induced in a person by subjecting him to "a series of abasements, degradations, humiliations and profanities of self".[3] The inmate's pre-prison identity is undermined by his having to give up his clothes and his possessions, having to be deferential to his keepers, and having his privacy invaded in all sorts of ways. Goffman adds that for most imprisoned persons, mortification and curtailment of the self is very likely to involve acute psychological stress.[4] Note here that, as mentioned in earlier chapters, autonomy is a feature of the personal identity of adult humans, and therefore assaults on identity can undermine autonomy and vice-versa.

A common feature of the total institution is a system of control which involves a set of "house rules", and which permits keepers to dispense minor privileges and relatively severe punishments. For the inmate, these privileges and punishments force him to play a small-child role with which he must psychologically cope.

If a prisoner develops the kind of dependent "personality" described by Goffman, then he or she may no longer have the emotional resources and the will to develop his or her potential. If so, then there has been a profound loss of individual autonomy.

---

[2] Irving Goffman, *Asylums* (London: Penguin, 1961).

[3] *ibid.*, p. 14.

[4] *ibid.*, p. 48.

While prison restricts and undermines autonomy – and bearing in mind that the various freedoms are both intrinsically good, and good as the means to other human goods – none of these freedoms is an *absolute* good. Accordingly, there are times when autonomy comes into conflict with other values, and is justifiably overridden. More specifically, the freedom of an individual needs to be restricted under certain conditions, notably when the individual seeks to seriously harm others, e.g. by murdering or assaulting them, or by stealing from or defrauding them.

So it is obvious that while imprisonment infringes the autonomy of those imprisoned, it is nevertheless necessary in relation to *some* offenders and offences. We take it that imprisonment ought to be available only for serious criminal offences. Accordingly, the issue reduces itself to whether and under what conditions prison is an appropriate form of punishment for serious criminal offences.

Notwithstanding the possible ill-effects of a prison environment, it would still not follow that prison is not a just and reasonable form of punishment for *some* criminals who engage in serious crimes. Certainly from the perspective of retributivism, an argument can be made for imprisonment which is not defeated by the fact – if it is a fact – of pervasive corruption in certain prisons; perhaps criminals deserve to live in a corrupt environment. Moreover, consequentialists can make the point that while imprisoned, criminals cannot assault, steal, and otherwise harm the innocent individuals and the wider society. On the other hand, it is very difficult to see prison as an ideal environment for the rehabilitation of wrongdoers. Moral character-building does not seem to be a particular feature of prison life in many or most countries.

Naturally, there are many differences between prisons. If a prison has a relatively uncorrupt environment, a regime of discipline, and provides an array of educational and vocational options, then a prisoner may well benefit from being imprisoned; the goal of rehabilitation may well be furthered. We have simply sought to draw attention to some of the potential problems associated with imprisonment as a form of punishment for offenders.

One way forward at this point might be to consider the empirical evidence in relation to imprisonment of offenders. If imprisonment deters or otherwise influences offenders not to re-offend, then that would be a powerful argument in its favour. On the other hand, if prison could be shown to have a backfire effect – to increase the probability of offenders re-offending – then obviously that would be a powerful argument against it.

Whatever the empirical evidence one way or another, there is a growing view that prison is not the answer, or not the answer for most criminals, and that other responses to criminality need to be pursued. In this connection, the restorative justice movement is salient. Moreover, police have had an important role to play in relation to the deployment of restorative justice techniques.

Restorative Justice

The term "restorative justice" has come to mean many different things to many different people. So much so that we fear it is beginning to cease to have any clear reference. It is apparently being used to refer to an extraordinarily wide and diverse range of formal and informal interventions, including: (a) victim/offender conferences in criminal justice contexts; (b) discretionary problem-solving policing initiatives in disputes between citizens; (c) conflict resolution workshops in organisational contexts; (d) team-building sessions in occupational settings; (e) marital advice and counselling sessions; (f) parental guidance and admonishment of their misbehaving children, and; (g) apologising for offensive or otherwise hurtful remarks in institutional and other settings.

The scope of the term "restorative justice" has widened to the point that it now has within its purview – at least potentially – any and all harmful, conflictual or otherwise morally problematic actions, situations, or relationships. But even the term "justice" – let alone "*restorative* justice" – cannot sensibly embrace the totality of what is harmful or otherwise morally problematic. Many moral problems are not principally matters of injustice. A drug addict may well be doing great harm to herself, but she is not necessarily committing, or been in receipt of, any injustices. Interventions of various kinds may be necessary if a child is to undergo appropriate moral development, but such interventions are not necessarily in response to any injustice, and being developmental *ex hypothesi* they are not restorative or re-educative in any sense. Conflict may arise from a variety of causes other than injustice, including distrust, lack of sympathy, jealousy and ambition. Finally, many acts of wrongdoing are not principally acts of injustice. Murder is profoundly wrong, but it is not essentially wrong by virtue of being unjust. Naturally, many sorts of wrongdoing give rise to questions of justice. For example, it would be unjust for a murderer to go free. But many sorts of wrongdoing do not. Consider again the drug addict or the unreasonably jealous husband.

Sometimes the term "restorative justice" is used not to refer to these conflictual and other moral problems themselves, but rather to their solutions. But obviously the solutions are as diverse as the problems, and any given solution is not necessarily describable as a state of justice. Solving conflict amongst co-workers might merely require an independent referee to allow the various parties to have their say, and discharge some pent-up emotion. But the solution is not necessarily a state of justice; the predominant values in question might be trust, or even just good order. Moreover, there may well be no offender or victim *per se*, and no injustices may even have taken place.

Perhaps a more plausible way to delimit the notion of restorative justice is to focus not on the problems or the solutions to the problems, but rather on the methodology for solving an admittedly wide array of problems. But it is by no means clear that there is in fact such a single method, or unified set of methods. Certainly it is difficult to see from our above list just what this method or set of methods is. In some quarters a negative definition is apparently on offer. Restorative justice, on this view, is defined as any non-punitive method for resolving moral problems or repairing moral relationships. But there are too many non-punitive methods for this suggestion to be a helpful one. And in any case, as we will see below – and has been forcefully argued by many philosophers over centuries, including recently by Charles Barton[5] – punishment cannot be eliminated as an element in restoring justice. Consider, in this connection, murder. The person who has suffered the wrong – the deceased victim – cannot be dispensed any restorative justice. Retributive justice is called for. This is not to say that restorative justice has no part to play in relation to, for example, the victim's family. For instance, in one of the case studies below, we discuss Terry O'Connell's filmed conference with a murderer and the victim's family, which displays the potential role that a restorative justice mechanism can have in relation to a murderer, and the friends and relatives of the person murdered. In so doing, of course, it does not remove the need for retributive justice. Far from it.

In the light of the above, we have decided to restrict our use of the term "restorative justice" to contexts in which moral rights – as distinct from other sorts of wrongdoing or harm-causing – have been, or might potentially be, infringed, and there is a need for redress or repair in relation to these infringements. Moreover, we are especially concerned with those moral rights that the criminal justice system has been designed (however inadequately) to protect, e.g. rights to protection from force, fraud and theft. Other kinds of problems, including many conflict situations, are no doubt in various respects similar to cases in which moral rights have been infringed, and no doubt sometimes also susceptible of treatment by similar methods, but we doubt that this is typically or even very often the case. Nor should we be taken as necessarily rejecting the value or efficacy of any or all the methods that are used under the banner of restorative justice. There does seem to be a need in our society to explicitly confront moral problems and to revive a variety of formal and informal mechanisms for exposing and resolving them. At any rate, on pain of losing our grip on the topic of restorative justice, we have opted for our narrow definition.

The general concept of justice is complex, and embraces notions of procedural justice, e.g. fair trial, and distributive justice, e.g. fair wages, as well as the notion of justice of greatest interest to us, namely commutative justice or justice in the sphere of punishment, rehabilitation, reintegration, and the like. In relation to punishment, there are an array of theories on offer, including consequentialist and retributive theories.[6] A third category of theory are so-called "restorative justice" theories. According to consequentialist accounts, we ought to punish only to promote good consequences; including deterrence of would-be wrongdoers, rehabilitation, incapacitation, and the like. Retributive theories emphasise the deserts of the wrongdoer; those who do wrong deserve to be punished, irrespective of consequentialist considerations of deterrence, prevention of future harm, and so on. Restorative theorists emphasise the moral education of the wrongdoer and his/her reintegration into the community.

---

[5] Charles Barton, *Getting Even: Revenge as a Form of Justice* (Open Court Publishing Company, 1999), Chapter 8.

[6] For a useful survey of available theories, see C. L. Ten, *Crime, Guilt and Punishment* (Oxford: Clarendon Press, 1987).

We want to stress at the outset that we do not believe that these general accounts are mutually exclusive. Indeed, in our view elements of all three kinds of theory are required if a satisfactory theory of commutative justice is to result. Surely consequences, including harm reduction, are important considerations, and deterrence – based on a credible threat of punishment – does in certain circumstances work. Consider the enforcement of anti-speeding and anti-drink-driving laws. On the other hand, the evidence suggests that many restorative justice programs in relation to juvenile offenders also work. So restorative justice in certain circumstances works. Moreover, reintegration might itself be a consequence to be aimed at. So restorative justice is not necessarily an alternative to all forms of consequentialism. Finally, some retributivist principles, such as that the guilty ought to be the ones to be punished or the ones to compensate victims, need to be maintained in many circumstances. Indeed, as we will argue in detail below, retribution ought to be a component element in many restorative justice programs. In short, we are pluralists. Moreover, *qua* pluralists, we do not accept that any unitary theory, be it consequentialist, retributivist or restorative, can adequately accommodate the plurality of moral considerations in play. For example, in our view even sophisticated consequentialists do not in the final analysis succeed in reducing or otherwise accommodating retributivist considerations.[7] As pluralists we do not disregard, attempt to explain away, or otherwise downplay moral consequences, the importance of deterrence, or the internal moral dynamics of reintegration, merely because we are also committed to punishment as desert. Nor do we see workable deterrence-based or restorative justice programs as being able to jettison retributivist principles. Non-pluralists, we suggest, end up either with the irrationality of punitive retributivism, the sentimentality and ineffectuality of restorative justice proponents who have jettisoned punishment, or the dangers of Benthamite social engineers who have embraced consequentialism.

In Australia, restorative justice, or at least its applications in criminal justice contexts, has been associated with the work of John Braithwaite and Terry O'Connell.[8] They and others have developed and implemented institutional mechanisms such as youth conferencing, and in so doing have in effect resurrected the institution of confession and (implicitly) the theoretical moral framework which underpins it. They have, of course, developed other sorts of restorative justice programs that are not predominantly confessional in character. For example, O'Connell's work in the behavioural change program in the NSW Police Service in local area commands seems to have been principally an exercise in resolving workplace conflict and team-building.[9] As such, it required voluntary participation,

---

[7] For a sophisticated consequentialist account, see John Braithwaite and Philip Pettit, *Not Just Deserts: A Republican Theory of Criminal Justice* (Oxford: Clarendon Press, 1990).

[8] John Braithwaite, *Crime, Shame and Reintegration* (Melbourne: Oxford University Press, 1989).

[9] Terry O'Connell has delivered a number of papers on restorative justice issues at conferences, e.g. "Dawn or Dusk in Sentencing", delivered in April 1997 to the CIAJ National Conference in Quebec, Canada.

open and frank discussion, agreement on procedures and goals, and presupposed some framework of shared moral principles.

Moreover, confession has been used in a wide variety of situations in which moral principles have been infringed, but not any moral rights. So the device of confession has been used in contexts above and beyond what we have been calling restorative justice contexts. Nevertheless, we believe that confession is a central element in many restorative justice programs, and the exploration of it may assist in the process of providing a philosophical foundation for, and taxonomy of, the varieties of restorative justice programs.

Here it is also important to point out that restorative justice in general, and many of its associated institutional mechanisms, are not something new and exotic. They have been part and parcel of systems of justice for thousands of years, both in western and other cultures. For example, the institutional device of confession is a mechanism of restorative justice. Moreover, confession in one form or another has existed in most societies, including Christian, Japanese and Maori societies.[10]

At any rate, in order to focus our discussion we shall outline three Australian conferencing case studies. We have chosen one example of what we take to be a successful conference, a second example which is a manifestly unsuccessful conference, and as our third example, a conference the success or failure of which is somewhat unclear.

Case Studies

Case Study 6.1 David's Story[11]

David was 16-years-old and lived in a large rural town. He had lived with his retired parents, both of whom were very supportive. He had two sisters; both had left home. One sister, Peta, had worked as a police officer in the same town. Up until 15-years-old, David was considered a regular young lad, but then began committing (with others) some minor crime. Having experienced the normal police cautions and court appearances, nothing seemed to make a difference. David became involved in more serious crime, including motor vehicle theft and house burglary. His final series of offences included theft of the complete contents of a house, including the motor vehicle. This was the second occasion David had broken into this house. He was remanded in custody, then released for assessment prior to being sentenced to six-months detention in a juvenile remand centre. David's sister Peta negotiated to have a conference conducted just prior to the court (sentence) hearing. The conference was not proposed nor intended to have any bearing on the court outcome.

---

[10] See, for example, M. Hepworth and Bryan S. Turner, *Confession: Studies in Deviance and Religion* (London: Routledge and Kegan Paul, 1982).
[11] O'Connell, "Dawn or Dusk in Sentencing", *op. cit.*, p. 10.

David's Reflection

David was interviewed on national radio about the conference process. When the interviewer asked David about whether he would commit crime again, David replied, "I would not even think of spitting on the footpath. I have learnt so much and now I have got a job, I feel that I will never get into trouble again."

When asked what was the most important thing to come from the conference, David said, "Just understanding how my behaviour affected so many. I don't think I could have coped with being locked up for six months if I hadn't been in the conference. It is a great process, but a very hard one."

David's Family

Life has been difficult for David's family with David continually getting into trouble. Nothing made a difference and his family were frustrated, not knowing what to do. For Peta, being a police officer had its own special problems. It seemed that she was not able to influence David. The conference was at least worth a try.

After three hours of strong emotional engagements, David and his family felt a great sense of relief. Finally it appeared that something had worked. David began to understand that his family, apart from being badly hurt, did actually care for him. David's radio interview, which took place approximately 12 months after the conference, allowed David to reflect on where he had come from – quite some distance.

David's Many Victims

The sense of loss and violation on the victim's part was all too real. The family whose house was broken into twice by David had since experienced a separation and divorce. For that victim's family, there were so many unresolved emotional issues that it was not surprising to hear the mother (from that family) say with such feeling, "If I had a piece of four-by-two (timber), I would smash your head in."

All the victims spoke about their sense of loss and grief, and their feelings of "not being safe" were very painfully expressed. Towards the end of the conference, the dynamics had changed from anger and disgust to interest and hope. Each victim began to describe David as "not a bad young bloke". Some were prepared to help David beyond the conference, offering themselves as contact people if David needed someone to talk with.

Beyond David's Conference

David spent six months in juvenile detention and then began living with his sister Peta. He is now employed in the area of his choosing. The conference was a significant event in David's life. His family have an increased confidence that David will not re-offend. Relationships have generally improved in David's family, and for the victims, the conference gave them an opportunity to be heard and validated. The conference did bring a sense of closure for many who had experienced isolation and disconnection.

Case Study 6.2 Drink-Driving[12]

An early-twenties single mother with a pre-school child had been randomly selected for "diversioning" in respect of a 'Drive with Prescribed Concentration of Alcohol' offence (drink-driving). She attended the diversionary conference with her mother and father, with whom she resided, and had brought along her boyfriend (not the child's father). There was conflict between the parents and the boyfriend, but inasmuch as the boyfriend sided with her against her parents, he was the only supportive person the young woman saw she had present.

On the evening of the initiating offence, the young man had been engaged in his usual practice of drinking with companions at a club. Intoxicated and fearful of being stopped by police for a random breath-test, he had his girlfriend drive him home in his car. Randomly stopped by the police, she was breath-tested and arrested; she had then been equally randomly selected for diversionary conferencing.

It emerged during the conference that she had had her infant child in the car at the time of the offence – something of which her parents had been unaware. The parents entered into recrimination. Responding angrily to their reaction, she said, "I didn't tell you because I knew you would go on at me."

The young woman was an ostensibly independent adult – yet as her behaviour attested, she obviously still cared to some degree for her parents' good opinion. That existing relationship was where the conference's emphasis should have been placed. The opportunity of allowing the young woman to observe the effect of her dangerous behaviour on her elderly parents was largely disregarded.

The admonitory episode began with a video show, a road-safety horror film. To a kid raised on video splatter-flicks, the effect was minimal. There followed a dressing-down from an "imported person", a uniformed ambulance driver, who tried to shame and scare the young woman with stories of dead children pulled in pieces from car wrecks. "Imported" persons are used in respect of "victimless" offences such as drink-driving to ape the adversarial legal system in which the courts act as the "nominal" defendant.

Use of persons such as the ambulance driver to deplore the subject's behaviour and shame them include members of the arrest area's Community Consultative Committees, and survivors of drink-drivers' victims, who are encouraged to upbraid the subject for driving whilst intoxicated. There was no part in this punishing activity, other than as passive witnesses, for the subject's intimate group.

The diatribe of the "ambo" (ambulance driver), incoherently delivered in comments such as, "If the cops don't get you, we will", failed to elicit any response from the angry-faced and intransigent young woman; but then it wasn't an interactive process – it was something that was being done to her. Then they heard

---

[12] This case study was written by John Blackler and based upon an actual conference that he attended.

from a little man in a dark suit who had been sitting quietly – he was revealed to be an undertaker. His sad tale didn't elicit any response from the girl – and then it was the convening police officer's turn to deplore her behaviour. The approach taken was intended to pierce her only defence – stubbornness – and was aimed at generating a shame-response. They were purposive only of her degradation; their effect can only counter-productively have been destructive of any notion of self-worth.

She was the imperfectly-parented daughter of familially-inept parents, and a person also in a harmful relationship with an uncaring and anti-social man. Her limited social skills, and low levels of intellectual attainment and self-esteem, should have precluded her from diversionary conferencing. She was not a suitable subject for a simple diversionary conference in a family group setting – not suitable without preparatory and supportive activities, that is.

The present problem was that nobody was taking a proper "read" on her situation and tailoring their approach accordingly – at this stage, nobody seemed interested in her response. She merely represented a pilloried subject who was to be castigated and shamed, and whose behaviour was to be semi-publicly deplored.

It was then time to decide what penalty the young woman should pay. What about donating a pint of blood to the Blood Bank? What about two pints of blood? The young woman reared back and looked fearfully at the ambo, as if expecting him to advance on her and extract the penalty on the spot; she regarded the undertaker narrowly. A penalty was eventually decided upon, without much reference to the young woman.

The punishment-rite was not concluded with an end to the shaming; it remained open-ended and ongoing, and, in respect of her prior experience, probably cumulative. The acrimonious relationship that existed prior to the conference still obtained as the angrily muttering participants left.

Case Study 6.3 Murder

This conference was conducted by Sergeant O'Connell at the Central Industrial Prison, Malabar, in 1999.[13] The conference related to the 1994 murder of Michael Marslew, a gratuitous and unprovoked shooting in the course of the armed robbery of the Janalli Pizza Hut.

The arrest, trial and subsequent conviction of the four young male offenders – the legal process, that is – left a range of unmet needs amongst the murdered youth's workmates, friends, relatives and parents – and also amongst the convicted offenders. They expressed a need to be understood by each other in ways that had not been possible within the legal system as it is currently constituted.

Two of the offenders, Karl Kramer and Douglas Edwards, agreed to participate in the conference conducted by Sergeant O'Connell. Although neither Kramer nor Edwards had possessed firearms, both acknowledged their participation in the

[13] The conference was recorded on film by Dee Campbell, and was presented to the Reshaping Australian Institutions Conference at the Australian National University, Canberra, on 17th February, 1999.

crime, and their shared culpability with the offender who fired the fatal shot. They desired also to acknowledge the harm and pain they had caused, and sought an opportunity to express regret and contrition, and to offer apology to the deceased man's intimates and parents.

The offenders would gain nothing in way of parole benefits or remission of sentence from their participation – neither did they sensibly expect forgiveness from the friends or relatives of the deceased. What appeared to have been directing the offenders' participation was the more important, and as yet unresolved, emotions flowing from a finding of guilt in the trial of themselves being conducted in the court of their own consciences.

On the part of the deceased's parents, there was a desire to gain some insight and find anwers to some of their questions regarding the seemingly meaningless death of their son. And whilst the deceased's parents hoped to move from the hopelessness of their current existence to some hope for the future, there could be no hope for forgiveness from them. Joan Marslew, Michael's mother, benchmarked her requirement; she would forgive the offenders anything, but only if her son could be restored to life. Ken Marslew, the deceased's father, remained furiously angry – an emotion that appears to have largely powered his creation of the pressure group Enough is Enough.

The death of the child, which inflicted overwhelming, incapacitating grief on his mother, fuelled an implacable wrath in the father, which he vented in furious activity. Despite the retributive stance this would seem to infer, Ken Marslew remains an active supporter of restorative justice – not least because of his own experience with the existing criminal justice system.

The circle of victims of course included the intimates of the offenders; Douglas Edwards' mother Joanne expressed sorrow for her son's actions and admitted to feeling guilt; the deceased's parents immediately reassured her that she should not feel that way.

Ethical Analysis of Restorative Justice Conferencing

As mentioned above, in our view the kind of conferencing illustrated in the three case studies above is not only a quasi-institutional embodiment of principles of restorative justice, it is in fact the resurrection, or continuation, of that ancient and widely-used paradigm of restorative justice mechanisms, namely the institution of confession.

Confession ideally consists of: (a) voluntary but painful confrontation of an individual with his or her moral failing; (b) truthful communication/expression of this moral failing to an/other person(s), such as a person's so-called "significant others" and/or the rest of the social group, and/or (in relevant moral offences) the victim; (c) feelings of shame in respect of those moral failings; (d) emotional release from the burden of bottled-up guilt, and; (e) resolve or commitment on the part of the individual to refrain from wrongdoing and to try to make amends for past wrongdoing.

Confession presupposes: (a) the existence of social norms which the individual has voluntarily infringed, but which the individual accepts; (b) that the moral worth of an individual is something that the individual believes and feels to be very important to him/herself; and; (c) that the moral approval of others is very important to the individual.

Finally, confession can result in: (a) behavioural change in the light of this moral watershed, and; (b) moral reaffirmation by the moral community (and perhaps in some cases, reintegration of the wrongdoer back into the moral community to which he or she belongs).

If this is what confession consists of, and presupposes, it is easy to see that David's conference (Case Study 6.1) is essentially the deployment, albeit in a contemporary secular setting, of the institutional device of confession. It is also clear that the other two case studies are similarly attempts to deploy this device.

In our view, the drink-driving conference (Case Study 6.2) exemplifies some of the dangers inherent in the use of confessional devices. First, there was an ambiguity in the young woman's wrongdoing. After all, she was cajoled into driving drunk by her boyfriend in order to protect him. Second, the process was not such as to get any purchase on her own independent moral judgment in relation to her actions. It was rather a heavy-handed and ham-fisted attempt to mobilise social disapproval in order to shame her into submission and confession. Third, there was in fact no commitment on her part to refrain from wrongdoing in the future, and genuinely to try to make amends for her past actions. Fourth, there was no closure in the sense of a negotiated resolution that all parties could live with.

The murder conference (Case Study 6.3) exemplifies not so much the dangers as the limitations of confessional devices. The wrongdoers are sincere in their expressions of remorse and contrition. The family and friends of the victim appear to want restoration. But there is an insurmountable barrier. The victim is dead. The wrongdoing can never be undone. The substantive moral damage can never be repaired. On the other hand, there was a certain restoration of the moral relationship between the victim's family and friends on the one hand, and the mother of one of the offender's, on the other.

We can conclude that confession has proved to be a powerful device for moral transformation and reconciliation with victims in many different times, places and contexts, including criminal justice contexts. However, it is a device which has important limitations and can be misused. For example, it can be deployed simply as a means to undermine moral autonomy and to ensure submission to authority. Accordingly, even if restorative justice and its associated institutional mechanisms are as successful as their proponents in Japan, Australia and elsewhere claim, there are some important qualifying and somewhat deflationary points that need to be made concerning confession.

First, confession can be used solely as a mechanism for social control by those who happen to be in charge of the processes. Indeed, historically confession has often failed, been misused, and indeed at times served grossly immoral purposes. Consider confessions extracted from heretics by religious zealots in the Middle Ages. Consider also the communist show trials of the 1930s. Confession can simply be an exercise in social control for its own sake, and have as its main effect the destruction of the moral autonomy of the individual. Accordingly, the use of confessional devices cannot be given a general endorsement either in non-religious, non-political restorative justice settings or elsewhere.

Second, and relatedly, restorative justice mechanisms should involve moral reflection and moral judgment-making – we don't mean judgmentalism – directed to the truth; they ought not simply be the occasions for socially-imposed, uncritical triggering of emotions – such as shame – emotions that have been unhinged from cognitive states grounded in moral reality.

Third, restorative justice mechanisms might have problems in relation to crimes in which the victim does not exist or exists only in a diffuse form. For example, in the case of murder, the victim has ceased to exist; so in what sense can any important moral relationship be restored? Again, in the case of many crimes, such as drink-driving and fraud, the "victim" is somewhat nebulous, or it is a corporation or government organisation or – in the case of tax fraud – the community as a whole. Accordingly, there is no specific human victim who can confront the offender, and no easily identifiable moral relationship that can be restored.

It might be replied that in the above sorts of case, it is the moral relationship of the offender to the community at large that is at issue, and this can be restored by, for example, having community representatives (in the case of drink-driving, fraud and tax evasion). Unfortunately, the presence of such representatives does not seem to generate the requisite moral emotion, and for good reason – they are only victims in an attenuated sense. On the other hand, in so far as compensation can be paid, and the community is accepting of that as a morally adequate response, then reintegration may well be possible. However, such a process of reintegration is based on "paying one's dues" – hardly a notion exclusive to restorative justice.

Naturally the presence of significant others can powerfully affect the attitudes and behaviour of offenders, and do so across a range of offences, including perhaps murder. But this misses the point. We are here speaking of the moral relationship to be restored, not the means by which it might be restored. There are of course crimes directed against significant others – and these might be especially susceptible to treatment under the auspices of a restorative justice scheme. However, these are a minority of crimes in the community.

Restorative Justice and Retributive Justice

As has already been mentioned, among the proponents of restorative justice there is a strong tendency to contrast restorative justice and retributivism, and to disparage, and indeed strongly disrecommend, the latter in favour of the former. This disrecommendation is often based on the following two claims. First, it is claimed that retributivist, but not restorative, conceptions are punitive. Second, it is claimed that the restorative justice program, unlike the retributivist criminal justice system, emphasises informal processes that place the moral relationship between the victim and the offender at centre-stage. By contrast, the retributivist system involves a formal process of applying abstract principles of justice by state functionaries to offenders. The victim has no part to play. Let us first respond to the latter claim.

We need first to remind ourselves of the fundamental role the criminal justice system is supposed to have. We leave aside the question as to whether or not it is in fact succeeding in that role.

The criminal justice system is ultimately based on social norms. Social norms are a society's accepted moral principles. As such, social norms are fundamental to social life. Thus, social norms against random killing enable cooperative economic and family institutions. Again, social norms of truth-telling and of providing evidence for statements are necessary for institutions of learning. Moreover, social norms are in large part enshrined in the criminal law or its equivalents. Theft, assault, murder, rape, child molestation, fraud and so on, are actions which violate social norms in contemporary societies, and they are also criminal acts. Indeed, it is because they are held to be profoundly morally wrong that perpetrators of these acts are held criminally liable. Moreover, some of these actions are regarded as morally worse than others, e.g. murder is morally worse than theft. Accordingly, the punishment meted out for murder is in general greater than for theft. In short, the criminal law is essentially a formalisation, regimentation and attempted objectification of society's most basic moral principles. Individuals can afford to disagree about, and indeed infringe with impunity, many moral principles; but not those moral principles enshrined in the criminal law. In effect, these moral principles are agreed by the society to be objectively valid. Moreover, these moral principles include not only prohibitions against specific forms of behaviour, but also moral principles in relation to moral responsibility and punishment. One example here is the principle that moral responsibility consists in part in having an intention to commit a wrong. Another is the principle that only those who are responsible for crimes should be punished and that the wrongdoer should be the one to pay compensation.

Accordingly, the point to be made here, in relation to the ambitions of some proponents of restorative justice to replace (substantially) the current (allegedly) retributivist justice system, is that criminal justice systems have developed complex sets of moral principles of the kind described above over long periods of time. Some of these principles are doubtless questionable or imperfectly applied. Moreover, there may well be a need to make greater use of informal processes, and to give victims a greater role in both formal and informal processes. However, the point we want to stress here is that any system of justice – whether based on principles of restorative justice, retributivist justice or some other conception – that has pretensions to substantially replace existing systems would also need to provide its own complex set of principles. Having an array of processes is hardly sufficient. In short, the so-called "restorative justice paradigm" is in its infancy if it sees itself as something more than simply an adjunct to the existing system.

Let us finally turn to the much discussed issue of punishment. Restorative justice is often contrasted with retributive justice on the grounds that the latter is held to be committed to punishment for its own sake, the former to abandoning punishment in favour of shame, reconciliation and forgiveness. We will argue that there is an ineliminable role for principles of retributive justice, including punishment, in the concept of restorative justice. We will further argue that the concept of shame is more closely related to punishment than might have been thought. Consequently, shame and punishment are not alternatives, but go hand in hand within an acceptable restorative justice framework.

Let us first introduce some distinctions. First, there is the suffering in the form of painful feelings of shame experienced by an offender who undergoes a restorative justice process. Secondly, there is the restitution that an offender might be called upon to provide to his victim, e.g. returning stolen goods. This is a burden imposed on the offenders; it is not simply restoring of the victim's prior circumstances by some third party, e.g. the taxpayer. Third, there is the compensation that might be paid by the offender to the victim to make up for the harm done, e.g. the psychological suffering inflicted by the knowledge that one had had one's goods stolen, or the loss of not being able to use the stolen item for a period. Again, this is a burden imposed on the offender, and is a burden above and beyond that comprising the restitution. Fourth, there is the punishment that might be imposed on the offender for his wrongdoing. By "punishment" it is not here meant simply restitution or compensation. For example, a thief might not only need to pay back the money he stole (restitution), and make some further payment for the harm done to the victim (compensation); he might also need to be punished for doing wrong. To see this, consider a thief who is very wealthy, and would remain unpunished if he simply paid back the money he stole and paid a sum sufficient to compensate the victim for the harm done. It is important to note that in some cases punishment might be included in compensation. A fine paid to the victim might both compensate the victim and punish the offender.

Armed with this fourfold distinction, let us consider suffering in relation to confession. Confession necessarily involves suffering on the part of the confessor – minimally it involves the painful feelings of shame generated by his own as well as others' knowledge of his wrongdoing. So punishment, at least in the sense of painful feelings, is part and parcel of the restorative justice process, including in the case of confession. Part of the point of confession is to get wrongdoers to confront the fact of their wrongdoing, and that is necessarily a painful process.

Moreover, a wrongdoer accepts the community's principles of justice in relation to restitution, compensation and punishment. Accordingly, a wrongdoer will typically accept the proposition that he or she – rather than some third party, such as the taxpayer – ought to provide restitution and compensation. Accordingly, restorative justice entails the imposition of burdens on the guilty above and beyond the suffering associated with shame. To this extent, it embraces a retributivist principle.

But what of punishment – as distinct from the suffering of shame or the burdens of restitution and compensation? If punishment is an accepted moral principle in the community, then the wrongdoer will also accept that he or she should be punished. But this still leaves the question of whether punishment should in fact be inflicted. Here there are two questions that need to be kept separate. These are whether the guilty should suffer and/or be made to redress the results of their wrongdoing, and, if the guilty should suffer, who should inflict the suffering. In general, suffering is a bad thing to be avoided and not to be inflicted on oneself or others. But we have already seen that the suffering of the guilty is justifiable, indeed mandatory, within a restorative justice framework, to the extent that it is involved in the shaming process, and in restitution and compensation. But could there be a justification for some further infliction of suffering, namely punishment for doing wrong? Suppose a man is hell-bent on making his wife suffer, by (say) continually beating her up. For her part, she is an innocent victim. A court case ensues and he is found guilty. He is very wealthy and able to pay an amount to her by way of restitution and compensation. The wife's physical health returns, and she is no longer fearful of him, since they divorce, go their separate ways, and the magistrate's threat to lock him up next time deters him from any further actions. However, he has gone unpunished, for the money he paid to her was of no great consequence to him, given his wealth. Nor does he accept that he has done anything wrong. As far as he is concerned, he would cheerfully do exactly as he did, given the same circumstances. After all, it gave him a certain amount of pleasure to be able to dominate and inflict suffering on his wife. Again, consider an initially unrepentant murderer whose victim – his wife – has no relatives or friends. Assume also there is no justification for punishment on the basis of deterrence, since he hated his wife and was driven to murder her; but no-one else is at risk, and other would-be murderers of their wives would not be deterred if he were to be punished. There is no painful feelings of shame, and no burden of restitution or compensation to be paid. Should he go unpunished? More specifically, if he or the wife-beater are to be reintegrated into the community, could this be done without some form of punishment? Here, Hegel, Simone Weil and Reinhold Niebuhr, and more recently, Eric Reitan and Charles Barton, are instructive.[14]

What this kind of case serves to illustrate is what might be called "the moral bond" between individuals. After all, morality is predominantly concerned with interpersonal relationships, including relationships to strangers and to members of the community. Offenders breach these moral bonds. On a reintegrative theory, punishment is necessary for the purposes of reintegration, and it is necessary for reintegration by virtue of the fact that the punishment: (a) "washes away the stigma of the crime"[15] that is a barrier to restoration of moral bonds, and; (b) educates the moral judgement of the criminal so that he conforms to the requisite moral principles. In the case of our two examples, it is hard to see how either of these two goals could be achieved in the absence of any punishment.

An important additional point to be made here is that, as Niebuhr puts it, the punishment should not belittle or degrade, but rather inspire repentance and reintegration.[16] Accordingly, punishment should comply with moral principles that

---

[14] G. W. F. Hegel, *The Philosophy of Right*, trans. T. M. Knox (Oxford: Oxford University Press, 1942); Simone Weil, "The Needs of the Soul", in *The Need for Roots* (New York: Putnam's Sons, 1952); Reinhold Niebuhr, "God's Justice and Mercy", in R. M. Brown (ed.), *The Essential Reinhold Niebuhr* (New Haven: Yale University Press, 1986); Eric Reitan, "Punishment and Community: The Reintegrative Theory of Punishment", *Canadian Journal of Philosophy*, Vol. 26, No. 1, 1996; Barton, *op. cit.*

[15] Niebuhr, *op. cit.*, p. 29.

[16] *ibid.*

the offender can agree with, and as a consequence, the offender can come to accept his punishment as just and reasonable.

Conclusion

In this book, we have argued that the central and most important purpose of the institution of the police is the protection of moral rights, but that the use of harmful methods in policing is both routine and inescapable. In Chapter 1, we elaborated and defended this philosophical theory of policing. In Chapter 2, we discussed in detail a variety of problems concerning police authority and discretion. We considered the problematic nature of the relationship between police organisations and governments, and specifically the issue of police independence from government. We also explored and offered a qualified defence of the notion of the original authority of the office of police constable in the UK and Australia.

In Chapters 3 and 4, we looked at a range of moral problems that arise from police use of harmful methods. In Chapter 3, we considered police use of deadly force, and argued that the moral justification for police use of deadly force was somewhat wider than that available to ordinary citizens; in particular, it was not restricted to self-defence and the defence of the lives of others, as is commonly supposed. In Chapter 4, we discussed police use of surveillance and related methods that infringe individual privacy. In Chapter 4, we also discussed the related issue of entrapment, and argued for a restricted use of that particular policing method.

The topic of Chapter 5 was police corruption, including an outline of the nature and causes of police corruption, and the phenomenon of noble cause corruption. We provided an original philosophical analysis of the concept of corruption, according to which corruption is both a causal and a moral concept; an action is corrupt because it has a morally bad effect on some institutional process, purpose or role. Within this general analysis of corruption, we also offered a distinctive analysis of the species, noble cause corruption.

The final chapter of this book, Chapter 6, consists of a discussion of restorative justice in policing. Perhaps the most obvious harmful method deployed by police is arrest and imprisonment; the infringement of individual freedom or autonomy. The restorative justice movement is in part a response to a perceived failure of imprisonment to reform or deter criminals. We argued for a conception of restorative justice according to which it is an attempt to redress the moral imbalance that occurs when the moral rights of victims are violated by offenders. This conception resonated with some of our earlier discussions, including our objectivist yet relational theory of the moral justification for killing in self-defence.

Bibliography

Alderson, John, *Principled Policing*, Winchester: Waterside Press, 1998

Alexandra, Andrew, "Dirty Harry and Dirty Hands", in Tony Coady, Steve James, Seumas Miller and Michael O'Keefe (eds.), *Violence and Police Culture*, Melbourne: Melbourne University Press, 2000

Alpert, Geoffrey P., and Dunham, Roger G., *Police Pursuit Driving: Controlling Responses to Emergency Situations*, New York: Greenwood Press, 1990

Barton, Charles, *Getting Even: Revenge as a Form of Justice*, Open Court Publishing Company, 1999

Benn, Stanley I., *A Theory of Freedom*, Cambridge: Cambridge University Press, 1988

Bittner, Egon, *The Functions of Police in Modern Society*, Cambridge, Mass.: Gunn and Hain, 1980

Bradley, David, Walker, Neil, and Wilkie, Roy, *Managing the Police*, Brighton: Harvester Press, 1986

Braithwaite, John, *Crime, Shame and Reintegration*, Melbourne: Oxford University Press, 1989

Braithwaite, John, and Pettit, Philip, *Not Just Deserts: A Republican Theory of Criminal Justice*, Oxford: Clarendon Press, 1990

Bringing them Home: Report of the National Inquiry into the Separation of Aboriginal and Torres Strait Islander Children from their Families, Commonwealth of Australia, 1997

Bronitt, Simon, and Roche, Declan, "Between rhetoric and reality: socio-legal and republican perspectives on entrapment", *International Journal of Evidence and Proof*, No. 4, 2000

Bryett, Keith, Harrison, Arch, and Shaw, John, *An Introduction to Policing*, Vol. 2, Butterworths, 1994

Cohen, Howard, "Overstepping Police Authority", *Criminal Justice Ethics*, 6 (2), Summer/Fall 1987

Cohen, Howard, and Feldberg, Michael, *Power and Restraint: The Moral Dimension of Policework*, New York: Praeger, 1991

Cohen, Stanley, *Visions of Social Control: Crime, Punishment and Classification*, Cambridge: Polity Press, 1985

Daley, Robert, *Prince of the City*, London: Granada, 1979

Davis, Frank, *Blackburn: A Forensic Disaster*, Sydney: Harry the Hat Publications, 1990

Davis, Kenneth Culp, *Discretionary Justice: A Preliminary Inquiry*, Baton Rouge, LA: Louisiana State University, 1969

Delattre, Edwin, *Character and Cops: Ethics in Policing*, Washington, DC: American Enterprise Institute, 1994

Denning, D. E., and Baugh, W. E., "Encryption and Evolving Technologies as Tools of Organised Crime and Terrorism", US Working Group on Organised Crime, National Strategy Information Centre, 1997

Devlin, Patrick, *The Enforcement of Morals*, Oxford: Oxford University Press, 1965

Doyle, James, "Police Discretion, Legality and Morality", in William C. Heffernan and Timothy Stroup (eds.), *Police Ethics: Hard Choices in Law Enforcement*, New York: John Jay College, 1985

Duff, A. (ed.), *Philosophy and the Criminal Law*, Cambridge: Cambridge University Press, 1998

Dworkin, Gerald, *The Theory and Practice of Autonomy*, Cambridge: Cambridge University Press, 1988

Dworkin, Ronald, *Law's Empire*, Oxford: Hart Publishing, 1998

—, *Taking Rights Seriously*, Cambridge, Mass.: Harvard University Press, 1977

Etzioni, Amitai, *The Limits of Privacy*, New York: Basic Books, 1999

Foreign Corrupt Practices Act of 1977, Public Law 95-213 (5305), December 19th, 1977, United States Code 78a, Section 103

Goffman, Irving, *Asylums*, London: Penguin, 1961

Goldstein, Herman, *Problem-Oriented Policing*, New York: McGraw-Hill, 1990

—,"Team Policing", in Steven G. Brandl and David E. Barlow (eds.), *Classics of Policing*, Cincinnati, OH: Anderson Publishing Co., 1996

Griffin, James, "Human Rights", in Tom Campbell and Seumas Miller (eds.), *Human Rights and the Moral Responsibilities of Corporate and Public Sector Organisations*, Dordrecht: Kluwer, 2004

Hallenstein, Hal, *Investigation into the Death of Gary John Abdallah: Coroner's Findings*, Melbourne: State Coroner's Office, 1994

—, *Investigation into the Death of Hai Foong Yap: Coroner's Findings*, Melbourne: State Coroner's Office, 1994

—, *Investigation into the Death of Gerhard Alfred Paul Sader: Coroner's Findings*, Melbourne: State Coroner's Office, 1994

Heffernan, William C., "The Police and their Rules of Office: An Ethical Analysis", in William C. Heffernan and Timothy Stroup (eds.), *Police Ethics: Hard Choices for Law Enforcement*, New York: John Jay College Press, 1985

Hegel, G. W. F., *The Philosophy of Right*, trans. T. M. Knox, Oxford: Oxford University Press, 1942

Hepworth, M., and Turner, Bryan S., *Confession: Studies in Deviance and Religion*, London: Routledge and Kegan Paul, 1982

Hill, Richard S., *Policing the Colonial Frontier: The Theory and Practice of Coercive Social and Racial Control in New Zealand, 1767-1867*, Wellington, NZ: Government Printer, 1986

Hindess, Barry, "Good Government and Corruption", in Peter Larmour and Nick Wolanin (eds.), *Corruption and Anti-Corruption*, Canberra: Asia Pacific Press, 2001

Hobbes, Thomas, *Leviathan* (any edition)

Hogg, R., and Hawker, B., "The Politics of Police Independence", *Legal Service Bulletin*, Vol. 8, No. 4, 1983

Hopkins, Jonathan, "States, markets and corruption: A review of some recent literature", *Review of International Political Economy*, 2002

Jabbra, J. G., and Dwivedi, O. P., *Public Service Accountability: A Comparative Perspective*, Kumarian Press, 1988

Johnston, Les, *The Rebirth of Private Policing*, London: Routledge, 1992

Kleinig, John, *The Ethics of Policing*, Cambridge: Cambridge University Press, 1996

Kleinig, John, (ed.), *Handled with Discretion: Ethical Issues in Police Decision Making*, Lanham, Maryland: Rowman and Littlefield, 1996

Klitgaard, Robert, Maclean-Abaroa, Ronald, and Parris, H. Lindsey, *Corrupt Cities: A Practical Guide to Cure and Prevention*, Oakland, Calif.: ICS Press, 2000

Klockars, Carl B., "The Dirty Harry Problem", reprinted in A. S. Blumberg and E. Niederhoffer (eds.), *The Ambivalent Force: Perspectives on the Police*, New York: Holt, Rinehart and Winston, 1976

Kneebone, Susan, "The Independent Discretionary Function Principle and Public Officers", *Monash University Law Review,* Vol. 16, No. 2, 1990

Locke, John, *Second Treatise on Government* (any edition)

Luban, David, *Lawyers and Justice: An Ethical Study*, Princeton: Princeton University Press, 1988

Lusher, The Hon. Mr. Justice, *Report of the Commission to Inquire into New South Wales Police Administration*, Sydney: NSW Government Printer, 1981

Lustgarten, Laurence, *The Governance of the Police*, London: Sweet and Maxwell, 1986

McKenzie, Ian K., and Gallagher, G. Patrick, *Behind the Uniform: Policing in Britain and America*, Brighton, UK: Harvester/Wheatsheaf Press, 1989

Manning, Peter K., "Rules, Colleagues and Situationally Justified Actions", in R. Blakenship (ed.), *Colleagues in Organisations*, New York: Wiley Press, 1978

Miller, Arthur, *Miller's Court*, New York: Houghton Mifflin, 1982

Miller, Seumas, "Self-defence and Forcing the Choice Between Lives", *Journal of Applied Philosophy*, Vol. 9, No. 2, 1992

—,"Killing in Self-defence", *Public Affairs Quarterly*, Vol. 7, No. 4, 1993

—,"Privacy and the Internet", *Australian Computer Journal*, Vol. 29, No. 1, 1997

—,"Corruption and Anti-Corruption in the Profession of Policing", *Professional Ethics*, Vol. 6, Nos. 3 & 4, 1998

—,"Noble Cause Corruption in Policing", *African Security Review*, Vol. 8, No. 3, 1999

—,"Judith Jarvis Thomson on Killing in Self-defence", *Australian Journal of Professional and Applied Ethics*, Vol. 3, No. 2, 2001

—,"Shootings by Police in Victoria: The Ethical Issues", in C. A. J. Coady, S. James, S. Miller and M. O'Keefe (eds.), *Violence and Police Culture*, Melbourne: Melbourne University Press, 2000

—,"Human Rights and the Institution of the Police", in Tom Campbell and Seumas Miller (eds.), *Human Rights and the Moral Responsibilities of Corporate and Public Sector Organisations*, Dordrecht: Kluwer, 2004

—,"Social Norms", in G. Holmstrom-Hintikka and R. Tuomela (eds.), *Contemporary Action Theory* (*Volume 2 – Social Action*), Synthese Library Series, Boston: Kluwer, 1997

—,"Authority, Discretion and Accountability: The Case of Policing", in Charles Sampford, Noel Preston and C. Bois (eds.), *Public Sector Ethics: Finding and Implementing Values*, London: Routledge, 1998

—,"Individual Autonomy and Sociality", in F. Schmitt (ed.), *Socialising Metaphysics: The Nature of Social Reality*, Lanham, Maryland: Rowman and Littlefield, 2003

—,"Noble Cause Corruption in Policing Revisited", in Robert Adlam and Peter Villiers (eds.), *A Safe, Just and Tolerant Society: Police Virtue Rediscovered*, Winchester: Waterside Press, 2004

—,"Creating Good Policing", paper presented in July 1995 at the Ethics/Professional Standards Seminar, Masonic Centre, Sydney, as part of NSW Police Service Development Program.

—,"Privacy, Encryption and the Internet", in A. D'Atri, A. Marturano, S. Rogerson and T. Ward Bynum (eds.), *Proceedings of the 4th ETHICOMP International Conference on the Social and Ethical Impacts of Information and Communication Technologies* (CD format) Rome, 1999

—,"Corruption: Some Theoretical Issues", appeared in the *Proceedings of the National Conference of the Australian Association for Professional and Applied Ethics*, Melbourne, 2003

—, *Issues in Police Ethics*, Keon, 1996

—, *Social Action: A Teleological Account*, New York: Cambridge University Press, 2001

Miller, Seumas, and Blackler, John, *Police Ethics* (Vols. 1-4: *Case Studies for Street Police; Case Studies for Detectives; Case Studies for Police Managers; Bibliography*), Charles Sturt University and NSW Police Service, 2000

—,"Restorative Justice: Retribution, Confession and Shame", in J. Braithwaite and H. Strang (eds.), *Restorative Justice*, Aldershot: Dartmouth Press, 2000

Miller, Seumas, Blackler, John, and Alexandra, Andrew, *Police Ethics*, Keon, 1995

—, *Police Ethics*, Sydney: Allen and Unwin, 1997

Miller, Seumas, Roberts, Peter, and Spence, Edward, *Corruption and Anti-Corruption: An Applied Philosophical Approach*, Prentice Hall, 2004

Miller, Seumas, Biles, David, Green, Tracey, and Ratcliffe, Jerry, *Report on Drug-related Complaints Against the NSW Police* (Australian Research Council-funded SPIRT Grant, 2001)

—,"Drug-Related Complaints against Police: Some Findings from a NSW Study", *Policing: An International Journal of Police Strategies and Management*, March, 2005

Montague, P., "Self-defence and choosing between lives", *Philosophical Studies*, Vol. 40, 1981

Moore, David, and Wettenhall, Roger (eds.), *Keeping the Peace: Police Accountability and Oversight*, Canberra: University of Canberra, 1994

Nagel, Thomas, *Concealment and Exposure and other Essays*, Oxford: Oxford University Press, 2002

Neyroud, Peter, and Beckley, Alan, *Policing, Ethics and Human Rights*, Cullompton, Devon: Willan Publishing, 2001

Ni Aolain, Fionnuala, *The Politics of Force: Conflict Management and State Violence in Northern Ireland*, Belfast: Blackstaff, 2000

Niebuhr, Reinhold, "God's Justice and Mercy", in R. M. Brown (ed.), *The Essential Reinhold Niebuhr*, New Haven: Yale University Press, 1986

Noble, Tom, *Untold Violence: Crime in Melbourne Today*, Melbourne: John Kerr, 1989

Noonan, John T., *Bribes*, New York: Macmillan, 1984

NSW Crimes Act, no. 40, section 352, sub-section 2(a) (1990)

Nye, Joseph, "Corruption and Political Development: A Cost-benefit Analysis", *American Political Science Review*, Vol. 61, No. 2, 1967

O'Connell, Terry, "Dawn or Dusk in Sentencing", paper delivered in April 1997 to the CIAJ National Conference, Quebec, Canada

Pearson, Zoe, "An International Human Rights Approach to Corruption", in Peter Larmour and Nick Wolanin (eds.), *Corruption and Anti-Corruption*, Canberra: Asia Pacific Press, 2001

Police Service Act 1990, No. 47 (reprinted as in force at January 24th, 1994 to include all amendments up to the *Statute Law (Miscellaneous Provisions) Act (No. 2) 1993*, No. 108), Section 213 (1) 'Protection from personal liability'

Rashid, Ahmed, *Taliban: The Story of the Afghan Warlords*, London: Pan Books, 2001

Reiman, Jeffrey, "The Social Contract and the Police Use of Deadly Force", in Frederick Elliston and Michael Feldberg (eds.), *Moral Issues in Police Work*, Totowa, NJ: Rowman and Allanheld, 1985

Reiner, Robert, *Chief Constables: Bosses, Bobbies or Bureaucrats?*, Oxford: Oxford University Press, 1992

Reitan, Eric, "Punishment and Community: The Reintegrative Theory of Punishment", *Canadian Journal of Philosophy*, Vol. 26, No. 1, 1996

Rose-Ackerman, Susan, *Corruption and Government: Causes, Consequences and Reform*, Cambridge: Cambridge University Press, 1999

Royal Commission on the Police: *Cmnd. 1728: Final Report*, 1962

Ryan, Cheney, "Self-defence, Pacifism and the Possibility of Killing", *Ethics*, Vol. 93, 1983

Scarman, Lord, *The Scarman Report*, London: Penguin, 1981

Shue, Henry, *Basic Rights*, Princeton: Princeton University Press, 1996

Silber, Laura, and Little, Allan, *Yugoslavia: Death of a Nation*, London: Penguin, 1997

Silvester, John, Rule, Andrew, and Davies, Owen, *The Silent War: Behind the Police Killings that shook Australia*, Sydney: Floradale, 1995

Sinnott-Armstrong, Walter, "Entrapment in the Net?", *Ethics and Information Technology*, No. 1, 1999

Skolnick, Jerome, *Justice Without Trial*, New York: Macmillan, 1966

——,"Deception by Police", *Criminal Justice Ethics*, Vol. 1, No. 2, Summer/Fall, 1982

Skolnick, Jerome, and Fyfe, J., *Above the Law: Police and the Excessive Use of Force*, New York: Free Press, 1993

Teichman, J., *Pacifism and the Unjust War*, Oxford: Blackwell, 1986

Ten, C. L., *Crime, Guilt and Punishment*, Oxford: Clarendon Press, 1987

Thomson, J. J., "Self-defence", *Philosophy and Public Affairs*, September, 1991

Uniacke, S., *Permissible Killing*, Cambridge: Cambridge University Press, 1994

United Nations Code of Conduct for Law Enforcement Officials

Violence: Directions for Australia, Canberra: National Committee on Violence, 1990

Waddington, P. A. J., *The Strong Arm of the Law*, Clarendon Press, 1991

Warwick, D. P., "Ethics of Administrative Discretion", in J. L. Fleishman (ed.), *et al.*, *Public Duties: The Moral Obligations of Public Officials*, Cambridge, Mass.: Harvard University Press, 1981

Wasserman, D., "Justifying Self-defence", *Philosophy and Public Affairs*, Vol. 16, 1987

Weil, Simone, *The Need for Roots*, New York: Putnam's Sons, 1952

Whitton, Evan, *The Hillbilly Dictator: Australia's Police State*, Sydney: ABC Enterprises, 1988

Wood, Justice James, *Final Report: Royal Commission into Corruption in the New South Wales Police Service*, Sydney: NSW Government, 1998

World Bank, *Helping countries combat corruption: The role of the World Bank*, Washington DC: World Bank, 1997

Index